Please remember that this is a library book,
and that it belongs only temporarily to each
person who uses it. Be considerate. Do
not write in this, or any, library book.

The self in early childhood

The self in early childhood

Joel Ryce-Menuhin

*'an association in which the free development of each
is the condition of the free development of all'*

Free Association Books / London / 1988

First published in Great Britain 1988 by
Free Association Books
26 Freegrove Road
London N7 9RQ

British Library Cataloguing in Publication Data

Ryce-Menuhin, Joel
  The self in early childhood.
  1. Child psychology
  I. Title
  155.4   0136271

ISBN 1 85343 002 1 (hb)
ISBN 1 85343 003 X (pb)

Phototypeset by Input Typesetting Ltd, London SW19 8DR
Printed and bound in Great Britain
at the University Printing House, Oxford

Dedicated to Dr Violet de Laszlo-Staub, Zurich, who has understood and lives the centrality of selfhood in friendship.

'. . . the evolution of science reflects a basic polarity to nature itself: differentiation and integration.'
Koestler (1972)

'. . . the evolution of ideas appear[s] as a succession of repeated differentiations, specializations and reintegrations on a higher level – a progression from primordial unity through variety to more complex patterns of unity-in-variety.'
Koestler (1968)

Contents

viii

Contents

Contents

I wish to thank Dr Elizabeth R. Valentine of Royal Holloway and Bedford New College, University of London, for her acute supervision of the earlier form of this work as a thesis, and Dr Karl Figlio, who has been an invaluably brilliant in-house editor to its revised and expanded version at Free Association Books.

Grateful thanks are also due to Wolfgang and Gabriele Somary, Zurich, for their patronage during my postgraduate studies at London University. I wish to thank my wife, the pianist Yaltah Menuhin, for sharing me with the wide-ranging efforts the writing of this book entailed during eight years of its preparation.

The author is grateful for permission to reproduce a diagram from Jolande Jacobi's *The Psychology of C. G. Jung*, published by Routledge & Kegan Paul in 1962, and Kenneth Lambert's diagram from his book entitled *Analysis, Repair and Individuation*, published in 1981 by Academic Press.

1. Introduction

In my own childhood I became acutely aware that I was 'more than' the sum of my parents' psychologies. By 'more than' I do not mean 'better than' but simply that my way of being could not be reduced entirely to my genetic predecessors. The childhood psychology of my personal self-development as a musically gifted child also could not be reduced to the environmental influences as a whole within which I grew up and lived. These realizations were not based on a rebellion or just the outgrowing of the universal oedipal complex through which each of us passes in infancy; nor were they based on attitudes of omnipotence after my fourth year. It was the desire to understand why my ambition for further and further self-expression never abated over the years that made me decide to enter Jungian analysis, as Jung's psychology has a self theory. What was 'self', and how could it be studied or realized? I entered Jungian analysis when I experienced a mid-life crisis and its resultant depression led me on to further and further search towards 'selfhood', whatever that might be.

Throughout the ensuing seventeen years' study of psychology and ten years' experience as a Jungian analyst and sand-play therapist working with the self-material of others, I have become even more aware that we are only at the dawn of comprehension concerning self/ego processes in psychology. Not very much is

known about these processes and their theory and application to
our psychological understanding of self and of other selves.

When I left an artistic life as a concert pianist to study psychology
at London University, I was nearly forty. It was not too late to
add, during these studies, some improvement to my perception
of the sciences, which had not been well enough developed earlier.
My childhood education was thorough, but one shared with a
career as a public performer. This work at university filled out
my education to one balanced both by the arts and by the science
and philosophy of psychology.

In this time of appraisal and learning during my psychological
studies, much was made by my university lecturers of the
conflict between depth psychology and academic experimental
psychology. However, I came to realize that more than conflict
was implied between depth psychologists, using theories of Freud
and Jung and the extension of that work with its unconscious/
conscious dimension, and the laboratory experimentalists who
often could not comprehend what depth psychology was offering
for experiment. It seemed to me that as academic experimentalists
could rarely construct a way to experiment with the empirical
claims of depth psychologists or make much of an approach to
the ground of ego/self study, there were difficulties; but were
they insurmountable? I have come to believe that these difficulties
can be solved. This movement towards a solution would need to
be facilitated by an explanatory method that clearly stated the *a
priori* philosophic position forming the boundary for the ground
of study in human psychology and its formulation. It would need
a reappraisal of work from depth psychology and experimental
psychology in an area that tried to formulate a hierarchical system
of self. This would be a study structure in which the totality of
human psychology must theoretically be included. Could these
two approaches learn from each other and utilize more successfully each other's discoveries in a more common effort?

I continued the personal analysis of my own childhood with a

Jungian analyst well versed in Freudian and Kleinian theory while I worked at London University for a scientific degree and wrote a postgraduate theoretical paper. Thus childhood study was re-experienced simultaneously in depth analysis and in the study of experimental work in child psychology. This resulted in a psychological sense of union in me between differing approaches to childhood psychology, rather than the feeling that they were split from one another which persists in many of my student and later professional colleagues. I decided to go on dealing with my inner realization by writing a book which would outwardly and scientifically express my ideas about these problems. Over time I continued to realize that ego theory needed much more empirical explanation and if an analyst could do that, partly using experimental findings in support, experimental psychologists could respond with further empirical testing with their laboratory and other methodologies. I have become more and more aware of this potentially unified scientific development in theory and in practice, and have chosen the empirical self psychology of Jung as the ground or framework in which to place and clinically defend a further theory of the infant self.

The postulation of my new theory requires a strong conjecture to be put forward as scientific and defended within the present knowledge of psychology. In the past experimenters have rarely been sufficiently close to the work of depth psychologists to comprehend what is being claimed in theories about self and ego and to determine if it is testable by experiment.

This book is an attempt to remedy that historical situation, which in my view is not based on any final incompatibility between the approaches but, often, on ignorance of psychology itself. Basically, depth psychologists cannot be blind to human experience or convert it very easily into a laboratory setting. Individual experience and its detail is important to them. 'Individual' implies that a self involving a total personality is what needs to be tested by experimenters in broadly based psychometric

4   approaches. If experimenters could work more effectively with
depth psychologists and analysts, it might be possible to begin to
quantify depth psychology with carefully designed research and
strictly controlled experiments. The chief problem has been that
the postulates of depth psychology are difficult to frame in an
experimental design. To do so, experimenters have often so
altered the meaning of behaviour to be tested as to be testing
something other than the postulate under question.

Using Jung's work to define self psychology, which will be
fully surveyed in Chapter I, I shall argue that this self theory in
an updated form should be the principal framework for human
reflexive psychology as a whole. For all psychological work is
reflexive in the sense that the psyche is talking about and working
with the psyche. This implies that a totality within attempts to
look at a totality without and to study the psychological interaction of each to each. That includes everything that can occur to
the psyche, all of which must occur within some self or selves.
To bring back the self theory to its inherent position of importance
would be a significant goal for the future of a total psychology,
one that includes the richness of the unconscious and its manifestations in conscious experience. In a hierarchical self theory – to
which this book contributes by extending ego theory within self
theory – we have suitable levels of study that could begin to form
a bridge connecting approaches to the psychology of the self to
many of its ramifications. We must begin at the beginning: what
self does the child 'come in' with? In what sense could one use the
word 'self' within a study of the infant?

The verbal formulation for this starting point has often
confounded both depth psychologists and experimental workers
in the laboratory. Perhaps this is partly because it is true that the
etymologies of most words standing for the concept of the self
(as used in everyday language) are obscure or unknown. The base
of Anglo-Saxon is *selbha* (Pokorny, 1959), which contains within
its root the symbolic union of separation and of belonging. *Selbha*

is compounded of *se*, meaning away, separated, for, or by, itself;   5
and *bho*, which refers to cohesive totality – compare Gothic *sibja*.
Old High German *sippe* (kin, kinsfolk, totality of one's own
people), English dialect *sib* (related by blood), Latin *Sabini*
(members of the clan), Indo-European *suebho* (belonging to
one's own people, free): hence Russian *o-soba* (person) and Old
Ecclesiastical Slavonic *svoboda* (freedom, originally meant as the
status of the members of the clan).

The other important root is *poti*, or self in the Indo-European
languages. Thus Old Indian *pati* (lord or master), Greek *posis*
(mighty), Old Latin *potic sum* (I can), *potoir* (I seize upon).

Two striking motifs emerge in the etymology of the self
concept: one, that of belonging to a clan but, associated with
this, the notion of freedom and individuality; the other that of
omnipotence of the individual self.

For psychology, etymology cannot be more than a sign-post
for what ordinary people mean when the self as an idea is
mentioned. Psychology needs an overall conceptual definition
from which it can argue and make theory. This would include a
reassessment of the contribution from cognitive, behaviourist
and psychodynamic schools, bearing in mind recent relevant
evidence from physiological studies and from the philosophy of
psychology. The most broadly based conception from which to
extend elements of self theory is that postulated by Jung, the
Swiss psychiatrist and analytical psychologist. Jung's theory and
that of the Freudian school will be thoroughly evaluated in this
book and a new model of the self's ego-processes attempted,
grounded on theoretical ideas from both major schools of depth
psychology. The critical and empirical influence of other historical
contributions to self theory will be considered. More specifically,
the empirical evidence of infant and child psychology will be
culled as supporting evidence for a new self/ego model.

Jung worked throughout his life in reformulating a description
of a theoretical self concept, and in 1959 stated one of its problems:

6   The concept of psychic wholeness necessarily implies an
     element of transcendence on account of the existence of uncon-
     scious components. Transcendence in this sense is not equi-
     valent to a metaphysical postulate or hypostasis; it claims to be
     no more than a borderline concept . . . (Jung, 1959b, p.143)

Another problem for a concept of self in Jungian psychology is
that the archetypes of the collective unconscious, as projected into
consciousness, are thought to bring affects which influence the
formulation of psychologists' self postulates in both self-
experience and in the study of the self. Jung derived the idea
of the archetypes from the archetypal images represented, for
example, by the gods in mythological systems. Archetypes
generally were introduced to account for regularities observed in
dreams and imagination. Although Jung worked mainly with
adults, Michael Fordham (1976) observed that in studies of
children evacuated from London during World War II the child's
psyche was seen to be making a separate archetypal contribution,
divorced from an intrusion of the parents' unconscious into the
child's dream life. Moreover, the evacuated child's range of
neurosis, behaviour disorder, psychosomatic diseases and
psychoses suggested that more than the home, past or present, was
responsible. Fordham has published his collection of children's
archetypal dreams in *The Life of Childhood* (1944) and developed
this theme in *Children as Individuals* (1969). Images of the self can
be easily observed in children's symbolic material and are widely
reported by many therapeutic schools.
     Fordham believes that the Jungian theory of archetypes brings
body and psyche together because the archetypes are described as
unconscious states or entities having two poles: one an expression
of instinctual force and drives, the other expressed in the form of
fantasies. The instinctual drives would be relatively few in number
and fixed, while the fantasy component 'has wide and flexible
applications'. Therefore one is stating theoretically that a child

has a predisposition for developing archaic ideas and feelings which are neither only introjects, nor implanted. Suitable imagery enables the unconscious archetypal ideas to find expression in consciousness.

Education presumably influences archetypal ideas, and parents build on the child's archetypes when they mediate the culture patterns within which a developing organism is living. So there is both an outer (projective, introjective, identifying) and an inner (archetypal) influence which gives regularity to the affect associated to archetypal images. This interaction between unconscious archetype and traditional environmental components causes a reinforcement between the two aspects.

It will be necessary, in tracing back the archetypes to early infancy, to show how they are reflected in early physical object relationships. The infant is first concerned with what is transmitted to his body, the quality of that experience and what he can do with these objects. But what may the infant be bringing to this early experience from his own psyche?

In this study I assume a neo-Kantian position: from birth, or shortly before, the mind brings meaning-framing 'premises' or categories of understanding to what Rychlak (1976) describes as a 'proforma' or going towards a formal sense. These are precedent categories, conceptual and not necessarily primarily constituted as in the Lockean model of *tabula rasa* upon which a stimulus-response set is built up into a hierarchy of behavioural habits. The Kantian theoretical position and that of Jung when dealing with support of the idea of the self as a central archetype are very similar. Both Kant and Jung argued that we must bring things in the mind down to empirical test. This allows, however, for a contribution from mind to the empirical result. A purely material and efficient-cause description – that is, a mechanist explanation – is here rejected for a humanistic approach which comments from an introspective perspective in an attempt to 'see things the way the conceptualizing intellect sees them' (Rychlak, 1976).

8   Humanism contends that the individual self contributes to the flow of events and makes a difference. This contention is fundamental to this study of the self/not-self polarity in the early development of childhood.

I shall introduce a new model of the ego-processes as a framework for further research. This self/ego model postulates an original conception of 'integrates' which have special dynamic relation to the ego-processes.

In initiating a more extended theory of the ego, two ideas were fundamental: (1) that existing ego theory was not sufficiently related to contemporary empirical studies, and these areas needed to be brought together; (2) that the relationship of the ego-process to the self concept as a paradigm for individual psychology needed further elucidation, defence and theoretical amplification. To the extent that this study achieves its purpose, a further step will have been taken towards the full clarification of the self as it constellates its ego-process.

Psychologists have been diffident in recent times about extending ego theory. The disarray in the field concerning the postulates of ego-function is marked. In proposing a model for the ego-process, carefully elucidated and growing out of the most substantial historical work in ego psychology that precedes it, I have attempted to confront the psychological professions with systematic and thoroughly argued theory. I attempt to define the terms 'ego' and 'self' with clarity and to make formulations parsimonious throughout. Presentation of the ego-process in a flow diagram follows the precept that scientific explanation should demonstrate the 'most with the least'. A theory should be a simplifying statement.

In searching for the ways in which the infant ego conceptualizes its inputs I came to discover, for reasons I will explain later, that an integrating or clustering pattern of ego subsystems builds up; these I have named 'con-integrates'.

The 'con-integrates' theory, my new theory about self-integrates in ego-process, is postulated to show how a large number of apparently different inputs to the ego system have much in common in their processing within the ego-process structure and become integrated as separate structural components in my new ego-process model. The possibilities for predictability studies should be much enhanced by my theory of the con-integrates and their related memory systems. Empirical work must contain the context that gave it its motivation for study: man's subjective experience of self and its ego-processes. The theory of the self objectivizes this subjective set of facts in a hierarchical construct – parsimonious and partially testable in that its postulates are open to falsification – which provides an exciting heuristic orientation to ego psychology of great explanatory power.

The reader should not be concerned about new words being introduced here; they will all be carefully defined and discussed in the body of the book. It seemed appropriate to indicate here and now, using these technical and formal words briefly without full definition at this stage, the area this book covers and the new elements it contains for further study and research.

2. Psychology and the self: the need for a self/ego-integrates theory

Most of the group of 'self' psychologists who worked in the United States after 1900 neglected the childhood self as the working basis of their theories. For this reason, of W. James, C.H. Cooley, G.H. Mead, R.B. Cattell, E.H. Erikson, A.H. Maslow, P. Lecky, A. Angyal, H.S. Sullivan, K. Horney, E. Fromm, C. Rogers, K. Goldstein, W. McDougall and G. Allport, only the theories of Sullivan and Allport and the work of Heinz Kohut (discussed in Chapter II, 3, b–5) closely relate to the body of work being extended here about childhood self.

Sullivan drew attention to the fact that subjects with differing available concepts focused on different aspects of the 'same' stimulus. For self-behaviour this is interesting, because two similar behaviours may not have similar self conceptions behind them. The monitoring of self by appraisal and the differentiation of self/not-self is well introduced by Sullivan (1953), but like the other workers in America he treated the self as merely persisting and consistent behaviour; this was his measure of the self throughout personal development.

My own model for the infant's early ego-development within the self/ego-integrates topography, proposed in Chapter VI, puts forward a system for processing information as part of an integrated self which is a process and dynamic consistent with empirical behaviour of infants but also contains enough flexibility through its repression, memory and deintegration processes to allow theoretically for all behaviours: Sullivan's idea that consistent behaviour is a sufficient measure of self is repudiated by my work on infant self, which is psychologically grounded in the self theory of Jung and Fordham and contains my own extension in ego-integrate theory. This is prepared by the first five chapters of this book, and its structural/dynamic model is presented in Chapter VI. Chapter VII contains an illustrative and vivid clinical example of how my theory emerges in therapy with children. For now, I will briefly sketch Sullivan's line of thought about self and my objections to it.

Although Sullivan argued for consistency of behaviour as the teleological goal of self, I would argue that early archetypal infant behaviour provides the only area where some consistency can be observed. This is especially so during the infant's early ego-development when the baby begins making matches between inner and outer images which become the beginning of ego-integrate differentiation. I will be discussing and extending the theory of how the ego develops from the infant self throughout this book.

Later behaviour is much too varied and complex to be consistent, as measured by external means over time; Sullivan seems not to have considered this point. As the ego develops, together with its integrates, the range of self-behaviour would undercut any possible externally measured consistency of self across a large population except in extremely general terms, such as introversion-extroversion as a typology or the functional types (sensation, intuition, thinking and feeling).

Sullivan discussed the 'good-me' and 'bad-me' concept in babies and concentrated his interest on anxiety states picked up from the mother. He reduced all early experience at the breast to 'nothing but' a reactivity based on the degree of ego-security the child achieved at feeding. In not dealing with the archetypal images as a prefigurative read-out during self/ego development, Sullivan falls into the trap of supposing that the ego's only concern is defence. In relating my own extended theory of infant self to the ego I have tried to reveal an integral set of developing ego-areas that influence the developing self. All these may contain an element of defence, like an immune system in the body, but they contain many other dynamics as well, especially the archetypally influenced dynamics the reader will discover later on.

Allport (1961) looked at self in young infants and believed in a functional autonomy; however, his Freudian orientation precluded his understanding of Jung's collective unconscious and its important archetypal contribution to the child's self. This will be reviewed at length in Chapter I. Allport named all ego-functions the 'propriate' functions. He thought that the baby's self-experience during the first three years consisted of a 'self-body' sense, a 'self-identity' and a 'self-esteem'. He described the role of the ego by stating that no self/ego acts as an entity distinct from the remainder of the personality. In the archetypal sense – with which Allport never dealt – this is true, for unless the collective and personal unconscious can be adapted to ego-behaviour through image-matches that build up and reintegrate into the ego's conscious process, the personality disintegrates. However, the ego can function at a conscious level independently of its integrates in that it can use its repression system and control what enters the self for conscious dynamic use. This can prevent disintegration through self-defence within ego-defence systems.

My contention is that the ego is a process, not a complex, as Jung thought, and the flow-diagram (Chapter VI) of the ego's dynamics, showing its theoretical structural mechanism, is perhaps the solution to Allport's dilemma. For example, it should be possible to include all Allport's developmental self-functions in my model. Allport names those developing after the age of three as self-extension, rational thinking, self-image, propriate striving and the function of knowing. It is endemic as a necessity to the ego's deintegration–reintegration developmental pattern (discovered by Michael Fordham, see Chapter I) that a great range of ego-material is accepted by the self/ego system for use and storage.

The con-integrate ego system attempts to make clear how the ego-match to archetypal images and recognizable self-objects develops the personality from infancy. Such a system can theoretically operate to create the genius level of a Mozart or a Menuhin in infancy or the result at the other end of the same spectrum, the autistic infant (see Chapter III).

3. The research situation

The reader may need now to become more aware that as all activities, functions and structures of the psyche are subject to development, a theoretical requirement has been a clearer differentiation between ego and self and a more detailed developmental ego concept for the first years of life. My con-integrate theory modifies ego/self theory by suggesting that the ego-conglomerates are vital support systems for ego-processes; it is an extension of Jung's and Fordham's theories and an outgrowth of their work. It is also an extension of, and part of, the scientific series of theories explained in Chapter V as essential to science's own development.

How will other child psychologists support these theories? It is widely agreed that the development of ego-process depends on hereditary aspects, aspects pertaining to intrauterine and intraparture events and early postnatal experience. In reviewing empirical studies, Schaffer (1971) proposes that the neonate has a structure that predetermines apprehension of the external world and a stimulus barrier affecting selection. Continuous adaptation transforms patterns of structure cognitively so that the baby changes his response patterns over time. By the tenth month, Schaffer suggests, an internal scan exists in children with which to match external image to internal image. Together with Fordham (1958b, 1969, 1976) I believe this match occurs during the first weeks of life and that the Fordhamian theory of deintegration-reintegration ego-process, which will be carefully restudied in Chapter I, is present early on in the baby. The development of an enmeshing, entraining intensity of interaction between self and other is empirically supported by 100 scientific papers quoted in just one review of child development by Shaffer and Dunn (1979).

It will be important to help the reader to understand that the work of depth psychologists like Jung and Fordham can be seen to gain support from experimental child psychologists like Spitz, Ende and Metcalf (1970) and Harmon and Ende (1971) quoted in the very next paragraph. I shall continue to combine this kind of contrasting but supportive evidence from different empirical workers at many places throughout the presentation of my argument.

A particular and relevant example of research is by Spitz, Ende and Metcalf (1970) who recorded a clearly defined change in babies in the third month. Quiet sleep, rapid eye movement states, changes in smiling patterns and the introduction of the adult form of the EEG sleep-spindle pattern started at this time. These changes would suggest empirical evidence for correlates with my theory of the initial and rapid development of the ego-integrates at the level I name as 'con-integrates'. These build up

14   through the deintegration–reintegration process, and the changes found in laboratory testing by Spitz *et al.* are actually a part of the ego-integrate development in the self. For example, exogenous smiling independent of the infant's endogenous needs begins to occur after six to twelve weeks. Actions of anticipation based on memory become present and directed action is seen by the third month. This third-month development suggests that some of the con-integrates which I shall be proposing are already starting to function. Whereas endogenous smiling is present in even a microcephalic infant with no functioning cerebral tissue (Harmon and Ende, 1971) and is believed to be mediated by the brain stem, the change to exogenous smiling between six and twelve weeks marks the increased function of the ego and its integrates between the inner and outer world of the baby.

The great challenge to empirical study of the con-integrates is that it is essential to include experimental criteria of what only the subject knows about his own behaviour, not just what another can measure. In the young child it is notoriously difficult to interpret experimenters' description and interpretation of early language, but archetypally projected images can be studied by photographing the child's art or sand-play creations while taping any spoken interaction and photographing the child's movements and manner of using toys. Where the function of the archetypes (Chapter I) is not included in the psychological study of early childhood, empirical work may remain full of disparate detail in hundreds of thousands of experiments unrelated to any complete theory of the self/ego, hence becoming both parenthetical and perseverative. Babies cannot be reduced to organism or process alone. They are persons, and however obscure the form of the personal has remained in psychology as a whole, the self/ego system is inevitably involved in behaviour. As the self is mediated by the ego's constructions and interpretations as agent, experimentalists run a danger of incompleteness in that statements about personality should include deductions both from laboratory data and from the self-evaluation of those tested, where age allows.

The predictive capacity of experiments is questioned in Chapter V because the individual self cannot predict itself. This will be discussed at length, as it suggests that experimentalists may need to revise the goals they are trying to achieve. The ego and the con-integrates have sufficient freedom of response within their archetypal framework to be simultaneous agents of the psyche. This precludes laboratory measurement of past behaviour as totally predictive of future behaviour. The influence of outside objects and their study neglects the fact that the self/ego system can adapt its interpretation and meaning concepts constantly so that over time the person's interactions change. The standpoint of the agent is in flux.

A parallel study to this idea, concerning the indeterminism of self-prediction, is found in Popper's work (see Popper and Eccles, 1977). While the probability of events may be predicted from precise information – provided that similar conditions are present for their occurrence – events between the subject and object and their closed system of interaction lead to unpredictability. Popper points out that it is impossible for a calculator to have up-to-date information about itself. I assert here that it may also be impossible for the self, in each ego-decision process, to be up to date with the present and complex incoming demands. Past states can be explained in detail. It is self-prediction while constantly interacting with an ongoing self-system that cannot be accurate. The interaction introduces into the system a disturbance whose magnitude is unpredictable.

If a standpoint within this total ongoing action of self – the self/ ego-integrates system proposed here – is not the paradigm for psychology, the alternative is a scattered, broken-up set of aggreg-ates of extreme psychological specializations lacking coherence or an organizing principle. That situation needs a scientific remedy. Disconnected data demand a self theory inclusive of

16   childhood leading on through to old age. Hypotheses need a
developmental procedure that is open to what persons of any age
can do and become. The self and the ego-integrates are the
processing systems which can include a knowledge of what the
person knows about his own behaviour as well as what others
observe that behaviour to be.

The amalgam of inner and outer experience of self/ego, including the
repeated experiencing of the archetypes, is the totality within which
psychology should be conducting its investigations.

Personality is not only what it seems to be for others, it is also
what one knows it to be oneself. It is both about what one can do
and about what is experienced in the doing. Action is experiential.
This gives two sorts of proposition that lead on to higher-order
theoretical propositions: one of the behavioural action and one of
the experience of the actor.

4. The philosophical position

In this reappraisal of the self concept I have assumed for
theoretical purposes that Kant's 'transcendental deduction' in
his _Critique of Pure Reason_ (1788) is a philosophical basis for
arguing the general approach I have used. A summary of those
elements of Kant's arguments with which the self concepts deal
would be:

1. all experience includes a plurality of sensory elements, and for
these to be seen as subsumed by a single consciousness it must be
possible to posit a self which is able to be conscious of itself;
2. judgements are required to bring elements together into a
potentially self-conscious experience so that experience is united
by a propositional form;
3. an equivocation about self-consciousness would be that there
are differing kinds: a. a minimal self-consciousness; b. a reflective
awareness during experience that one is having experience; c. a

full consciousness of a persisting self requiring inbuilt judgements about the self's past for its conceptualizing;

4. there is a structural element in the conception of experience that we can make intelligible to ourselves which is pervasive, based on experience and related to self as a way of functioning and of knowing or experiencing. (This is the self-totality framing the self/ego as its 'centre' control of action-interpretation.)

In the use of concepts to aid the interpretation which the self may use about itself, I refrain from citing Kant's belief in cause and effect as applicable to any and all experience: rather, I present the enlargement of the self/ego theory as the self's structural/dynamic system without touching on the philosophical arguments of strict causal theories. They are outside our direct concern. What can be said is that the self is a required unity if the psyche is to make experience coherently conceivable in a single consciousness. The subject may or may not ascribe each item of psychological experience to his own self-behaviour; although he must be able to do so in theory, he may not be so self-conscious as actually to do so (see Autism, Chapter III). Mental recognition that contains concepts requires a span of memory if experience is to become fully conscious and involve a duality of apperception of what the ego deals with and may record in memory within the stream of outer and inner input to it; and of concept in terms of a structural self-system in which the ego can allocate this totality cognitively within the flow of ego-process.

These representations of apperception and concept belong to ' . . . a single consciousness in the sense that they are remembered, compared, and so on . . .' (Mackie, 1974), but they may not be seen as belonging to a single consciousness in the psychopathology of self, as in the contrast between 'mine' and 'not mine' in object relations. Strawson sums up the position regarding the need for a self conception in *The Bounds of Sense*.

. . . any course of experience of which we can form a coherent

18   conception must be, potentially, the experience of a self-conscious subject and, as such, must have such internal, concept-carried connectedness as to constitute it (at least in part) a course of experience of an objective world, conceived of as determining the course of that experience itself. (1966, p. 117)

The con-integrates are proposed as the self's chief concept-carriers. They function under the direction of the ego and unify the self's objective input to its own subjective connectedness of experiencing. The influence of the archetypes is seen as that of the *a priori* categories of universal human experience as they read out in projection from the collective level of the unconscious. The archetypes contribute a degree of regularity within the self's innate propensity to interpret sequences of impressions as unity within complexity, but their influence over time will be altered by the ego's propensities.

5. *The author's map*

In approaching the path of this book's content, I wish to provide the reader with an ideational map which sets out clearly the terrain and direction of passage through the argument and scientific conjecture contained within it. I am indebted to the concept of convergence in scientific advancement of theory which Thomas Kuhn (1963) has elaborated. Kuhn describes convergent thinking as based on the best consensus of work within the scientific area under discussion. Then convergent thinking also leads on to new theory growing out of existing theory as branches grow out and upwards from a tree trunk. This manner of scientific advance is a step-by-step process.

Divergent thinking, or the freewheeling rejection of old solutions in psychology for a striking out in far-flung directions, is here put aside for convergent thinking about self theory in psychology and its extension through research which may over time diverge to more radical conclusions. This book attempts to move from a historically grounded reassessment of existing self theory in both the academic and the depth psychologists' fields to an extension of ego theory, the ego developing out of self and becoming self's agent of consciousness.

New theories about this process need a reason for being of value to scientific advance and to clinical application. What is wrong with existing ego theory? This will be appraised with a view to presenting a new explanatory model of the child's self in its ego-cognitive process with support drawn from many psychological approaches to show its potential and implications for a child's ego-development. This study is looking at the first three to four years of the infant self. In Chapter VII a case study will illustrate an example of the clinical use of the new theory of infant self from my analytic practice. This brings theory down to earth in its human documentation.

Self theory needs both theory and documentation. My map for the book has kept these two forces ever present along the reader's way. It is not, however, the task of the theoretician to provide complete empirical evidence. This volume does contain extensive evidence, and other workers in the field can continue to build that up.

I wish the reader a good trip – at the right pace, with sufficient time and concentration – through this book's known terrain and its newer, unknown terrain. The reader's own self will be the passport needed to traverse the borders it crosses. I hope this passport will have some blank pages in it on which can be stamped the reader's record throughout the reading tour. This journey has many implications for all readers interested in the pilgrimage of self every child must begin and which every adult has made psychologically, perhaps without 'knowing' or discovering all its ramifications. I hope this introduction has now prepared my reader for departure to begin the new adventure of *The Self in Early Childhood*.

Chapter I

The contribution of Jung and the neo-Jungians to self psychology

The words of a dead man . . . Are modified in the guts of the living.
W.H. Auden, 'In memory of W.B. Yeats'

1. The Jungian background

The history of depth psychology, as it evolved from the psychoanalysis of Freud to the analytical psychology of Jung, has shifted from ego as a separate theoretical entity without a self theory in which to be subsumed to an ego theory as a part of a total self-system. The neo-Freudians including Donald Winnicott and Heinz Kohut, will be treated at length in the next chapter, as they are a part of the bridge towards but not reaching the full exposition of ego/self theory which Jung's psychology of self had already built. Michael Fordham has extended ego theory as a systemic developmental process in which the ego separates from self and reintegrates as the operating centre of self-consciousness. This has clarified theoretically the relation of ego and self. In this chapter I will introduce the contribution of Jung and Fordham against which to compare other psychologies as an approach to understanding the development of self in early childhood.

As a background to my discussion of Jung and Fordham, it is important to recognize that Freud essentially looked at man in terms of his personal history and found in the child–parent interrelationships the elements which determined the healthy and/ or pathological development of the individual. This genetic and personalistic view led to an emphasis on childhood analysis. Jung, however, moved away from a preoccupation with only the personal to look at a transpersonal factor in the psyche – the archetypes of the collective unconscious – which in his theory determine man's development, aided or abetted by experience. A person's experience creates contrasts to, and conflicts with, the 'read-out' of archetypal material through the stages of life-development from birth to death.

If emphasis is laid purely on empirical and clinical factors in depth psychology there is a danger to the practitioner: he may be unconscious of his own theoretical preconceptions. Jung was an empiricist, but his theory of the psyche is constructed on both a grand and a rich scale. Conversely, when empirical material is almost unmanageable due to its complexity, as it is in the work about the psychology of early childhood, it pushes scientists to build theories that differentiate aspects or a part of the whole. But without a superordinate self theory it will be difficult to keep open the farthest parameters within which scientific inquiry can properly move in the dynamic study of the first years of life. The balancing act required in the avoidance of these two dangers in their extreme forms is one of my goals in writing this book.

a. The nature of archetypal image

As the subject and object of cognition are of the same nature in the science of psychology – that is, both are interpreted by one and the same psyche in a psychological manner and then also studied psychologically – it can be said that any or all psychologies must share this interpretative challenge. Jung came to the conclusion that beyond causal relations and manifestations in time and space within consciousness and the personal unconscious there must lie a transpsychic reality, or collective unconscious, where a relativization of time and space occur. Physics has investigated the discontinuities in subatomic processes and has also, within modern science, been confronted with the problem of the relativity of time and space.

Analytical psychology, formed on Jung's contribution and

widely extended by others both before and since his death in 1961, is based principally on the study of the archetypes. Jungian psychology has an object to study and a method by which to study it. The object is the 'objective psyche', which Jung originally referred to as the collective unconscious. This part of the unconscious is held to differ fundamentally from more personal material which has been repressed into the 'personal unconscious' because of incompatibility in terms of its acceptability from the conscious standpoint. The personal unconscious is what Freud emphasized in his model of the unconscious (see Diagram 1 for the Jungian schema of the unconscious). In the objective psyche or collective unconscious there is a second kind of material, expressing primordial collective forms that influence the way conscious material is experienced and which Jung compared to a crystal:

> The form of these archetypes is perhaps comparable to the axial system of a crystal which predetermines . . . the crystalline formation in the saturated solution, without itself possessing a material existence. This existence first manifests itself in the way that ions and then the molecules arrange themselves . . . The axial system determines . . . merely the stereometric structure, not . . . the concrete form of the individual crystal . . . and just so the archetype possesses . . . an invariable core of meaning that determines its manner of appearing always only in principle, never concretely. (Jung, 1939, p. 79)

Jung views this unconscious material as fundamentally objective in the sense that its image in consciousness can be studied. When aspects of the collective unconscious become conscious, they can be discussed as elements of the objective psyche. Jung sees the psyche as just as suitable an object for scientific study as is the world of outer material fact. The archetypes or universal patterns of perception are contrasted in definition with the term 'archetypal images', which means symbolic manifestations and the pictorial

Diagram 1

1. The ego
2. Consciousness
3. The personal unconscious
4. The collective unconscious

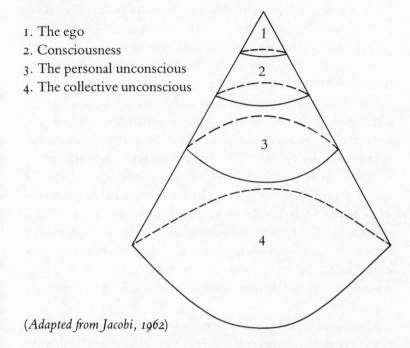

(*Adapted from Jacobi, 1962*)

expression of the archetypes: 'These belong to the knowable realm of consciousness and occur as analogous motifs in myths, fairy tales, dreams, delusions, etc., at all times and in all parts of the world' (Jaffé, 1972, p. 51).

In 1936 Jung presented an unpublished paper at Bedford College, London, in which he elaborated his view of the collective unconscious. The archetype *per se* is an unknowable factor in the collective unconscious which underlies archetypal images and contents and arranges them into typical images and groupings. Such a structuring element would be comparable to a 'pattern of behaviour' in biology which also underlies recurrently typical life-situations such as birth, change, illness, love or death. The phenomena of the collective unconscious are, unlike repressed material, transpersonal; unlike repressed contents which have

24   once been conscious, they have never been conscious before but
emerge as new to consciousness from the collective unconscious
and are represented in images. 'The hypothesis of a collective
unconscious is no more daring than to assume there are instincts'
(Jung, 1936, p.44). Instincts are likewise unconscious in functioning and transcend personal considerations.

The theory of the collective unconscious and its organs, the
archetypes, is based on an assumption that the fundamental
structure of the psyche is uniform. If we could eliminate the
conscious, Jung believed, there would be little or no difference
between one human being and another (in the original unconscious psychic content). So Jung has postulated an unknown
'x', a psychoid archetype in nature, unconscious and having a
hypothetical vital principle directing the behaviour of organisms
out of which consciousness grows. When it appears consciously
it is an archetypal image which is seen to be the mental representative of instinct and which transposes the instinct into a conscious
experience.

Mindful of the distinction between the personal and the collective unconscious, Jung criticized Freud's explanation of Leonardo
da Vinci's picture *St Anne with Mary and the Christ Child*. This
was based on the fact that Leonardo had two women who served
as mother to him. Jung, in the paper entitled 'Dual mother' in
Symbols of Transformation (1956), asserted that the dual mother
theme is widespread, having motifs of rebirth, the dual descent
or twice-born, in which the culture hero has a double birth, one
human and one divine. Jung's examples in amplifying this idea
include myths around Heracles, the Pharaohs and Jesus: the rebirth
ritual was used in medical healing at the dawn of civilization; it
is found in mysticism and in infantile fantasy and is a central
concept in medieval occult philosophy. Jung concluded: 'it is
absolutely out of the question that all the individuals who believe
in the dual descent have in reality always had (or experienced)
two mothers . . .' (1959 a, p.44). He also argued, using a neurosis

where a patient appears to be deluded that he has two mothers, that the neurosis under review is not personal but a collective manifestation.

Jung began his formulation of archetypal theory in his work between 1908 and 1910 when he encountered in his patients unconscious contents which resisted integration into consciousness. This material was made evident in their dreams, symptoms and fantasies. Jung was accustomed to receive from patients a projection of archaic motives on to himself as physician. These took the form of a transfer on to the doctor of the figure of the medicine man or magician. These primordial images – a designation Jung took from a letter (*circa* 1855) from Jacob Burckhardt to a student, Albert Brown, in which Faust and other 'genuine myths' were first described as 'primordial images' – were seen to have four regularly appearing qualities which Jung thought to be: repetition as a universal across races; constancy within the races; a fascinating effectiveness or numinosity setting archetypal images apart from other images; and regularity within each individual's life.

In Latin, 'arche' is the beginning or primary cause and 'type' is imprint. 'The religious point of view understands the imprint as the working of an imprinter; the scientific point of view understands it as the symbol of an unknown and incomprehensible content' (Jung, 1944b, p. 17). Jung was not the first to be concerned with archetypal images. In the *Symposium* Plato described images, schemata and inherited functional possibilities such as knowledge of universals that are supposed to be innate. In ethnology Adolf Bastian (1860) was the first to draw attention to the widespread occurrence of certain 'elementary ideas'. Hubert and Mauss (1898) called *a priori* thought-forms 'categories': 'They exist ordinarily as posits which govern consciousness, but are themselves unconscious.'

Jung thought it a mistake to suppose that the psyche of a

26   newborn child is a *tabula rasa* or blank slate in the sense that there
       is absolutely nothing in it:

> In so far as the child is born with a differentiated brain that is
> predetermined by heredity and therefore individualized, it
> meets sensory stimuli coming from outside itself not with
> general aptitudes, but with specific ones, and this necessarily
> results in a particular, individual choice and pattern of appercep-
> tion. (1959a, p. 66)

Jung developed this idea when speaking of the 'child archetype':

> It is not the world as we know it that speaks out of his [the
> Australian aborigine's] unconscious, but the unknown world
> of the psyche, of which we know that it mirrors our empirical
> world in accordance with its own psychic assumptions . . .
> The archetype does not proceed from physical facts; it describes
> how the psyche experiences the physical fact . . . (1959a, p. 154)

Archetypes contain essentially mythological facts which have
numerous centres, or nodal points. These essential groupings
display themselves over and over again with the same ideas and
functions. Some of the archetypes are the 'shadow', the 'wise old
man', the 'earth mother' and the '*puer aeternus*'. They are best
described metaphorically. The archetypes occur at ethnological
level as myths, and their effect is strongest where consciousness
is weakest and most restricted and where fantasy can overrun the
facts of the outer world:

> . . . this condition is undoubtedly present in the child . . . the
> archetypal form of the divine syzygy (or conjunction of male
> and female) first covers up and assimilates the image of the real
> parents until, with increasing consciousness, the real figures of
> the parents are perceived – often to the child's disappointment.
> (Jung, 1959a, p. 67)

The psyche is seen as a self-regulating system, the unconscious having compensatory capabilities to correct deficiencies in conscious adaptation.

The technique of analytical psychology has been to find means to raise the contents of the collective unconscious to consciousness and to interpret their meaning. The techniques of free association and dream analysis are too well known to need amplification here. Active imagination, used by the Jungian school, needs more definition as it is not widely understood. If imagination runs free a person may create a drama in which he plays a part, or a dance or a vision. This can also be expressed through the media of clay modelling, sand-plays, painting, carving and drawing. Interpreting this material, which contains symbolic projections, necessitates its amplification by analogical method: Jung used the knowledge and viewpoint of antiquity to throw light upon the unconscious products of modern man. In a similar way the meanings of Egyptian manuscripts have been decoded by referring to archaeological finds of antiquity which occur in the symbolization of later language. Such insights and amplifications are used by Jungians to interpret symbols produced in dreams and fantasies. It is clear that Jung has expounded a theory of the unconscious and its interpretation totally different from that of Freud, who conceived of the unconscious as an infantile phenomenon. By infantile I mean that which belongs to a person's infant consciousness and is developmentally limited to this psychological material. In an interesting analogy, Fordham (1944) points out that in physiology nobody would assume that because both man and child have a heart, it is an infantile organ. In tracing back adult fantasies to childlike roots, would the Freudians discard those experiences as merely infantile deposits?

It is here, with fantasy, that Freud and Jung and their 'schools' part company. Jung asserts that the whole of fantasy life is not infantile; parts of it are an attribute of man in general in the manner of Fordham's analogy: that the heart is an organ common to the human race at all ages:

28   The unconscious bases of dreams and fantasies are only appar-
       ently infantile reminiscences. In reality we are concerned with
       primitive or archaic thought-forms, based on instinct, which
       naturally emerge more clearly in childhood than they do later.
       (Jung, 1956, pp. 28–9)

These archaic thought-forms may contain personal factors, but
impersonal motives may have great significance as well (Freud
and Jung, 1974; see Jung's letters to Freud of 15 November 1909;
10 January 1910; 30 January 1910). Jung argued that there are
ageless motives in myths, fairy tales and folklore, including ever-
repeated themes which point to the existence of symbols common
to all humanity. This led him to assume that there were impersonal
nuclear processes in the unconscious psyche – he confirmed this
on the basis of collective archaic patterns, the archetypes.

a–1. Hereditability and archetype
Freud had studied the phenomena of the unconscious entirely
within the terms of his theory of repression. He studied unconscious products historically and personalistically, falling in line
with the current contemporary view that mind was an ontogenetic
phenomenon, acquired in the course of individual development.
Jung rejected the developmental source as the only basis of the
archetypal images. He argued that archetypal themes in an
individual could not have been in his consciousness before they
emerged from the unconscious; they were not the consequence
of nurture alone. He published extensive empirical proofs to
support the contention in 'The concept of the collective unconscious' (1936).

    It is with great caution, however, that Jungian psychology calls
the archetypes hereditary factors. The notion that archetypes
are the deposits of racial experience is emphatically denied by
Weismann's (1893) theory of the continuity of germ plasm. As
the body is a by-product of the germ plasm created by the union

of the male and female cells, nothing acquired in a lifetime, in   29
body or mind, has any effect whatsoever upon germ plasm – that
is, all acquired characteristics die for ever with the body. Thus
inherited body-structure changes or change in psychic organization originate only in variable gene combinations or their structural mutations. The environment does contribute to the appearance of physical characteristics in that if an unfavourable environment occurs in the interuterine development, anomalies result.
The structurally inherited factors are those within the fertilized
ovum; psychosomatic development in addition to inherited structural factors is the product of the inherited factors and the
environment.

a–2. Instinct and archetype
In this section I want to defend a nonreductive notion of instinct,
making it more compatible with archetypal theory than I believe
it is with behaviourism. Behaviourism itself will be reconsidered
fully in Chapter V.

Jung saw that if instincts are taken to be innate patterns of
behaviour, then archetypal images are comparable with and partly
represent the instincts in consciousness. In *The Study of Instinct*
(1951), Tinbergen investigated 'sign stimuli' which release
patterns of behaviour which are initiated by a stable perceptual
system within the animal – for example the baby gull – called the
innate releasing mechanism (IRM). This selects suitable stimuli
from the perceptual field and releases the instinctual response. As
the whole behaviour system is determined by this functional
selection system, it cannot be reduced to a reflex mechanism.
Reflexes are accepted as innate. In addition spontaneous rhythmic
activities of the brain, the spinal cord and the autonomic nervous
system take part. The central nervous system does not contribute
special movements from its stimulation but its rhythmic activities
are released from an inhibitory influence by the sign stimuli acting

30 through the IRM. Thus an innate neuroendocrine system is the basis of instinctive behaviour.

Since archetypes are perceived in terms of acts and images, the organization of the brain may reveal a close relation to the organization and function of the archetypes. Neurologists have not always operated with the concepts of a neurophysiological substrate on the one hand and consciousness on the other; in the history of the eighteenth and nineteenth century several neurologists, physiologists and psychologists, following Charcot's studies in 1878 of dissociation at the Salpêtrière, became interested in the possibility of unconscious brain influence. In 1868 Despine published the view that an automatic cerebral activity manifests itself without the participation of the self (*'le moi'*), whereas the self is manifested by conscious cerebral activity. These theories of 'unconscious cerebration' as a physiological explanation for varying functions in different layers of cortical grey matter were picked up by Luys, Huxley and Maudsley. They were attacked by Bernheim (1884, 1888), since he found traces of '*le moi*' still operative as a personal style in somnambulists and suggested that this might be explained better by an increased speed of translating suggested image into action than by an unconscious cerebration.

This debate had begun already at the dawn of the eighteenth century when Bichat had distinguished between central and autonomous nervous function. Du Bois-Reymond and Helmholtz studied the transmission speed of nervous impulse and learned that the stimulus impact and its registration are not simultaneous. Reflexes, studied in the nineteenth century, emphasized the unconscious aspect of reflex action in the subject. Bernard and Brücke, as well as Du Bois-Reymond and Helmholtz, referred to unconscious homeostatic processes whereby body maintenance is regulated for biological equilibrium. Breuer, Fechner and Spencer used the notion of physiological equilibrium as well as the psychological aspects of its effect.

Flügel (1955), in discussing Spencer's psychology, mentioned the homeostatic principle in so far as 'adaptation of inner relations to outer relations' aims at a state of equilibrium. Galton (1879), in analysing word associations, inferred the importance of unconscious cerebration. Thus many eighteenth- and nineteenth-century scientists preceded Freud and later schools of depth psychology in postulating various forms of unconscious activity.

Concepts of cerebral activity – including the idea that the cortex, with the subcortical ganglia and the network of association fibres, acts as a whole – were put forward by Flourens in an 1842 paper, 'Recherches expérimentales sur les propriétés et les fonctions du système nerveux dans les animaux vertébrés'. His work on lower animals – for example rabbits, chickens, hens and pigs – enabled him to study general faculties but not individual differences. On the basis of experimental results using ablation, he postulated a unity of the cerebrum proper and its functional abilities. Localization of perception, however split up or localized this might be when mapped on the brain, was found to be dependent upon the cerebral cortex as a whole. Lashley confirmed Flourens' generalization a hundred years later.

More recent work carried on research into concepts of wholes. A study by Head *et al.* (1920) showed that patients with cerebral cortical lesions which distorted their appreciation of posture and body-image used a standard against which to measure all postural change that was not a visual or motor image; rather it lay outside consciousness and entered consciousness already in a relation to what went before, and was directly perceived as a measured postural change. A whole body schema is postulated as necessary for understanding body-image generally. Body-image was defined by Head *et al.* as an unconscious physiological disposition used as an ongoing standard of comparison for postural change.

Perception of wholes or universals relates to cybernetics (Wiener, 1948) in a brain conceptualized as dynamic and purposeful and described in terms of reverberating circuits,

32   negative feedback, scansion and oscillation. Wiener defines rever-
      berating circuits as a closed chain of neurons which can be set into
      impulse by a single incoming impulse. This impulse passes
      around the circuit until other incoming impulses change it or the
      metabolism no longer supports it. Negative feedback indicates a
      system where activity is modified when some part of the output
      returns as input.

      Wiener uses the term 'scansion', derived from television, to
      mean a rhythmic sweep of impulses through the cortex: alpha
      rhythm, for example, has been thought of as the 'smoke' of the
      rhythmic sweep. Oscillation, as opposed to rigidity, is the correct
      feedback state in a servomechanism where feedback is set to
      maintain the system in an equilibrium:

> Not only has extrapyramidal function and dysfunction been
> given a new explanation, but what is more important . . . a
> physiological interpretation has been suggested for psycho-
> logical processes, such as perception of universals . . . (Meyer
> and McLardy, 1950, p. 285)

These newer concepts of cerebral activity suggest that where
higher, more psychic activities of the brain are concerned the
cortex, the subcortical ganglia and the network of association
fibres act as a whole.

   If the theory of instincts leads to a concept of a nervous system
containing innate patterns of energy (not only reflexes), then the
analysis of the nervous system restricted to terms of reflex
mechanisms is outdated; physiologists have introduced the
concept of 'spontaneous' or self-activated rhythmic activity of
brain cells. This has been correlated, for example, with the
rhythmic activity of the infant's earliest sucking activities. With
so many higher brain activities now known to operate as a whole,
this indicates even more strongly than does the co-ordination of
muscular activity that a selfhood is implied psychically and cannot
be left out of psychological theory.

a–3. Human evolution and archetype
The evolutionary theory of Darwin brings up two problems which relate to the theory of archetypes. What origins do archetypes have, and have they undergone any evolutionary change? Jung (1953, p. 192) believed that '. . . their [the archetypes'] origin can only be explained by assuming them to be the deposits of the constantly repeated experiences of humanity'. It is clear that on present biological theory these experiences cannot be inherited. The manner of experiencing the world, however, may be the result of changes in the germ cells. To align archetypal phenomena with what is known about heredity, one can say that primitive man experienced the world in terms of archetypal images as a consequence of archetypal activity in the unconscious. Once evolution is applied to man, the enormous development of consciousness is striking. Unlike most animals, in whom evolution may fairly be described as almost 'blind', man has transmissible variants which genetically produce anatomical changes (the upright posture), new physiological processes and new instinctual patterns. Variants survive or fall by natural selection.

Since transmissible knowledge is noninheritable, schools have developed everywhere to make secure the available traditions and influence the consciousness of history. Elliot Smith (1933) of the diffusionist school of anthropology, in postulating that all the essentials of civilization began in Egypt and then diffused outwards from this single centre, forgets that diffusion depends upon the local consciousness of any area. If that consciousness is not developed enough to make use of advances from elsewhere, there is no soil for the seed. No explanation of the way assimilation of new concepts takes place is as convincing in the present state of knowledge as the Jungian school's theoretical redefinition of the problem: the conscious originates in the unconscious in its evolutionary sense. It has its first expression in images, dreams,

34   inspirations, etc. The archetypal images take a major place and
      eventually become systematized as knowledge.
         Jung believed that scientific theories themselves can be based
      on quasi-mystical experiences. Pauli (1955) discusses the influence
      of archetypal ideas in Kepler's scientific theories. He argues that
      scientific ideas and theories have developed beyond the possibility
      of experience. Accordingly it becomes necessary to question the
      nature of the bridge between sense data and their conceptualiz-
      ation. Pure logic has not been able to construct the bridge, so
      Pauli suggests that the process of scientific discovery is not based
      upon perception on the one hand and the elaboration of logical
      construction on the other:

> The process of understanding nature . . . seems to be based on
> a correspondence, a 'matching' of inner images pre-existent in
> the human psyche with external objects and their behaviour.
> (1955, p. 152)

He believes that the 'inner images' relate to archetypal image and
that scientific theory is the abstract equivalent of these archetypes:

> . . . the archetypes thus function as the sought-for bridge
> between the sense perceptions and the ideas and are, accord-
> ingly, a necessary presupposition even for evolving a scientific
> theory of nature. (1955, p. 153)

These ideas retain reason and logic in scientific discovery, but
throw into question its rationalistic basis. Rationalism has kept
this bridge between sense data and conceptualization unconscious,
and Pauli uses Kepler as an example of a religious nature that ran
side by side with abstract scientific concepts. At the root of
discovery lies an archetypal form that does not change: what does
change is the form or image it is given. Kepler's scientific
discoveries reflect religious doctrines of great antiquity. What
matters is where man's consciousness is: '. . . dream the myth
onwards and give it a modern dress' (Jung, 1949, p. 79).

b. Symbolization and mythology

Jung observed attempts at myth-making in children; from these he originated the hypothesis of a creative urge towards mythology in the psyche, a condition to which Freud objected. Jung saw a profound tension of opposites in the meaning of symbols (such as God and the Devil). In a dynamic context this led to transcending the opposites, while in content the presence of analogies facilitated symbol formation. Jung was unable to accept Freud's hypothesis that fantasy was composed of distorted phenomena. He found the Freudian conceptual framework uncomfortable:

> Besides the obvious personal sources, creative fantasy also draws upon the forgotten and long buried primitive mind with its host of images, which are to be found in the mythologies of all ages and all peoples. (1956, p. xxix)

The content of any particular image raises questions that are reflected in the use of the word 'symbol'. Stein (1957) points out the derivation of the word:

> . . . sym, i.e. *syn*, which means 'together, common, simultaneous, with, according to', and *bolon* which means 'that which has been thrown', from *ballo*, 'I throw'. 'Symbol' thus means something perceptible as the result of an activity which throws together such things as have something in common, and in such a way that one thing somehow accords with another not presented to the senses and is synchronous with it. (p. 73)

Definition is difficult. Recently neurophysiologists have called images symbolic. When it was discovered that the stimulated neurons in the brain form patterns on the cortex unlike the shape of an object under observation, it was realized that a perceptual image was inferred, and thus symbolic. In Ancient Greece symbols were tallies. This brings us closer to Jung's definition of symbol. Tallies were

36   halves of two corresponding pieces of a bone, coin, or other object which two strangers . . . broke between them in order to have proof of the identity of the presenter of the one part to the other . . . The symbol, the broken off part, is not a separate element, but carries with it and points to wherever it goes, the whole in which it has participated as well as the situation in which it was broken in half; when it is 'thrown together' and matched with the remaining half the whole has value because the symbol grips the two opposites together and so can convey – not create or apply – this value. (Stein, 1957, p. 77)

This prepares us for Jung's definition of symbol:

> . . . the symbol always presupposes that the chosen expression is the best possible description, or formula, of a relatively unknown fact; a fact, however, which is none the less recognized or postulated as existing. (1921, p. 474)

Another aspect of perception is myth. Kerenyi (1951) discusses the concept of mythologem, a word denoting the core-concept of a single myth or a class of myths. An example of a mythologem would be the 'divine child', under which Kerenyi subsumes Buddha, Cupid, Dionysus, Jesus, Krishna, Hermes, Strong Hans, Tom Thumb and others:

> In a true mythologem . . . meaning is not something that could be expressed just as well and just as fully in a non-mythological way. Mythology is not simply a mode of expression in whose stead another simpler and more readily understandable form might have been chosen. (1951, p. 3)

Jung (1950) takes the position that the psychological meaning in myth comes from the archetypes as expressed in the archetypal images corresponding to Kerenyi's mythologems. But Jung goes further and suggests that the archetypal image alone is not the symbol. He thinks that the conscious is also involved, as data from every psychic function enter into its composition. In Jung's view a symbol prevents a clear-cut observational and intellectual process as the observer gets drawn into his objects and they invoke his whole conscious activity until he is 'thrown together' into a unity. The symbolical experiences of wholeness revive again and again. This wholeness is not known outside symbolic expression, but it can be thought to relate to child images and the self-images. The root meaning of symbol does carry a reference to the concept of wholeness 'as an integrate of all those contradictory and incomprehensible elements, which when thrown together, make the whole man' (Fordham, 1957).

Children can be studied in relation to their parents and to the mythological world as well. As the child grows nearer to his inner nature via experience with the archetypes, adults can see these developments as part of the child; at first, however, they are felt as something quite other than himself. The child does not have the necessary control over these unknown symbolic forces he feels, and parents need to mediate the child's experience of the unknown; this includes both the influence of outer objects and events and the inner influence of archetypes and myths. All these factors make up the growing personality.

All analytical schools would accept that the fundamental goal of a child's development is to establish himself in the world. The goal of childhood can be compared to the goal of individuation.

c. Individuation in childhood
Jung wrote:

> Over against the polymorphism of the primitive's instinctual nature there stands the regulating principle of individuation. Multiplicity and inner division are opposed by an integrative unity whose power is as great as that of the instincts. (1960, p. 51)

Jung always retained a concept of the total personality. He was concerned with the relationship between the partial and total personality, and envisaged a totality so as to understand the particular from the whole. Thus he saw the tension between the tendency to dissociate and the inclination towards unity characteristic of life-processes. Jung's investigation of fantasies arising from the unconscious enabled him to become convinced that the image sequence not only exhibited a disorderly variety of dissociated fragments but at the same time showed a tendency towards a gradual integration. In 1934 he defined individuation again:

> It is the process of forming and specializing the individual nature; in particular, it is the development of the psychological individual as differentiated from the general collective psychology . . . Before individuation can be taken for a goal the educational aim of adaptation to the necessary minimum of collective standards must first be attained. (pp. 448–9)

At individuation, a person has to withdraw the projections of the collective psyche so that they can be considered in relation to the individual and not just accepted passively as what everybody does, thinks and feels.

The child, however, does not need to give deep consideration to what is generally accepted (Fordham, 1944). Thus he can leave a large part of his psyche projected into the world. Young children may fight social, political, military or religious views for personal reasons but not because they actually believe that their individuality (except in its collective image) is at stake. Children tend to take a collective or one-sided view, as an individual standpoint involves becoming free from one-sided tendencies through a symbolic solution which would require that opposites be given complete equality. If one were to give opposites the exact same ego-participation, a suspension or arrest of the will would result. Jung proposed a reconciling function which can move beyond the opposites and is one aspect of the psyche's individuation capability.

Individuation is contrasted with the goal of childhood, which is strengthening of ego-development; adult individuation requires a relativization to self, allowing further ego-integration with the self. In the adult, as in the child, individuation can otherwise be expressed as the realization of the self. Individuation strives towards wholeness and totality, developing the specific potentialities that form the particular personality. This unconscious dynamic matrix lies waiting for the ego to understand and incorporate these potentialities. It is entirely possible that a child may be conscious of symbolic images of the self, but cannot realize their implications. The dynamic development of self is seen as dependent upon the reaction of the unconscious to what is primarily ego-activity. I would agree with Fordham (1976) that individuation can be seen as an extension of the ego reaching out and assimilating the archetypal movements of the unconscious, as well as separating subject and object and then consciously integrating-deintegrating this potential which is postulated to contain the symbolical solution pointing towards individuation.

In *Psychological Types* (1921) Jung describes individuation as a process of differentiation, with its goal the development of the individual personality:

> Individuation is practically the same as the development of consciousness out of the original state of identity which is . . . the original non-differentiation between subject and object. (pp. 449–50)

Fordham (1976) argues that by the age of two the infant has achieved a state of physical control over body activities which are 'correlates and sometimes the expression of psychic operations'. After birth the infant, during the first weeks, develops a state of 'identity' with his mother and the environment. This identity is not primary, but develops through fusion with the mother. It is

40   inferred that the baby fuses only with those parts of the environment that correspond almost exactly to his needs; other events appear not to exist for him. This is confirmation of the theory that the primary unity of the self (expanded in section 3) exerts a conservative influence.

This phase is superseded by the omnipotence of object relations over all else as archetypal forms deintegrate more clearly out of the self and gain expression in perceptual imagery. The mother-infant unit is the most important area of study, and in the section to follow on deintegration its development is discussed at length. Here it will suffice to say that the days have passed when the infant could be thought about either as only a physiological unit or simply as an autoerotic being. He is now seen as a psychosomatic unity, relating increasingly through the first two years to all objects with his libidinal and aggressive drives. The infant uses his developing imagery by deducing and evaluating experiences with his thoughts and feelings:

> The achievement of a physical control over bodily activities means that the two-year-old has also grown psychically out of the state of identity into a separate being with an individual unit status. (Fordham, 1976, p. 39)

On this basis it can be asserted that by the age of two an infant can achieve the essential elements of childhood individuation:

> . . . he has emerged from a primitive, ruthless way of living to become a person who can show concern for others; he has known love, hate, fear, grief, sadness; he has the basic rudiments of a conscience, and he has developed a clear distinction between internal and external objects, which he evaluates as good or bad; he distinguishes an inner world from the outer; . . . he has developed true symbols that express his inner life. (Fordham, 1976, pp. 39–40)

Thus Fordham makes a strong case for using the term 'individuation', which Jung introduced referring only to the adult stages of development, for the developmental process in the first two years of childhood.

2. Jung's theories of the self

a. Self-as-totality

Jung developed two theories of the self: (1) a 'totality' theory and (2) the 'self-as-archetype' theory (1951, p. 167). The origin of the totality theory of self came from oriental formulations concerning *atman*, which is regularly translated as 'the self' in English. In *Psychological Types* (1921) Jung discusses *atman* in a footnote: 'Brahman is the designation generally applied to the Supreme Soul (param*atman*); impersonal, all-embracing, divine essence, the original source and ultimate goal of all that exists.' Putting the oriental view into a psychological frame of reference makes the self an organized wholeness of the personality. This is expressed in symbolic experience which is transpersonal and transcends the incompatible opposites of which man both psychically and physically appears to be composed: psyche, soma; ego, non-ego; inner, outer. Another source for the self-as-totality concept seems to grow out of Jung's idea of a transcendent function:

> The shuttling to and fro of arguments and affects represents the transcendent function of the opposites. The confrontation of the two positions generates a tension charged with energy and creates a living, third-thing – not a logical stillbirth in accordance with the principle *tertium non datur*, but a movement out of the suspension between opposites, a living birth that leads to a new level of being, a new situation. (1916, p. 90)

This is manifested as a quality of conjoined opposites and is closely related to the theory of the symbol, which by uniting opposites becomes the union of the conscious with the unconscious.

Jung sees one functional aspect of the self to be the meeting-place of all opposites and their synthesis. Redfearn, a neo-Jungian, states:

> The image of opposing entities meeting, with the liberation of great energy, good or bad, is so all-pervasive that it is hardly possible to exaggerate its universality and importance. This is the energy underlying, for example, primal scene excitement at its most archaic level, schizoid splitting and defences, the illuminating or blinding properties of the God image, and the individuation process. (1977, p. 140)

An example analogous to this general idea would be how easy it is today to see in society how little people are able to let the other person's argument count, although this capacity is fundamentally indispensable to a peaceful national or international community. To the degree that one does not admit the validity of the other person one denies the 'other' within oneself the right to exist, and vice versa. The inner dialogue of conscious and unconscious, which the transcendent function can enable, is a 'touch-stone for outer objectivity'.

> Thus, in coming to terms with the unconscious, not only is the standpoint of the ego justified, but the unconscious is granted the same authority [e.g. in Jungian interpretation during psychotherapy]. The ego takes the lead, but the unconscious must be allowed to have its say, too – *audiatur e altera pars*. (Jung, 1916, p. 88)

As early as 1921 the totality definition had discriminated between the ego and the self. Jung states that the self 'embraces and includes the ego' as well. It is important to distinguish the empirical ego – the ego as experienced – from the spontaneous images of imagination, or non-ego. Thus Jung saw the ego as a part system, that is, one system among others of a different kind. His formula expanded to 'self equals ego plus archetypes', which equates with

the usual definition of the self as a combination of the conscious
(ego) and the collective and personal unconscious (archetypes and
personal repressed material).

To clarify this position, I quote from Fordham:

> If the self is the whole psyche, then it cannot be observed as
> such by the ego, since the ego is contained in it as a part and
> there is hence no observer. It is only when the unity is
> deintegrated and when some part of the ego stands separate
> from or only participates up to a point in the rest of the whole
> that data about the self can be collected. The data are called
> 'symbols of the self'. (1963, p. 11)

The self as 'unknowable' became a position taken by Jung in a
passage in 'The holy men of India':

> India is 'prepsychological': when it speaks of the 'self', it posits
> such a thing as existing. Psychology does not do this . . .
> though very well acquainted with the self's peculiar and
> paradoxical phenomenology, we remain conscious of the fact
> that we are discussing . . . something essentially unknown and
> expressing it in terms of psychic structures. (1944a, p. 580)

However, by deriving inferences from the data of each incomplete
symbol, it does seem on reflection that a theoretical construct,
not testable more directly than with the derived symbolic
material, can be made. The self as a whole would then remain
inexperienceable rather than unknowable in a theoretical sense.
There is, too, the question of hypostatizing a scientific thought –
treating a scientific inference as if it were a known empirical fact.
Jung implies hypostatization when he describes individuation as
'realization of the self'. He seems to mean that inner experiences
are to be given equal status with the facts of the external world.
It is clear and fair to say, I think, that the self as a concept of
totality is particularly difficult to construct, as the archetypal
images cannot be the actual self but only representative of it.

44   These images or approximations can represent only states of relative wholeness. Only if bits of the ego are split off and function as observers of these images can the self be inferred.

A further problem may well remain: the relation of the ego or conscious 'knowledge' to introspection and its report, such as in association with dreams or other images people discuss, and Freud's famous fear that introspections are rationalizations. Nisbett and Wilson (1977) find evidence that suggests that there may be 'little or no direct introspective access to higher cognitive processes'. Subjects tend to give reports based on *a priori*, implicit causal theories, or to judge if what they report seems 'plausible'. Nisbett and Wilson conclude that introspection will be more accurate if influential stimuli are salient as plausible causes of the responses they produce. Tversky and Kahneman (1974) agree that if a stimulus seems 'representative of the kind of stimuli that influence the response in question, the stimulus is reported to have an influence on the response, otherwise it is thought to be non-influential'.

Wason and Evans (1975) assume two processes: a type I process underlying behaviour and unavailable to consciousness (like Jung's archetypes) and a type II process underlying protocols and available to consciousness (like Jung's ego-bits that interpret the archetypes in the earliest ego-development in infancy). The relationship between these two processes is theoretically developed by Fordham's deintegration theory (see section 3). E. Valentine (1978) points out that the relation between these two types of process (unconscious and conscious) is one of the least investigated problems in psychology. It has, of course, been the underlying theoretical and empirical preoccupation of Jung and later his 'school' of analytical psychology since about 1920, but is often ignored by other workers in psychology.

Another aspect of conscious report is the influence of subliminal perception in introspection. Acceptance of subliminal perception has largely rested on laboratory methodological innovations in the forum of signal detection techniques and dichotic listening procedures with different stimuli given to each ear of the tested person (Wilson, 1975). Persuasive theoretical arguments have been put forward by Erdelyi (1974) which derive the subliminal phenomena from notions of selective attention and filtering. Many more stimuli are apprehended than can be stored in short-term memory or transferred to long-term memory, so subliminal perception, which has previously regarded as paradox – how can one perceive without perceiving? – would be a logical consequence of selective filtering. We can perceive without remembering. Some stimuli may affect ongoing mental processes – including higher-order processes of evaluation, judgement and behaviour initiation – without being registered in short-term memory or, in any case, without transfer to long-term memory. This also indicates that where subliminal perception is operating subjects might not be aware of influential stimuli, and therefore that these stimuli are unconscious: this brings us back full circle to Wason and Evans' type I process, unavailable directly to consciousness, and to Jung's archetypal construct of the collective unconscious.

b. The ego–self relationship

The ego–self relationship needs further elucidation. Ego theory has been much argued by and among Jungians. Basically, Jung (1921) described the ego as a 'perceptual system which has affective roots in the unconscious'. He defined the ego as a relatively independent centre of consciousness, the agent of repression and of both the internal and external defence systems. Jung postulated an unconscious ego, or 'shadow', using this metaphorical term, as he always did, as his specific 'jargon' for unconscious contents.

This systemic relationship between ego and its unconscious ego-shadow as always having the possibility of permeating ego for its integration and psychic equilibrium, in Jungian formulation, is in sharp contrast to Freud's ego-repression system. In Freud's

46 theory, ego can repress ego-material into the unconscious as 'bad' (as opposed to 'good') objects for the ego to survive in psychological equilibrium at a given time. But because in Jung's theory the ego innately emerges at least in part from its own shadow, which is at both personal and collective levels of the unconscious, Jungians believe that early in childhood the perceptual and integrative functions of the ego become differentiated from the essentially unconscious archetypal structure. Jung's postulation of an unconscious ego-shadow is a radical departure from Freudian ego theory, and ego-shadow in my own theory of ego 'con-integrates' (Chapter VI) is claimed as a further extension of Jungian ego-shadow from the study of childhood development.

Arguments have arisen over the way Jung uses both metaphor and abstraction in his description of the self and the ego:

> The term 'self' seemed to me a suitable one for the unconscious substrate, whose actual exponent in consciousness is the ego. The ego stands to the self as *the moved to the mover*, or as object to subject, because the determining factors which radiate out from the self surround the ego on all sides and are therefore supraordinate to it. *The self,* like the unconscious (archetypes), *is an a priori existent* out of which the ego evolves. It is, so to speak, an unconscious prefiguration of the ego. (1958, p. 259)

Fordham (1960) points out that the phrase above (which I have emphasized for clarity of reference), '*moved to the mover*', is metaphorical and that the phrase 'The self . . . is an *a priori* existent' is an abstraction. This distinction is important. For Neumann (1955) began writing about the ego and the self as two separate entities. If the ego is defined as a part of the self, it cannot be a separate entity. What Neumann does is to *abstract Jung's metaphor* in his theory so that the self does not equal the ego plus the unconscious, but the ego is discussed as an independent aspect not contained within the self. Neumann selects one aspect of the ego's selection to self and hypostasizes it.

Following in this theoretical confusion, Edinger (1960) describes the task of the child at first as one of separating out the ego from the self. He then suggests that there is a repeating tendency to alternate between self–ego union and self–ego separation. Thus all development is seen as a continuous dialectic between ego and self, leading paradoxically to both greater separation and greater intimacy. This implies that the ego has functional autonomy, which Neumann also believed. The paradox would be that if the ego is autonomous it would become 'inflated'; on the other hand, if it is dependent and determined by a superordinate force, it remains 'irresponsible'.

But Fordham (1960) points out that the paradox may be removed by considering the self not so much as a total integrate – both conscious and unconscious – but as an ordered number of systems that result from division of the integrate into part systems, all subject to the functioning of the organism as a whole. There is assumed to be a total integrate in infancy which may be considered the original state of the self. This deintegrates in instinctual experience conceived as a release mechanism:

> The result is intense perceptual stimulation and as one result the ego starts to separate out and develop. At the end of any particular instinctual experience the organism integrates again and in this way the experiences become built into the whole organism. (Fordham, 1957, pp. 12–13)

In the Jungian view the archetypes, being the instincts and their unconscious fantasy representations, are also thought to separate out from the integrated whole, as does the ego, in the instinctual experience. They also integrate again afterwards.

Piaget, in *Insights and Illusions of Philosophy* (1972), is critical of prereflective experience as a notion and sees a contradiction between the idea of prereflective experience as the origin of knowledge and the unchanging background for acts of interpretation (such as archetypal material) and the idea that intentional

48   consciousness (ego) is continually creating new meanings during development. Jung, however, saw no real contradiction in that Jungian interpretation of the symbolic images of archetypes is rightly determined by the developmental status of the individual and the appropriate level given the interpretation within this development. With this qualification of interpretation there is no problem *vis-à-vis* an unchanging unconscious archetypal given as the theoretical source behind symbolic material. The Jungian view is that the self-images symbolize a central integrative system and the self is thus seen as something like a central ordering system. Jung contended that the ego might be able to take over all of the pattern contained in the self briefly, but that it is ultimately subordinate to it.

c. The self-as-archetype theory abandoned
The second of Jung's theories of the self, the 'self-as-archetype', causes a contradiction. In *Aion* (1951) Jung writes: ' . . . the self is the real organizing principle of the unconscious, the quaternity, or squared circle of the self.' He ambiguously implies here that the self is an archetype of order which may be seen as an organizing principle, or it may be the totality of the archetypes. The question immediately raised is: does Jung mean that the self is not the whole psyche-soma, as the ego is left out altogether in the self-as-archetype theory? The ego has been specifically differentiated from the archetypes in his general theory of the psyche (self equals ego plus archetypes). In tracing his confusing discussion between these two definitions of the self, we see that in *Aion* (and also in 1944b, 1954 and 1959b) he refers to the self as an archetype (the second definition) repeatedly but also says: 'I have suggested calling the total personality which, though present, cannot be fully known, the self. The ego, is, by definition, subordinate to the self and is related to it like a part to the whole' (the first definition: self-as-totality).

    Curiously, the concept of the self as an archetype began after the idea of it as the totality of the psyche in Jung's writings. The archetypal theory was published in 1919, two years before *Psychological Types*, where the first definition of the self appears: ' . . . the self is my totality . . . hence it includes the unconscious psyche'. There have been several attempts to deal with the two definitions. Perry (1957), in studying schizophrenia, recorded self-images related neither to integration nor to individuation. He argues that the archetype lying behind the images should be termed 'central archetype'. Jung (1958) considered this ' . . . a central archetype . . . which I have called the archetype of the self'. He observed that self-images occur in abnormal chaotic states when the relation between the ego and archetypal images gets diffused and the play of fantasy may go beyond normal psychological limits.

There are passages where Jung combines the idea of self-as-totality with that of the self-archetype. In *Aion* he writes:

> . . . definable psychic contents emerging from the unconscious indicate the psychic totality of the individual. They indicate the presence of an archetype of like nature, one of whose derivations would seem to be the quaternity of functions that orient consciousness (thinking, feeling, intuition and sensation). But, since the totality exceeds the individual's consciousness to an indefinite and indeterminable extent, it invariably includes the unconscious in its orbit and hence the totality of all archetypes. But the archetypes are complementary equivalents of the 'outside world' and therefore possess a 'cosmic' character. (1951, p. 196)

Throughout his writing Jung mixes metaphor and abstract statement and slides from one level to another. Nevertheless, neo-Jungians have considerably cleared confusion by careful study and re-evaluation of his ideas. What is perhaps most important in the Jungian theoretical definitions of the self is to bear in mind that the self contains opposites. This is not a paradox, since the

50 whole is not an opposite of its parts, but it is true that formulations about opposites may need to be stated paradoxically. Actually neither the totality theory nor the archetypal concept refers to the contents of the self directly, but to its place in the theoretical model of the psyche.

A possible revision concerning Jung's two theories of the self has been suggested by Fordham (1960). The self-as-totality theory is seen as an abstract theory of the whole personality. In dealing with a whole, we define a totality which can be seen in several different states such as integration, deintegration and dis-integration:

> The self as a totality also gives a theoretical limit to life, i.e. the organism starts from a unity (the original state of self in infancy) and ends as a unity at the end point of individuation; these two states are outside experience. (Fordham, 1963, p. 19)

The total self theory can form a basis for a full developmental theory in that it persists through life.

To supplant Jung's unsatisfactory self-as-archetype theory, Fordham (1963) proposes a central archetype of order. A central concept of ordering would indicate an archetype that deals with the succession of acts or events and attempts theoretically to place the disposition and array of the psychological substrates into a somewhat regularized rank, grade or class of scale in being. The centrality of such an archetype would indicate that it could establish, or begin to establish, some system within archetypal structure as a series of ranking or of parts subject to a uniform or eventually established hierarchy of archetypal ordering. A central archetype of order would bring meaning or meaningful premises to bear on its images in consciousness.

It is assumed that each archetypal image contains an ego-fragment which renders it conscious. This ego-fragment can become linked with the ego-centrum (or ego as the centre of consciousness in Jung) in a process which involves unconscious integrating functions. The advantages of a theory of a central archetype of order – postulated as the unconscious system behind conscious ego-formation and as a part system of the self – to replace the self-as-archetype are several. It leaves the ego a position in theory which it has always had throughout Jungian work. A central archetype can theoretically be included among the other archetypal images in consciousness, operating with the same ability for these images to be introjected, projected, assimilated to other unconscious elements, or identified with the ego consciously, etc. The central archetype would express itself in images depicting wholeness and transcending and uniting opposites in close relation to the central ego. (Its role in development will be discussed in section 3.) The self-as-totality would remain the principal definition for Jungian self theory and the self-as-archetype would be abolished in favour of the more subsidiary central archetype of order. This would be included within the basic archetypal structure Jung has proposed, and the separate ego-structure, that make up the self.

I believe Fordham offers the best theoretical solution to the contradictions in Jung's writings about self theory. I now want to introduce Fordham's ego theory, since it is the foundation on which I base my further contributions to such theory.

3. Fordham's deintegration concept

a. The childhood ego in Jungian thought

Inclusive to this view of the central archetype – but deserving attention in its own right – is Fordham's (1951) view of deintegrates, a term he created to extend the self theory into its development during infancy. In considering the background to the deintegration concept it will be helpful to develop the Jungian view of the ego's origin in childhood.

Jung (1954) saw the psychic development of children centring

52 mainly around ego-formation within natural growth. He believed
that the origin of the conscious ego was the unconscious:

> The greatest and most extensive development takes place
> during the period between birth and the end of psychic
> puberty . . . This development establishes a firm connection
> between the ego and the previously unconscious psychic
> processes, thus separating them from their source in the uncon-
> scious. In this way the conscious rises out of the unconscious
> like an island newly risen from the sea. (1954, p. 7)

The archetypes, as organs of the unconscious and possibly bound
up with the functioning of the central nervous system, are assumed
to be formed before birth, when the brain is formed. Jung
originally thought that archetypal images in children's dreams
and fantasies, because of their adult nature, related to the parents'
psychology. Later, however, he came to believe that children
were expressing their own archetypal images, which had an
apparently adult character. In *The Development of Personality* he
writes:

> The child's psyche, prior to the stage of ego consciousness, is
> very far from being empty and devoid of content . . . The
> most important evidence . . . is the dreams of three- and four-
> year-old children, among which there are some so strikingly
> mythological and so fraught with meaning that one would take
> them at once for the dreams of grown-ups, did one not know
> who the dreamer was . . . these archetypes of the collective
> psyche . . . are the dominants that rule the preconscious soul
> of the child and, when projected upon the human parents, lend
> them a fascination which often assumes monstrous
> proportions. (1954, p. 44)

Archetypal images in childhood dreams, play and fantasy and
pictures and sand-play are relevant to children themselves. Children unceasingly demand repetition of fairy stories and folk tales.

This natural phenomenon represents the activity of archetypes within the child, and has little that is pathological or especially adult about it. It is very hard to eradicate, in much parental experience. Jung described children under the influence of archetypes as preconscious, here designating a state of consciousness in which the ego is very weak. He also believed that the images that represent unconscious vitality are high in libido. The general Jungian concept of libido is that it includes all available psychic energy and does not refer only to sexual energies, as in Freudian terminology. Jung described these highly energized archetypal images as 'numinous'. With a more developed or organized ego-formation, a more strongly coherent and conscious mind emerges. A progression is postulated from unconscious to preconscious to an organized conscious mind.

Jung thought that the unconscious and preconscious stages in the child included a primitive identity, which he called 'participation mystique'. He proposed that since identity derives at the start from the unconsciousness of the small child, this suggested a nondifferentiated state. Without a clearly developed ego, the child cannot distinguish whether events belong to him or to another. This concept of primitive identity should not be confused with narcissism or being 'ccaught' within the ego in a restricted or morbid sense of turning back on the self in an exclusive self-identity. 'Primitive' here refers to the collective unconscious level in Jungian theory, where archetypal images are raised in the first formation of the ego by an image-match of outer perception to the inner 'read-out' of archetypal givens. However, I wish to delay the detailed concrete evidence about this here and simply state that in the earliest stage of the ego's formation, 'identity' in this matching process of inner and outer would naturally and inevitably be primitive or lacking in a more differentiated ego-consciousness. This is because the baby is largely unconscious or in a pre-ego state of pre-participation with the collective unconscious or self-as-totality at birth. The term 'participation mystique' is confusing, as it would be more accurate to say that the baby is in a state of 'pre-participation' and therefore it feels like a 'mystique' to an observer because so little ego is present in the baby's initial behaviour.

All that is felt by the child, in Jung's view, is that someone should be affected by emotional reactions which become infectious to anyone in the vicinity, often involuntarily. The weak ego-consciousness does not allow the child yet to say: 'I am not reacting as you are because I am not you'. The child does not know clearly his own ego-separateness, so this primitive identity enables the unconscious of parents to enter the child's psyche, where children act out or interiorly live through their parents' problems. Thus the concept of ego-boundaries is hazy in the early stage of primitive identity, and no boundaries of the self are apparent. This is clearly different from later, more conscious identification with parents as a part of cognitive development and emotional feeling.

Jung traced libido in infants as manifesting itself initially in the nutritional zone. In sucking, food is drunk with rhythmic movement. Contiguous with the first period of breastfeeding there is rhythmic movement of arms and legs. This model of rhythmic movement spreads to other functional zones and produces pleasure, with sexuality its ultimate goal. Other body-openings become an object of interest, then the skin. Rhythmic movements extend to picking, boring and rubbing. Rhythm may influence the sexual zone, and the first attempts at masturbation begin. Jung saw the period from birth to the first clear manifestations of sexuality as the 'presexual stage'. When the rhythmic activity no longer relates to breastfeeding in the nutritional phase, it transfers itself to sexuality.

It is assumed that in the act of suckling and while excreting, infants experience various fantasies which they cannot separate out from the physical experience. Jung saw these fantasy systems as preconscious and expressing archetypes. Libidinal zones, on this basis, are seen as preconscious centres of awareness having primitive images that form themselves into the first ego-fragments. A linkage between libidinal zones is necessary for differentiated ego-functions. These zones or preconscious centres will be described below as aspects of the original self which Fordham has named 'deintegrates', which have a tendency to unite in reintegration to ego, as they are derivatives of the archetypes of wholeness.

It is justifiable to set out these arguments as if there were no real parents or real environment, because we are discussing infants' states of awareness. To the baby, the concept of having parents develops very gradually, as an image. They have not appeared within the infant's scene as persons distinctly apart from himself.

Fordham (1957) argues that the development of consciousness in the child violates an original condition of wholeness and postulates, theoretically, a primary integrated state at birth. Although psychologists are ready to recognize that infants' important reactions are total ones of 'self-reactions' in the undifferentiated but complete sense, the current dichotomous nature of biological and psychological concepts makes it difficult to conceive of a state previous to descriptive units like psyche, soma; self, environment; mind, body; ego, non-ego; conscious, unconscious.

It is because ego/self boundaries do not at first exist in the baby that Fordham's ego-deintegration theory fits the empirical situation so well, as it suggests a self from which the ego must begin to delineate its boundaries over time as a developmental process. I shall argue in Chapter VI that this fits a wide spectrum of the experimental and observational empirical work on childhood development.

In this broad area of research into the pre-ego consciousness states in the baby, both neo-Freudians like Donald Winnicott and Heinz Kohut and neo-Jungians like Michael Fordham and

56 Kenneth Lambert have emerged as main figures in the recent development of ego theory in infancy.

Winnicott writes:

> Let us assume that health in the early development of the individual entails continuity of being . . . The early psyche-soma proceeds along a certain line of development provided its continuity of being is not disturbed. (1953, p. 89)

Winnicott then insists that a nearly perfect environment for the baby is at first essential. By this he merely means that if parents face the conflicts of the baby in a normal way, nothing else can go wrong psychically. 'Continuity of being' implies a condition of wholeness, but Winnicott is speaking of psyche-soma and environment which divides up the self even if the inner-outer fit be perfect. This 'continuity of being' implies time. Compared to Winnicott's concepts, Fordham's (1957) description, the original self, is theoretically a simpler heuristic start, getting rid of both the psyche-soma–environment duality and of time. The original self has retroactive evidence in that mature persons, when facing difficulties felt to be insurmountable, return to an original condition which can be named the original self or a primal condition of wholeness. Adults may approach this through memory or a regression.

b. Deintegration, disintegration, integration

In the development of consciousness, the child violates the original wholeness with a spontaneous division of self into parts. Fordham has proposed the term 'deintegration' as a property of the self behind ego-formation which is present first. This is distinct from the concept of disintegration, which presupposes an already formed ego which is split into a number of fragments. It explains the difference between Winnicott's view and Fordham's. Fordham sees the self as dividing itself up to form the ego and as being unintegrated or deintegrated from the level of the self until reintegration of the new formation. Winnicott sees a primary unintegrated state based on a viewpoint which is limited to ego psychology without a primal *a priori* self concept, but Kohut (1977) has put forward a theory of the self contained within a Freudian framework (see Chapter II, section 3b).

The Fordhamian position is that the self cannot disintegrate. Only the ego can be split or even destroyed. The ego integrates, then regresses. If the process is at a catastrophic level the ego does not integrate to an earlier level of its history, either because there is no other such level available, as may be the case in schizophrenia, or because the disintegration has a high anxiety factor which blocks a regression to an earlier ego-level. If the disintegration is at traumatic level, a simpler ego-integrate appears naturally and an earlier ego-stability is re-established.

Fordham's deintegration hypothesis proposes a spontaneous division of the self (see Diagram 2). Indirect evidence may be gathered from various sources. Jung believed that a new concept has certainly been reflected in ancient myths, and this can amplify the concept of deintegration. The cosmic creation myths may be a source of ideas parallel to the deintegration theory. In the Orphic cult in Greece we find the cosmic egg as ' . . . the symbol of what gives birth to all things and in itself contains all things' (Plutarch, quoted in Harrison, 1908). And again: 'Orpheus likened chaos to an egg in which was the commingling of the primeval elements.' Eros sprang spontaneously from the cosmic egg: he ' . . . revealed and brought to light everything that had previously lain hidden in the golden egg' (Kerenyi, 1951). The process is spontaneous, like the deintegration concept.

Jung discusses the scintillae of the alchemists, which he describes as 'seeds of light broadcast in the chaos, which Khunrath calls "the seed bed of the future world" ' (1960). Jung sees these scintillae as like the archetypes, since he implies that the origins of consciousness are in both. Scintillae could correspond to 'tiny

58   **Diagram 2:** Self/ego deintegration

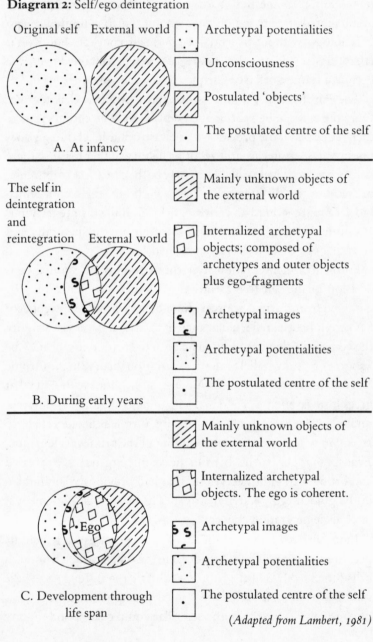

Original self   External world   Archetypal potentialities

Unconsciousness

Postulated 'objects'

The postulated centre of the self

A. At infancy

The self in deintegration and reintegration   External world

Mainly unknown objects of the external world

Internalized archetypal objects; composed of archetypes and outer objects plus ego-fragments

Archetypal images

Archetypal potentialities

The postulated centre of the self

B. During early years

Mainly unknown objects of the external world

Internalized archetypal objects. The ego is coherent.

Archetypal images

Archetypal potentialities

The postulated centre of the self

C. Development through life span

(*Adapted from Lambert, 1981*)

conscious phenomena' and be closely related to the concept of the deintegrates.

How could the first element of consciousness as a formal image arise? We can easily, but very incorrectly, infer this by taking the image found in small children's circles as the representation of the original self at birth. This is incorrect, because in Fordham's theory the original wholeness is imageless before the first deintegration achieves consciousness. Fordham postulates that a deintegrate may be described as a readiness to perceive and act which enables a correct perception to occur only if the object exactly fits the deintegrate, because only then is the state of affairs where the baby cannot distinguish between subject and object possible. If the correspondence between object and deintegrate is not exact, it may at first not be perceived, but a tolerance later develops of the object not fitting the deintegrate until the distinction between subject and object dawns upon the infant.

Fordham has as a hypothesis in the deintegration theory the idea that a perception is not a passive act but part of object-seeking activity. Piaget also postulates a clear need for the outer object to comply with what seem to be inner requirements. In the *Origin of Intelligence in Childhood* (1953) he concludes from studies of his own children that a schema lies at the root of imitation, play and intelligence. If we assume his schema to be a deintegrate, the deintegrate can develop through imitation in play and symbolic activity. Piaget describes his schema as unconscious elements upon which the psychic life of the infant is organized. These are 'global' reactions to which objects are assimilated. He postulates that only the resistances of the environment or the incompatibilities of the infant's activity in relation to it prevent this generalization from occurring:

> Now this schema . . . is not limited to functioning under compulsion by a fixed excitant, external or internal, but functions in a way for itself . . . From the point of view of

awareness, if there is awareness, such assimilation (sucking) is at first lack of differentiation . . . but from the point of view of action, it is a generalizing extension of the schema . . . (1953, p. 35)

Piaget, of course, bases his investigations on a set of theoretical concepts which differ from Fordham's. He believes that the infant's first reactions are reflexes and that the schemata represent reflex action. What is interesting is that Piaget sees imitation in the infant as built only upon schemata and says that the infant will imitate others' behaviour only if this behaviour corresponds closely to the schemata already expressed by the child. Inner requirements need to be met by the outer object. Here Piaget and Fordham are in complete agreement.

As the infant's unconscious, as well as his pre-speech period, contain much that has been incorporated into theoretical interpretation by Fordham, Klein (see Chapter II), Winnicott and Piaget, it is important to note the methods used empirically with infants. Diverse workers base their postulations on direct observation alone or on experimental results.

Kris's (1955) work in 'well baby clinics' broke ground because he made predictions of how a baby would develop and then did longitudinal studies of his mothers and babies to see if his predictions were valid. Escalona, in *The Roots of Individuality* (1969), studied babies at home, in the first four months of life, rather than in a clinical setting later, as Mahler *et al.* (1975) have done. The inclusion of very early life helps to round out a difficult area of study.

The psychoanalysts, more than the Jungians, doubted reliability in infant observation, fearing that projections of the experimenter might occur in the observation as well as in the experimenter's fantasies about infants. Some analysts thought it safer to wait until verbal communications gave information from which constructions about infancy could be made. Whatever anxieties remain about this, observation, while not totally reliable in giving exact information about internal psychodynamic processes, can provide hypotheses whose validity can be checked against further observations. In general one finds that theory abounds most where observation is least. Nevertheless, along with child analysis, infant observation can give a realistic picture of what mothers and babies do in the sense of the general relation of the infant to his mother and the building up of a timetable of changes within the infant self (Mahler *et al.* 1975).

One supporter of direct observation is Blackburn:

> The most reliable and effective knowing follows from direct and open confrontation with phenomena, no matter how complicated they are. Nature can be trusted to behave reliably without suppression of the manifold details of a natural environment, and nature's ways are open to direct, intuitive, sensuous knowledge . . . Since the self and the environment are inextricable (contrary to the philosophical stance of classical science), one can understand his surroundings by being sensitive to his own reactions to them. (1971, p. 1003)

Obviously, workers in the field of infant observation and child analysis attempt to observe the phenomena involved in a way that would ensure that another observer (in the same situation) would reach the same conclusion. Blackburn points out:

> Before conventional scientists (by this is meant workers outside psychoanalytic orientation) rush in with cries of 'subjectivity' in criticism of the sensuous approach (i.e. the response of the whole body, including the senses, to phenomena . . . dependent on factors such as mood and attention, but . . . undeniably a source of information about the world around us), they might stop to consider whether or not a person selected at random off the street could be asked to repeat their

highly sophisticated observations from laboratory experiments. (1971, p. 1003)

With proper training, they could. But this is exactly what the sensuous observer would reply is necessary for his method as well. Obviously the position of a pointer on a scale cannot be the only way of gaining quantitative knowledge, and there is other knowledge besides quantitative knowledge. The predators of *Homo sapiens* would have destroyed him if we ourselves were not instruments capable of understandingly confronting the 'messy' world outside the laboratory. This undermines value in the tendency to abstractions in laboratory studies, and points up the claim that laboratory science may be 'irrelevant' to the study of very young children because it does not fit their natural behaviour, as child analysts insist it must.

The pay-off for Fordham's theory based on Jung's self-as-totality theory is that the archetypal interpretative base in the reading of infant behaviour has led to definitive areas of agreement between Piaget's longitudinal infant observation and Fordham's ego theory: that is, that the infant is matching inner with outer from birth. I will be able to illustrate this further with empirical laboratory-based research that supports my extension of Fordham's theory below, in Chapter VI, and here with the Kellogg research.

A wide recognition of the importance of object relations has developed because children universally need objects as parts either of themselves or of others. This implies that perception becomes image. This is a development Piaget puts at about one year of age. Through objects, the child begins to see himself and other persons as a whole. The first image, separate from an immediate present object, is presumably linked up with the development from memory. Once images are formed apart from the object they can represent absent objects or, if taken hold of by the archetypes, can be used or altered to make up archetypal images.

The Kellogg (1969) research on 100,000 preschool children's early pictures and scribblings, which includes the author's theory of abstraction, may be correspondingly compared to deintegration. From twenty basic original scribbles, five diagrams or shapes were abstracted as most significant to the majority of the subjects; two forms of cross (+ and x), the square, the triangle, irregular-shaped enclosures and the circle. The children then made 'combines' of the diagrams. The mandala was the most frequent combine from which a human figure was later drawn by combining circles and a modification of the mandala. This study points out that the human figure is not copied from perception of it as a whole but grows through a process of combining and abstracting various forms, including the mandala image, which Jung saw as a representation of the self. This image was often transformed by the children into a human figure or ego representation. The abstraction of 'diagrams' from the scribbles can be likened to the deintegration process. The recognition of an external object (scribbles) releases an instinctual or unconscious archetypal response which separates out the image of the diagrams. Random activity plus abstraction or deintegration is followed by combination or integration.

In deintegration with the resulting images, we can speak of the preconscious state when fragments of ego-consciousness exist and unite to form an ego-centre. The self is seen as the integrator of the ego-fragments. Adler wrote:

> . . . in childhood . . . the non-ego has the upper hand at first, and the self charges the ego-function with sufficient energy for it to establish itself against the non-ego, so that it can fulfil the demands of adaptation to the outer world . . . the self operates as an image of potential wholeness behind the psychic processes and bends them towards realization of this wholeness, which appears as the synthesis of ego and non-ego, of conscious and unconscious, of the inner and outer worlds. (1951, p. 98)

64   Other psychic activities enter into the growth of the ego. Fordham
      (1957) suggests some examples: recognition of similarities,
      association in time, infantile logic, concept-building, instinctual
      drive aspects of the archetypes (for example infantile sex instincts),
      archetypal images having an integrative effect because the self lies
      behind them, and education.

      Integration of the self follows deintegration to form the ego-
      nucleus in a periodic manner. After the original self deintegrates
      spontaneously, perception and action may occur according to the
      patterns of the deintegrates. For this we are reminded that in
      Fordham's view a perfect fit with the environment is necessary.
      With this fit, reaction patterns develop based on preconscious
      image. These deintegrates grow into ego-nuclei which are
      brought together, through the integrating action of the self, into
      a single ego-centrum.

      The ego continues to develop through periodic deintegrative
      actions leading to specialized units of consciousness for which I
      propose to introduce the new term 'con-integrates'. Various con-
      integrates I would propose would be speech, defence-of-self, ego-
      persona, play, the aesthetic, the ego-ideal and the ego-shadow.
      The combination of abilities and perceptions required for these
      complex areas of behaviour – so universal across races as to imply
      an archetypal influence of a most fundamental and primordial
      nature – suggests a special case of unifying deintegrates, on a
      very complex and multitudinous scale, into 'con-integrate areas'
      within the integrated self. This results in the almost inconceivable
      ability, for example, to learn and speak the English language if
      the difficulties of doing so are analysed into detailed component
      parts and handled separately by the ego as 'bits'. The same may
      be said for infants' symbolic play, where concentration is required
      on all hierarchical levels of play difficulty.

      Body motility, similarly directed mostly from an unconscious
      level, suggests that con-integrates are huge, unifying, Gestalt-
      like complexes of deintegrates, conjoined to ensure survival

through effective performance and perception. Speech, play-work and body motility influenced by defence-of-self, the ego-persona and ego-shadow and the ego-ideal with the aesthetic, seem essentially basic to the psychological life of almost everyone and imply a vast co-ordination system between the conscious and unconscious mind.

While con-integrates are built by deintegration and are therefore a postulation subsumed by Fordham's theory of deintegration-reintegration, I maintain that my term 'con-integrates' helps to clarify a group of very large deintegrated aggregates which reintegrate in special systems of great biological significance. This concept adds clarity to Fordham's deintegration proposal by separating out certain reintegrations into this special category of con-integration and co-ordinating con-integrates into the overall neo-Jungian system. I am not, of course, implying that these areas should be called anything other than their ancient and regular names when being discussed outside the hierarchical framework of a new ego theory of the self and its development in early childhood. This conscious development runs parallel to an unconscious deintegrating into the archetypes of the collective unconscious, which become more discrete if individuation develops where the ego moves forward and the self is less apparent in the foreground of the child's personality.

The other important development with deintegration is that because the environment can exactly fit a deintegrate, so that at first there can be no differentiation between them, bits of ego develop, and where the environment fails to fit the deintegrate a separation occurs if the frustration involved for the infant is tolerable. The infant is assumed to tolerate more and more of these frustrations until a duality is established between the environment and the self, composed of the growing ego-nucleus and a whole body-image. Taking in and ejecting occurs in feeding and excreting, with later childhood development giving conscious psychic equivalents. As the ego increases in strength,

66   play, fantasies and dreams become less important, although these
preconscious conditions remain in the background. As the ego
develops clearer boundaries, the emotional environment also has
less influence. Theoretically it is only in the preconscious state,
or in the pre-ego state, that the environment cannot be psychically
handled by the child alone.

Children do not progress simply from ego-development to
integration, During this development some psychic experiences
may become disintegrated and repressed in the personal unconscious. Archetypes, as essentially unconscious constellations, can
never be totally integrated within the ego. Among the archetypal
images are those of wholeness and order, which have a controlling
influence over unconscious functions. Fordham (1960) has postulated a central archetype of order (discussed above) which is seen
as a potential integrate of the ego and the archetypes through a
general 'tendency to wholeness or a uniting of aspects of the
conscious and unconscious mind'. This kind of integration would
be different from ego-development or the growth of the conscious
mind alone. The symbolism of the comprehensive synthetic
process in adult subjects, concerning the general tendency to
wholeness, has been demonstrated by Jung in four works: *The
Secret of the Golden Flower* (1955), *Psychology and Religion* (1958),
Psychology and Alchemy (1944b) and *Gestaltungen des Unbewussten*
(1950). These studies demonstrate mandala symbolism in adults,
but Jung does not deal with this phenomenon in children.
Fordham (1947), however, deals with three studies revealing
mandala symbolism in one- and two-year-old children. Before
considering this empirical material, we need to consider further
the relationship of mandala symbolism to deintegration-
integration.

c. The mandala in childhood image projection
Jung (1953) writes of mandalas as magical enclosures which are
often but not always round. 'The round or square enclosures . . .

have the value of magic means to produce a protective wall . . . they prevent an outburst and a disintegration.' In addition to preventing disintegration, mandalas are drawn by people when they need to integrate a new element or as deintegration occurs. It is around mandala studies that the closer relationship and theory of integration, deintegration and disintegration was discerned. In mandalas, variable contents are always arranged about a centre. The most frequent number of divisions between the centre and the circumference is four or a multiple of four. In *Psychological Types* Jung puts forward the view that this fourfold division represents the fourfold structure of the psyche (thinking, feeling, intuition and sensation). The centre 'is simply unknowable and can only be expressed symbolically through its own phenomenology, as is the case, incidentally, with every object of experience.' The self is believed to be represented by the centre, by the surrounding contents and by the circumference jointly. The mandala is thus the most powerful symbol of the self known to Jungian psychology.

In children where ego-differentiation is not clear from self-manifestations, the self seems to prepare the ground for the ego's emergence. An example of this is Fordham's description (1957) of a one-year-old boy who was allowed to scribble on the walls of his nursery. After initially making squiggles, he became preoccupied exclusively with making circles. He continued this for a period of weeks, until upon discovering the word 'I', he stopped. The relation of the circles to the discovery of 'I' suggests that the circle represented a matrix of the self from which the ego arose. Stein (1951) had done research into the origin of the word 'I'. He agrees that 'The linguistic development [of I] . . . reflects a process by which the ego is separated from the self.' This is consistent with Jung's view that the circle is an archetypal non-ego. If the child identifies the word 'I' with the circle, he does not yet mean it necessarily as an organized ego but rather as an awareness or discovery of himself as a whole, complete, a circle,

68   a somebody if only for a moment. The circle probably also represents the boundary of the ego as well as referring to the integration of self-feelings.

Fordham (1944) describes the case of a girl of two-and-a-half. During analysis she would scribble while held on the analyst's knee, but upon drawing a circle she would get off and play elsewhere in the treatment playroom. In Jungian terms, when the circle appeared she became free to express her ego in action.

Another girl of two was brought for treatment of fits during which she became completely unconscious. She was very dependent on her mother and could not feed or dress herself. She displayed great fear of entering the playroom, but after scribbling with chalk made a circle and said 'me'. With this her frightened manner changed and she went about playing with toys. This was interpreted to mean that the circle was a picture of the self and ego in union, giving the child some – if only temporary – security. The relief of anxiety after drawing the circle was also seen as the tendency to unite with the mother (the circle united with the word 'me'). This was periodically necessary for the girl's balance at this stage. The concept of deintegration helped to make comprehensible the source of the fits, which were seen as the 'dismemberment of the ego by the deintegrating self, a process described as disintegration' (Fordham, 1957). Although pathological in itself, this disintegration made the girl have a regression to an earlier stage where mother and child once again represented the whole integrated self, from which the girl had been afraid to separate. Through spontaneous play, enabled by the analyst's presence giving a free and protected neutral space, the girl's ego began to develop separately through deintegration of the self, because once she had regressed to the earlier integrate of mother–child unity the energy formerly put into the fits was free instead to be directed into a progressive deintegration to establish the child's own ego-growth to a position of positiveness and separateness from the mother.

Fordham's theoretical basis for the discussion of these children's cases can be summarized in his own words:

> The danger [in these cases] is clearly from the child's psyche itself, and if it be accepted that he [or she] had made an image of the self from which the ego is budding off, then the danger to the ego can only come from the self. (1951, p. 83)

Theoretically, the self as a deintegrating-integrating system comes into this empirical material. The analyst sees deintegration as a danger to the ego, which can be split if separation of the two – ego and self – is not complete. This can be pictured as an insufficient ego-deintegration so that just when the self, at reintegration, begins to deintegrate again in a regular rhythmic cycle, the ego can be split, rather than progressively built, if it is not deintegrated out enough to be separate or to have separate ego-bits completed.

In the Jungian view, the circle is seen to represent a delimiting or magical area used to ward off danger from within or without, or in the inherent and dangerous condition of the ego-deintegrates as the ego comes into being. It is also possible, using analytic interpretation, to link circles and mandalas with the body-image experience of young children. Early experience of parts or of whole body-images may correspond to the impenetrability of the circle. It must be remembered that eyes, breasts and the principal body-orifices are all circular. Jungian psychology argues that it is not possible to account for circular imagery entirely on the basis of perceptual experience of external objects, since they can be images of the self which are symbolically observable in empirical situations like the analytical treatment of the children described above. Jungians would be the first to realize that children often use the 'magical omnipotence of the circle image' (Fordham, 1957) to simulate a control system inside which they can place and hold bad or terrifying objects. In the same way, precious or good objects are placed within the circle to protect them from outside dangers. Hence the mandala circle image can hold or contain the opposition.

d. Objects in symbol and meaning formation
Many features of symbolization in infancy require elucidation. An essential characteristic of a symbol is that it represents a relatively unknown influence. It is different from a sign in that its unknown part cannot be made completely conscious by getting rid of repression or by lifting its disguise by interpretation. In general symbols have a plurality of possible meanings, as they may combine opposites or transcend them in a unity which refers to the self. A small child knows that parents exist, but their nature is obscure. They are experienced through archetypal imagery. As the child grows up he sheds the symbolic image, if and when he is able to see his parents wholly without fantasy. A baby cannot take up a 'symbolic attitude' until he can pretend and take up an 'as if' quality. It is not known if there is an incipient capacity for the baby to hold its experience of deintegrated and integrated states until they are later represented symbolically, because the images depend on a certain degree of consciousness and on memory.

Presumably the infant's consciousness, in the sense of meaning formation, is initially vague and objects are only gradually constructed. At first these objects are not differentiated from the self, so everything is a self-object and the mother meets and satisfies all the self-objects' needs. The Jungian view holds that the self-objects are organized on archetypal models. Other sense data which are not self-objects are experienced as not-self when they integrate. These are at first attacked or rejected by screaming, crying and excreting or spitting and vomiting. These not-self objects form the basis for later bad objects. Since there is no capacity to sustain conflict between the opposites of 'good' self-objects and 'bad' not-self-objects, symbolization of objects does not occur.

Fordham (1976) postulates that the first grouping of experiences is in terms of their sameness. The case of Alan, which he discusses, shows how the self-object will tend to treat apparently very different objects as if they were identical. Segal (1957) calls this characteristic 'symbolic equations' and thinks that it relates to certain states of ego-fragmentation where projective identification is prominent. In Segal's view, based on Kleinian theory, a hallucination or a thumb is experienced firstly as the same as the breast, and eventually either may come to represent the breast.

An essential prerequisite for symbol formation is object-constancy or the ability to maintain an object in memory after it has been experienced. It is widely believed that infants do not at first have this capacity and cannot sustain an image of a feed after they have experienced it. For a symbol to influence experience, it must continue and develop so as to achieve a dreamlike or hallucinatory quality with archetypal characteristics which, in its image, the child may begin to deintegrate/reintegrate to ego. Since the archetypal, although it creates an image or self-object, does not control its persistence in time, the persistence or constancy of an object 'must be attributed to the development of consciousness' (Fordham, 1976).

With development, the child may relate symbolization to absence or loss of a valued object. The affect associated with this is mourning, and its early prototype is the 'depressive position' advocated by Klein (1948). Intially, the lost object is the breast. In the depressive position the child symbolizes the lost breast by an internal reparative act, using imagery and thought. This increases the perception of the real mother. To create a symbol, the self-object must be destroyed. Only then is the need for a creative act great enough. The breast, as self-object, is destroyed, but as the real breast is still existent the constructive act must abstract from the object; this abstraction is the symbol. The significance of the destructive fantasy must include perception of the breast as both a good self-object and a bad not-self-object.

72   When these two aspects are identified within one object, the
nature of the destruction changes. There is no feeling of loss if
the baby is attacking only the bad breast but if, at the same time,
the good breast is attacked there is experience of loss. Reparation
must be made if the self is to survive.

Once the child can pretend, fusion to self-objects becomes
sufficiently dissolved for them to become representational.
Winnicott (1971a) had discussed a special 'transitional object'
which helps to separate the fusion between the self and self-
objects. In first feeds, if a baby is satisfied at the breast, he
creates a breast through deintegration, over which he feels he has
omnipotent control. In reality the baby has no control except in
aspects of his interaction related to the length of feed. Gradually
the infant comes to recognize his mother as a separate object out
of his control. The need for omnipotence makes him stuff bits
into his mouth or thumbsuck. He does this because he can control
these actions. The bits stuffed into the mouth can be put to various
imaginative uses and acquire in imagination properties they did
not have before. At first, however, the thumb or bits are a true
self-representation in the sense that this is a demarcation area
between an inner psychic world (or omnipotence over the breast)
and 'the external world as perceived by two persons in common'.
This refers to a state where both baby and mother have a different
and a separate relationship to the breast as perceived by the child.
Later the thumb may represent only bits of mother, or the infant
himself.

The transitional object appears between four months and one
year. It is like a symbol in that it has a 'life of its own'; it contains
opposites and it can die by being relegated to 'limbo' if its
meanings become exhausted and/or assimilated into dreaming,
play, fantasy, thought and creative activities. The transitional
object discovers the not-ego (the mother) in a way that is not felt
to be alien or 'needing to be destroyed', as it would be at first as
the not-self. The processes underlying symbolization in separ-

ating out from the not-self are vital to the discovery and construction of reality. When deintegration makes the mother–object or not-self a part of the self, disillusionment gradually leads to a reappraisal by the infant and a not-self reality is discovered. The transitional objects help the child to use imagination and symbolization to contain parts of the self as they are seen to be actual not-self reality, a reality that is constructed piece by piece.

To summarize this section on deintegration: the self is seen throughout the discussion as a primary datum. This hypothesis assumes that the self is not reducible to anything else and is, on this basis, a parsimonious theoretical approach. The symbols depicting union of opposites in children refer to a state from which the infant began. Fordham has termed the first self-integrate in infancy the 'original self'. This suggests that the current concept of the mother as 'carrier of the self' is misleading unless it is restated to indicate that to the baby his mother is part (deintegrate) of the self. On this view the infant initially creates his mother in the light of his own needs and she represents, in this sense, a part of the infant-self. Without the concept of an original self, there is no basis for the persistent recurrence of integrative states.

The primary state of unity gives rise to later self-representations in the ego, expressed as 'unit states', and a sense of self in the baby at about two years of age (Fordham, 1969). Earlier derivations of self are a fusion experience where the infant treats his mother as part of himself rather than as a separate object. Although early perception may be global and cause fusion, it also suggests that fusion is due to the organization of perceptual input into a unitary perceptual system 'which only later deintegrates into specific and clear perception'.

The use of the term deintegration – corresponding to instinct defusion – is valuable because it keeps in mind the essentially interrelated activity of functional systems of adaptation and

74   provides a basis for ego-formation and for the periodic in-
     tegration of ego-fragments into what we know later is an
     organized ego-structure. (Fordham, 1976, p. 55)

The reader will now have a thorough knowledge of Jungian self
theory and of the exact details of how ego emerges from self in the
deintegration/reintegration which Michael Fordham postulated.
This begins the related series of theories, to which I shall later be
adding, to advance the concepts of Jungian psychology.

Chapter II

The contribution of Freud and the neo-Freudians

I pray you, school yourself.
Shakespeare, *Macbeth*, IV. ii

1. *The Freudian background*

In looking at Freud's work it seems important to me, within a Jungian book, to discuss quite fully the general scientific influence of his education and contribution. In 'The question of lay analysis' (1927b) Freud stresses: 'In psychology we can describe only with the help of comparisons over and over again, for none of them can serve us for any length of time.' Freud inferred causes from evolution and biology, especially early on in his writing, but Robert Young (1986) points out that psychoanalysis is using imaginative interpretation to infer hidden causes of hard facts. It is in the use of metaphor that Freud's work gives both a feeling for and an intellectual realization of what is meant. Bruno Bettelheim (1982) describes the term 'Oedipus complex' as a metaphor for a rich and suggestive idea related to dream and myth. It is not possible to turn the Oedipus complex as theory into a firm model, as in the physiochemical sciences. Young points out that Freud moved from thinking of psychic function as structured as in physiological terminology to the gradual use of terms from the somatic verbiage implying a more metaphorical function. In his psychophysical parallelism (that mind and brain work in parallel ways) Freud based a metaphysical position on a physicalist vocabulary as the clearest abstract language available. Holding the concomitance of the mental and physical in tension, I would agree that Freud used the language of his education as his base and enriched it with metaphors.

It is psychology's challenge that persons or former persons must be there to connect the idea of individual consciousness to reality, as psychoanalysis tried to do. Freud, however, stuck to a dualist, psychophysical parallelism and enriched this with metaphorical attempts to move freely within this correlation. My concern is that in moving from objects to persons, reductionist language constricted Freud from hitting upon the sense of a larger self concept within which to place his 'I' or ego-world of resonances.

I shall now look at the self concept as it partially emerges in the work of Ronald Fairbairn, Donald Winnicott and Heinz Kohut and other neo-Freudians. To prepare the ground, I shall outline below my conclusions about Freud's education and his major and lasting contribution to depth psychology. The work that followed Freud before Kohut's breakthrough to a self concept that is partially comparable to Jung's, although much more limited in its implications, is thoroughly described. It will then be seen that Jung's self concept can be better understood historically if one comprehends the full Freudian contribution, just as Christianity, for example, is better comprehended if its historically enabling vehicle, Judaism, is seriously studied. Precursors deeply influence the development of ideation literally, scientifically, humanistically and in the archetypal read-out of mythical images in the history of symbols as the carriers of psychological/cultural expression.

Sigmund Freud, the father-figure of psychoanalysis and a genuine pioneer, believed that neurotic symptoms could be explained in terms of the patient's life-history. He found that in the hysterical neuroses, symptoms could disappear if the patient felt secure with the psychoanalyst and reappear if that relationship became disturbed. In 1908, when Freud wrote 'Civilized sexual morality and modern nervous illness', he thought that instinct repression and sublimation – the diversion of instinctive energy to socially approved goals – created such difficulties that it forced many people into severe neurosis. His clinical observation turned up similar psychic experience in a wide variety of people.

Obviously Freud's discussion of fear, anxiety, love, jealousy, sexual desire, aggression, anger, hate and the way these may occur in the same person broke ground in clinical thinking about conscious experience and behaviour. In his theory, if turbulence is mentally suppressed the symptoms of psychoneurosis, whether physical or mental, arise. Not only may illness occur but antisocial behaviour may be acted out, or dream material and daytime fantasy may suggest meanings that are made intelligible by studying a person's life-history. Freud took as a resultant hypothesis that people apparently do not outgrow early childhood experiences and that early acute anxiety, anger and insecurity are repressed to the unconscious while the conscious self develops either conformity or rebellion or a mixture of the two as its day-to-day basis.

Freud's concept of ego-instinct [*Ichtrieb*] makes instinct a structure existent before the phenomenal relation of subject–object. Instincts are thought of as freed from a rigid reference either to objects or to the subjects and are seen to be variably directed. As objects may be exchanged by means of substitutions or displacement of cathexis, Freud discusses the self [*Selbst*] and self-regard [*Selbstgefühl*] only in this sense of redistribution of erotic cathexes (1914, pp. 73–102). He eventually saw the sexual instincts as most indicative of the primacy of aim over object and separated these instincts from ego- or self-preservative instincts. He posited a primal confusion between thing-love and self-love:

If one admits a narcissistic phase in which the external world is indifferent and the subject the sole source of pleasure, then the process of distinguishing between the external and the internal, between the world and the ego, is a process of economic division between what the ego can incorporate into itself and prize as the possession of the 'pleasure-ego' [*Lust-ich*] and what it rejects as hostile, as the source of unpleasure. (Ricoeur, 1970, p. 125)

Narcissism is introduced into psychoanalysis to include aims of instinct, the object and the ego, making the conception of instinct a more radical concept than subject–object relation by itself. Object-choice is seen as a departure from narcissism and economically, in the broadest sense, there are only departures from and returns to narcissism.

After 1924 Freud updated his topography to include the structure of ego, id and superego and conceived the idea that a displacement of narcissism brings about the formation of ideals. In the sense that the subject measures his own ego or self-regard by his ideal, this becomes the only sense in which Freud is dealing directly with a part of a visible 'self theory'. He ties this development to ego-changes in childhood in which a concept or primary narcissistic perfection is at first named the 'ideal ego':

> This ideal ego is now the target of self-love which was enjoyed in childhood by the actual ego. The subject's narcissism makes its appearance displaced into this new ideal ego, which, like the infantile ego, finds itself possessed of every perfection that is of value. As always where the libido is concerned . . . [the person] is not willing to forgo the narcissistic perfection of childhood; and when . . . he is disturbed by the admonition of others and by the awakening of his own critical judgement, so that he can no longer retain that perfection, he seeks to recover it in the new form of an ego-ideal. What he projects before him as his ideal is the substitute for the lost narcissism of his childhood in which he was his own ideal. (Freud, 1914a, p.94)

Here Freud defines how the *ego-ideal* grows out of the substitution from an earlier state of the *ideal ego*, when the child was his own ideal. These two terms, 'ideal ego' and 'ego-ideal', are totally different in their meaning and their place in the child's psychological development.

Freud leads us back from instinctual factors and their vicissitudes to their derivatives in consciousness. The object can be traced back only by understanding the economic distribution of the libido and its linked genesis with love and hate. Freud reduces all derived forms of instinct away from the first truth of reflection – 'I think' or 'I am' – to something altogether primitive and primordial named 'primary narcissism'. He thought that the resistance to narcissism which occurs in gaining self-knowledge was man's third humiliation by science, the first two having been the cosmological blow from Copernicus (that the earth is not the centre of the universe) and the biological humiliation of Darwin (that man's ancestry was recently most simian indeed)! Freud moved the description of consciousness to a topography involving psychical apparatus as description in order to include the complex nature of narcissism. Ricoeur (1970) remarks that in doing this Freud comes near to a point of phenomenological impoverishment, since consciousness becomes as obscure as unconsciousness. The 'I think' and 'I am' vacillate in Freudian theory. In introducing the interpretation of hidden meaning in apparent meaning, Freud found a way back to enrichment from this phenomenological impoverishment by linking the topographic-economic explanation to the work of psychoanalytic interpretation. The only way to justify relinquishing an obvious phenomenology [*Bewusstsein*] or self-evidence of being conscious, for a process of becoming conscious [*Bewusstwerden*] was to turn to the unconscious as a locality where ideas and representations reside, which will *mediate* the perception of the object, rather than to claim that perception is an immediate consciousness without unconscious participation. In *Cartesian Meditations* (1960), Husserl admits that at the heart of the certitude of the 'I am' there remains a question: 'How far can the transcendental ego be deceived about itself?'

By using the same language for both unconscious and conscious Freud allows affinities of meanings between the two: we can speak of unconscious ideas and conscious ideas. Apperception is no longer defined by the fact of just being conscious but includes the unconscious influence of the conscious in its perceptual life. The psychical cannot be defined apart from the possibility of becoming more conscious, as it is

> the only characteristic of psychical processes that is directly present to us . . . [it] is in no way suited to serve as a criterion for the differentiation of systems. In principle, psychoanalysis should translate the delimitation of meaning via the remote primary instinctual representatives back into a fuller conscious psychism. (Ricoeur, 1970, p. 115)

Freud sees the unconscious not as an absolute 'other' to the conscious but as interpretatively and reflexively homogeneous with it.

With the ego, superego and id, Freud postulated a structural topography later modified by the neo-Freudians. His theory of excitation and detensioning as basic to all experience and grounded on instinctual life constituted the foundation of economic theory. He proposed a position antithetical to the self concept in the sense that a progressive synthesis, inseparable from its production, cannot be posited in Freud's topography, nor can it 'appear among the vicissitudes of the instincts which constitute the theme of economics' (Ricoeur, 1970). The meaning of *Selbst* implies a self–other difference from which the self-identity surges. This ever-recurring separation of self and otherness resides in life-experience, inner and outer. Ricoeur suggests that 'it is life that becomes the other, in and through which the self ceaselessly achieves itself.' Freud takes unconscious archaeology as expressed in themes of instinct and narcissism and links these with a notion, whose exact themes are not clarified, of a teleology within the process of becoming conscious. Some of the themes involved include identification and sublimation of the self or parts of the self, which the neo-Freudians studied. Freud's use of *das Selbst* in his early work refers to and is almost synonymous with the ego. Later he defined the self as the totality of the id, ego and superego. He argued that the conscious has to develop ego-defences against unconscious conflicts which, if they irrupt into consciousness, cause anxiety symptoms which range from mild to severe. An important aspect of repressed childhood experience is that in adult life the sublimated emotions involved may 'transfer' on to an analogous figure through identification, causing disruption in friendship, marriage and politico-cultural choices.

Freud used a 'talking out' method of free association in which the patient voiced freely whatever occurred to him without losing the analyst's respect in discussing what previously seemed prohibited. Psychoanalysis relies on the analyst offering reliability, sympathetic objectivity and an attempt at genuine understanding within the theories Freud made explicit. Through free association the patient, theoretically having a trusting transference to the analyst, may integrate past difficulties and thus be enabled to make more appropriate relationships, to realize his or her own motives and to separate them from the motives of others through withdrawing projections. As independent self-knowledge enables a patient to withdraw projections, Jungians particularly would claim that self-knowledge *is* the route to withdrawal of projections on to others.

a. How original was Freud's contribution?
I would like to consider how Freud's view of a person emerges from his elaboration of and differentiation from a tradition in which the self notion was primordially existent but very unclear in formulation. Freud was extremely original in the method by which he began to see ego-consciousness as influenced by a

paradoxical unconscious. The way he refined his theoretical ideas over time is important.

Although Breuer's 'cathartic procedure' using hypnosis may be regarded as a forerunner of Freud's work, Freud discarded the hypnotic method altogether and introduced free association. He originated much that is really particularly characteristic in psychoanalysis. In *Studien über Hysterie* (1895), written jointly, Breuer and Freud claimed that the symptoms of hysterical patients are founded on traumata in their past life. Breuer obtained catharsis under hypnosis as therapy; in theory these symptoms represented an abnormal form of discharge for quantities of excitation which had not been disposed of otherwise via conversion. Breuer and Freud had different theories of the mental dissociation of hysteria, centring on the extent of the importance of sexual aetiology in neurosis. In his (1914b) paper 'On the history of the psychoanalytic movement', Freud clearly contends that his concept of repression was original to himself. He did not know (until Otto Rank pointed it out) that Schopenhauer, in *The World as Will and Representation* (1819) describes a similar phenomenon involving struggle against acceptance of a painful part of reality. Freud refused to read Nietzsche, as well as most other philosophers, during his later life because he wished to derive his ideas from clinical psychoanalysis, not from philosophy. He also claims that he had come to the central idea of his dream theory – that dream distortion could be reduced to an unknown conflict – before reading a similar idea from the engineer Joseph Popper, whose *Phantasien eines Realistin* (1899) was published under the pen-name 'Lynkeus'.

We must be rigorously specific about how far Freud was directly influenced by others. The generalizations about this in the literature are notorious. Ernest Jones (1953–57) states that Freud often quoted von Schubert (*Die Symbolik des Traumes*, 1837), and Reeves (1965) concludes that he had read von Schubert's dream theory. Von Schubert's concept of '*Zweideutigkeit*' or a double ambiguous significance like a Janus-face, which he found in nature, religious practice, prophetic insight, dreams and in somnambulistic behaviour, may have been an influence on Freud's pleasure-pain principle and concept of opposites.

Von Schubert mentions a striving or desire as the essential drive, with an opposing 'desire of spirit' directed to a world beyond the senses. Whether or not one disregards this as too metaphysical, the opposite concept of a desire that remains biological leads to an intense attachment to a more limited object of which von Schubert thought the reverse side to be destruction. On this view, aggressive destruction goes together with intense attachment, whether in the natural, biological or social world. The important point here is that resulting dissociation states were postulated which may have directed part of Freud's thinking on the subject.

Von Schubert believed in metastasis: that organs designed to function in one way may take over the function of another. This was important in dream interpretation because he postulated a metastatic linguistic confusion of reference in dreams as well as in myth, poetry and prophecy. He argued that the language of dreams followed laws of association different from those of everyday speech, using symbolic condensation so that one hiero-glyphic image might act as symbol for something more complex or unknown. Obviously von Schubert's contribution to ideas about unconscious functioning had some influence on Freud. The other influence, attested to by Freud in the posthumously published letters to Fliess, was his interest in Taine's *On Intelligence* (1871), which Freud would probably have known as he formu-lated the *Project* (Freud, 1895b; see also Pribram and Gill, 1976).

Since Taine probably influenced Freud's theory of primary and secondary processes which relate to his ego theory as stated in the *Project*, this material needs thorough consideration. The *Project* stresses an economic account of the organism as having limited energy; if one uses energy for one thing, Freud believed, there is

84 less for something else. He tied this idea to two proposed neurological principles: (a) neuronic inertia by which motor neurons keep the organism free of stimulation; (b) constancy, or the maintenance of equilibrium. Freud saw any action as reducing the tension of imbalance, so that pain and pleasure were defined throughout his theory in terms of tension and detensioning.

Of particular relevance to this view is Taine's idea of perception as 'veridical hallucination' containing antagonistic forces between 'sensations' and 'images'. He defined sensations as those processes that project outwards arising from the stimulation of receptors, sensory nerves and corresponding central areas. He believed that images are caused by a revival of the memory of a sensation. Where recollective images become hallucinatory, these could be neutralized by the external sensory input. This input, as a rival system of images, created a normal state. This idea of antagonistic and complementary nervous function seems fundamental to Freud's concept of primary and secondary processes.

Freud saw any deficit in hunger or sexual satisfaction, as well as a stockpiling of aggression, as creating an imbalance which produced tension. The primary process was immediately concerned with avoiding stimulation in order to achieve equilibrium; primary process involves a summation of the representations of externally induced change plus the immediate product of internal stimulation. The secondary process involves a toleration of some energy use in the process of satisfying the basic drives. In the neuronal theory of the *Project*, the psi neurons operate as a subsystem always energized to inhibit both internally produced images and motor actions arising from the primary process. Freud considered these responses, based on psi neuron inhibition, to be acquired or secondary.

In the *Project* the ego was this subsystem of neurons permanently cathected. The ego has two dangers to overcome: there could be a failure to separate hallucination from externally produced perception so that hallucinatory tension would not be reduced and, similarly, internal memory might overwhelm external perception. The *Project* contains a simple explanatory model which discusses the discrepancy between memory and perceptual image: (1) 'wishful cathexis' as neurons 'a' and 'b'; (2) 'perceptual cathexis' as neurons 'a' and 'c'; the ego halts action because 'b' and 'c' are discrepant and a search process is begun until a perceptual discharge equalling 'b' is achieved.

We have discussed the widely accepted theory that infants do not have a fully developed criterion for distinguishing external from internal image in the first weeks of life. Freud thought the ego was the natural criterion, as it could inhibit the intensity of internally produced imagery, but only through 'biological experience'. This would suggest that the ego needs to have a primary capacity for the whole organism to allocate stimuli associated with the past either to pleasure or to pain. Freud assumed that a baby has a very accurate memory-image of anything that has satisfied. We have seen that Michael Fordham, following Jung, postulates that the ego deintegrates out searching for a 'match' to fit the needs of the baby and that at first the baby can tolerate only a perfect fit without disintegrating. But Fordham was postulating archetypal givens as what at first is matched to outer experience; Freud was using a pleasure/pain ego–memory as the basis of the match. In the baby's long period of dependence, primary narcissism in the first two years of life would be a basic *a priori* assumption behind psychodynamic theory.

Freud has to acknowledge only a limited debt to the early ideas his teachers propounded. To defend this independent position, historical details of his life must be kept in mind. Throughout his life work, Freud was to use the prevailing ideas extant in Vienna during his training in new and extended ways. In his medical training he was taught by the physicalist group of Viennese neurologists who looked to Helmholtz and Mach. They tried to describe biological phenomena in terms used by natural science, helped by electrical stimulation and recording from biological

86   tissue and measuring its effects on neural activity and bodily chemical processes.

Jones (1953–57) traces Freud's work under Meynert and Brentano (see also Bernfeld, 1949; Merlan, 1949) and his tenure in Charcot's clinic, where trainees studied problem-solving behaviour by using hypnosis and observation of seemingly unrelated associations. It was a basic assertion of the training that action is intentional. This had been argued by Brentano and may have influenced Freud's distinction between what is perceived (real?) and what is conceived (only thought?). Although Freud's refusal to have much to do with philosophy is well documented, he did admit that the concept of unconscious determination in psychoanalysis is a psychological counterpart of Kant's philosophical views (Freud, 1914a). Rapaport (1960) sees the epistemological implications of psychoanalysis as closest to Kant.

Freud's teachers were living in a time when Central European thought was somewhat influenced by Schelling. He propounded 'Naturphilosophie' to be 'speculative physics'. All of nature was viewed as an organic, evolving unity with organic processes as the fundamental explanatory principles, thus reducing nonliving nature to the living. The strongest vogue for this thought was in Germany in the middle of the eighteenth century. Bernfeld (1949) points out emphatically that in Austria *Naturphilosophie* never had much power and was at minimal influence in Vienna. It would be true to say, however, that Ernst Brücke, who taught Freud his first courses in physiology was in reaction against J. Müller, a vitalist who always doubted that the velocity of the nervous impulse could be measured. Helmholtz, his pupil, succeeded in measuring it and formed the Berlin Physical Society (1842) with Brücke, Carl Ludwig and Emil Du Bois-Reymond, in order to destroy vitalism, Müller's fundamental belief. Vitalism explains the nature of life as due to a unique vital force different from all forces found outside living things.

It is doubtful if *Naturphilosophie*, although an attempt at monism in which mind might be the only reality, was actually exactly a vitalism. It did have a Heraclitean emphasis on 'becoming', common also to monism. In his sophisticated version of nature as 'unity', Kant postulated a uniting of the mechanical and the teleological. He thought that parts of the organism could be understood only in terms of their function for the whole. (In this theoretical approach he supports the theory of the whole as more parsimonious than reducing theory to separate bits or parts of the whole, and thus indirectly the idea of self as vital to theoretical framework and irreducible from this viewpoint of explanation.) Kant maintained that the existence of the whole implies an end. One cannot see in nature a visible purpose, but he thought one could understand an organism only if one regarded it as produced under the guidance of 'thought for an end'. Goethe picked up this influence and developed a more Platonic implication of this thought by postulating 'ideas' in 'God-mind' manifested as a limited number of patterns for the structures of organisms. The root of this was Plato's conception of the macrocosm of nature as reflecting the microcosm of man, and Kant restated this idea, believing that processes of mind reflect the processes of nature. Jung, in his conception of the collective unconscious, postulated the archetypes as carriers of the 'patterns' of psychological adaptation available to the organism.

Was Freud, after he entered university, concerned any longer with *Naturphilosophie?* Probably not. The only philosophy he studied was in five courses with Brentano, a classical and Aristotelian philosopher. The influence of Lenarch and Müller as vitalists had been overruled in 1842 and Freud did not enter medical school until 1873. By then the faculty was more analytic and the older philosophic style of broad, synthetic, deductive theory-formation no longer held sway. Freud is reputed to have heard Goethe's essay on nature read by Professor Carl Brühl at the Gymnasium although James Strachey, editor of many of Freud's publications in English, doubts that the essay was actually written by Goethe.

88   *Naturphilosophie* does not remain a part of Freud's mature inner *Zeitgeist* if one looks at a thorough review of the facts surrounding his university teachers: we know that Brücke, with whom Freud studied the nervous system for six years, was close to Helmholtz. Both Brücke and Helmholtz were Müller's pupils and founded a club together in Berlin. Helmholtz's contribution to physiology emulated physics and chemistry in its approach. His discoveries were many. One can mention the description of the peripheral nerve fibres, the principle of energy conservation, the measurement of the velocity of nerve conduction, the muscle heat production studies and the several visual and auditory studies.

Freud states that Brücke's influence (see Freud, 1925a) carried most weight with him during his studies. Brücke's assistant, Sigmund Exner, postulated, like Brücke himself, the accumulation of excitation at the cortical centres which Freud was to use in his theory. Theodor Meynert's Psychiatric Clinic, where Freud worked for five months after his clinical training, was another influence of sorts. He used this laboratory for several years.

Meynert's school tried to reduce all nervous function to physical reflexes. Mind as an efficacious agent was apparently eliminated. Meynert's model is important because Freud did have somewhat similar ideas and presented them, after much new elaboration, in the *Project* (1895b). Meynert attempted to work out a theory of how the cortex developed in response to its environment. By its environment Meynert meant both its own body and the external world. He saw excitation as pain-producing. The discharge of excitation was by the subcortical reflex system, but this would not stop the impingement of excitation, shown behaviourally in restlessness or convulsions. Meynert postulated a cortical image of an external agent which could stop the impingement of excitation. He thought that cortical innervation sensations were mediated through subcortical reflex pathways so that a cortical representation occurred at the end of impinging excitation.

Association fibres connected this system physiologically, and Meynert used a sucking infant as his example in lectures.

Before Freud, Meynert postulated the primary ego [*Ich*] as the 'nucleus of individuality' which by association was built up to a unique psychomotor intensity. He used teleology in his theory by defining ordered thoughts as 'goal ideas implanted in the ego':

> The goal-idea is, for example, the cessation of hunger, the means-idea which fits with it can be robbery, work, or someone else's hospitality. Which means-idea gains the force depends on the synergistic and antagonistic ideas which are already sufficiently well laid in the ego. (Meynert, 1889)

How far was Freud influenced by Meynert? It is fair to say merely that he also believed that all nervous excitation and the transmitting cortical pathways involved served the discharge of *all* impinging sensation; he also believed in an ego-structure.

The claims that Freud's *Project* was a rewrite of Exner's (1894) *Entwurf zu einer physiologischen Erklärung der psychischen Erscheinungen* are overstated. Exner's paper shares only in a vague way some of the background ideas of the *Project:* it compares to Brücke's lectures on neurophysiology and Meynert's work on cerebral function in the sense of using Brücke's fundamental mechanisms and Meynert's nervous mechanisms to explain complex psychological processes. The important thing to remember is that neither Meynert not Exner had physiological or anatomical postulates for their assumptions. Freud's *Project* changed this.

Via his own studies of aphasia, Freud began to see the speech area as less circumscribed than had his teachers. His case studies did not fit the cortical location of the speech apparatus which his teachers propounded. In the *Project* Freud added to the prevailing reflex concept by postulating, in addition, a mechanism on the cellular neuronic level which resulted in the transfer of excitation from one periphery of the neuron system to the other. Exner had

90 only assumed this transfer, without postulating a mechanism for it. Freud postulated the omega neurons, which received excitation only when the psi neurons did and assigned consciousness to these. His teachers had no such postulations.

The *Project* had several other innovations:

1. The theory of dreams as wish-fulfilments following on experiences of satisfaction in infantile sexuality has no equivalent in Freud's teachers; Freud argued that somatic sources of excitation were responsible for satisfaction in infantile sexuality, not only excitation from the afferent periphery, as he thought the latter insufficient to explain the considerable excitation involved.

2. The repression of hysteria contained a new concept of repressed ideas: Freud believed them to be isolated from association whether the ego functioned or not, whereas Meynert's 'amentia' involved a weakening of the ego so that hallucinatory ideas were cut off from associative processes.

3. Freud's therapy method was different from everyone else's and clearly innovative.

As for the influence of Freud's teachers on the *Project*, about all that can be said is that Freud generally regarded the cortex as an association mechanism, as they did. He then extended and modified these ideas to entirely original innovative concepts as early as 1895 and continually later on throughout his life. Rather than express his *Zeitgeist*, Freud used part of it as a launching pad for his new ideas, which were in sharp contrast to the available ideas of his teachers. It could be said that he was trying to apply thermodynamics to man and assumed that the nervous system is passive, having as fundamental function the removal of the energies fed into it.

More importantly, Freud included the unconscious within his theory. His work unveiled

. . . the meaningfulness of unconsciously determined behaviour as an indicator of a scientifically accessible process, whereas others had merely concerned themselves with the obvious, i.e. the conscious. (Pribram and Gill, 1976, p. 20)

Freud wrote:

> We at once become clear about a postulate which has been guiding us up to now. We have been treating psychical processes as something that could dispense with . . . awareness through consciousness, as something that exists independently of such awareness. We are prepared to find that some of our assumptions are not confirmed through consciousness. If we do not let ourselves be confused on that account, it follows, from the postulate of consciousness providing neither complete nor trustworthy knowledge of the neuronal processes, that these are in the first instance to be regarded to their whole extent as unconscious and are to be inferred like other natural things. (Freud, 1895b, p. 308)

This solution to the mind–brain–behaviour problem effectively smashed the *Zeitgeist* of Freud's time. Freud was a busy clinician making his living, with very little time to read outside his direct field. Although he was initially influenced by Charcot, Breuer and also probably by von Schubert and Taine, the academic interest in tracing his precursors has been misplaced, since he was an innovator drawing his conclusions from his clinical material much more than from what others thought. He actually represents very little of his *Zeitgeist* in the sense of the prevailing scientific opinion, because in psychoanalysis he applied a new interpretation to all this. The rampant sexuality of Vienna could hardly have been expected to lead him to a theory of repression! Pioneers cannot be 'placed' into historical perspective by the wishful thinking of tidy intellectuals who are afraid of originality in psychology and hence of nonperseveration. There is little point in reflecting that others partly paved the way for Freud. He simply did not know very much about most of them. He had not read many of the ideas similar to his before, during or after his major discoveries, with the exceptions discussed above. Surely Freud was an original genius.

Jahoda's claim (1977) that Freud suffered from cryptomania, or forgetting the source of an idea while remembering its content, is based on her reading of Dorer (1932) who claims that Freud's ideas were 'similar' to those of J. F. Herbart, who had distinguished dynamic from static states of consciousness, and Freud's teacher, Meynert. Freud himself denies this when, in his 'A note on the prehistory of the technique of analysis' (Freud, 1920), he acknowledges three predecessors who used free association as a means of self-discovery in creative writing (but not in the context of an analytic system): Schiller, in a letter to the poet Kerner (1819); Dr J. J. G. Wilkinson (1887) in his published verses, which were free associations on chosen themes, and the writer Börne (1858), who said that novels should be written after three days of associating. Freud, as usual, maintains that colleagues drew these sources to his attention after his own invention of psychoanalytic method, and unlike Jahoda I believe this assertion without reservation. Jahoda goes so far as to claim, in *Freud and the Dilemmas of Psychology*, that

> there can be little doubt that further work . . . restricted to European ideas, will uncover additional material (to be added to L. L. Whyte (1962) and A. F. Ellenberger (1970)), demonstrating that virtually every single idea of Freud's has been conceived by somebody else before him. (1977, p. 129)

What Jahoda seems not to consider sufficiently is that Freud was a divergent rather than a convergent thinker, in Liam Hudson's sense of the terms, and used the idea of free association as a *cure*, without hypnosis, for the first time. If he borrowed from von Schubert and Taine, he transformed this material into a much larger system of dynamic theory.

The essence of Jahoda's lack of awareness of Freud's innovative approach is revealed on page 135: 'Infantile sexuality, too, had been identified by many before Freud. Mothers and nursemaids must have known about it throughout the ages, whatever name they attached to it.' This may be so. The scientific point is precisely that no one before Freud had organized infantile sexuality into a causative concept or understood its interrelation to later development. Most writers before the nineteenth century display ignorance of infantile sexuality as a theoretical concept. Freud acknowledged two doctors: Lindner, who wrote on sexual thumb-sucking; and Bell, who collected more general observations of infantile sexuality. These ideas were tentatively put forward. Divergence rather than convergence characterized the development of Freud's ideas.

b. Freud's physicality theory and its implications for psychology

Freud began his working life as a laboratory scientist, but his experiences with patients led him to a study of dynamics in disturbed emotional, individual psychology, beginning with the relationship betwen parent and child. Initially he based explanation of physical factors on biology, following his medical training. He saw anxiety as sexual tension. It took twenty-five years for Freud to give this up for the psychological theory that anxiety is an ego–defence against some threat, relative to one's past self-experience. This shift from psychological instincts to ego – or self as Freud tended to see it – was important, but Freud oscillated between seeing the ego as the personal self and seeing it as a control system which was only a part of the whole.

This oscillatory confusion regarding how or what one reads in Freud has led Sulloway (1979) to describe Freud's work as a 'genetic psychobiology', arguing with an emphasis on Freud's tendency to use the physicochemical sciences as his early base for a model for scientific laws. As Freud had difficulty, even in his later psychoanalytic ontology, conceiving of a theoretical language for persons as organisms, Young points out that because Freud's ' . . . basic metaphysical position was psychophysical parallelism . . . he did not think organismically and did draw, throughout his life, on a physicalist vocabulary when speaking of mind' (1986, p.25).

In his abstract thought, Freud's language was of mind and of brain. Descartes's definition of mind as that which does not pertain to matter means that mind would have no separate language. But Strawson (1966) argues that one can think about minds only in a language that can connect material objects to persons in a corporeal sense or to former persons as formerly corporeal. This suggests that a whole-person system is what Jung came to in his self theory and what Freud could not include in his metapsychology, where ego was enough of a 'self'.

This question is of prime importance to psychology. Bronowski, during his work at the Salk Institute of Biology, held that man is both a machine and a self. This would allow for two qualitatively different kinds of knowledge: the knowledge of the machine or physical science, and the knowledge of the self, which Bronowski saw as 'outside' science.

But how can genuine psychological knowledge be left outside science? Burt (1968) cites Lord Adrian as commenting: 'For many of us still one thing seems to lie outside the tidy and familiar (materialist) framework – the "I" who does the perceiving.' He also cites Professor Mace: 'Freud seems to have been almost the first to take mental determinism seriously as a basic explanation in psychology.' Burt maintains:

A man's conscious life forms just one continuous event . . . [this] unity and continuity strongly suggest that the constituent events are related to some permanent and central entity, an entity of a special non-material kind, in short a personal self, who owns these events (by reflection) and refers to them as *my* conscious experiences or states, and describes himself by the proper name of 'I'. (1961, p. 145)

If one adds to Burt's 'conscious mind' the 'unconscious' of Freud, the field of psychoanalytic investigation becomes a mental psychology actually called for within the climate of thinking in physical science. Freud's work from 1890 to 1938 gives one a basis for the study of the psychodynamics of the human personality. Psychodynamics as defined by a neo-Freudian, Guntrip, is

. . . the study of the motivated and meaningful life of human beings, as persons shaped in the media of personal relationships which constitute their lives and determine to so large an extent how their innate gifts and possibilities will develop . . . (1971, p. 17)

Salzman (1967) points out that there are two coexisting strands in psychoanalytic history. One concerns the vicissitudes of 'a theory of behaviour in the then prevailing model of energy mechanics and oversimplified concepts of causality . . .'. The other history of psychoanalysis revolves around efforts to

move personality theory closer to a valid statement about man and his psychology . . . The physical models which have been offered to date do not adequately encompass man, who functions through a system of values as well as physiochemical changes. (1967, p. 12)

Freud's ideas fall into two main groups: (1) the id plus ego-control apparatus, and (2) the Oedipus complex of family object relationship. The first group of ideas pictures the psyche as a mechanism for securing homeostatic organization. The second tends to a personal psychology of parents and children. The oedipal work led Freud beyond the study of sex, with its biological basis, to aggression, with its social concomitants of depression and guilt, and into the concept of the superego, an aspect of

96   psychic life traced not biologically but on the basis of identification with parents. Freud believed that once identification with parents occurred, the Oedipus complex was largely overcome.

Freud's hydraulic model or apparatus for the control of id-drives is much more impersonal than his oedipal ideas, with the object-relational life of meaningful and motivated relations between persons as its basis. Freud tended throughout his work to keep these two aspects of his own dynamic drives – the biochemical and the psychological – in oscillation. On the one hand he put forward the mechanistic theory, with the economic and topographical points of view. On the other he presented the personal dynamic theory worked out on the basis of psychological processes within family relationships.

Mechanism had been exemplified in Du Bois-Reymond's manifesto of 1892:

> . . . No other forces than the common physical-chemical ones are active within the organism. In those cases which cannot at the time be explained by these forces one has either to find the specific way or form of their action by means of the physical-mathematical method, or to assume new forces equal in dignity to the chemical-physical forces inherent in matter, reducible to the force of attraction and repulsion.

Freud partially rejected this mechanistic doctrine of physicalistic physiology and created an abstract, hypothetical psychic apparatus in place of the nervous system, in which the operative quantity was psychic, not physical energy. This was not a 'pure' psychology but a convenient abstract theory, based on the brain as he saw it and probably intended eventually to be reunited with anatomy and physiology: 'We must recollect that all our provisional ideas in psychology will presumably some day be based on an organic substructure' (Freud, 1914a, p. 78). In *Beyond the Pleasure Principle* (1959) Freud puts forward his views about the pleasure principle. It gives us an example of underlying confusion between the mechanistic and the psychological:

> The course taken by mental events is automatically regulated by the pleasure principle . . . the course of those events is invariably set in motion by an unpleasurable tension . . . it takes a direction such that its final outcome coincides with a lowering of that tension – that is, with an avoidance of unpleasure or a production of pleasure. (1959, p. 1)

Here Freud uses 'automatically' as a mechanistic term with an unclear psychological meaning. In addition, the terms 'pleasure' and 'unpleasure' may have a psychological significance which he did not fully consider:

> We have decided to relate pleasure and unpleasure to the quantity of excitation that is present in the mind . . . and to relate them in such a manner that unpleasure corresponds to an increase in the quantity of excitation, and pleasure to a diminution. (1959, pp. 1–2)

These views stem from psychophysiology:

> The facts which have caused us to believe in the dominance of the pleasure principle . . . find expression in the hypothesis that the mental apparatus endeavours to keep the quantity of mental excitation in it as low as possible or at least to keep it constant . . . the pleasure principle flows from the constancy principle. (1959, p. 3)

The constancy principle is defined as the tendency to maintain intracerebral excitation at a constant level.

Freud's use of 'endeavour' in the phrase 'the mental apparatus endeavours' suggests purposive teleological striving. This would need a motivated psychic self, which suggests that we are not dealing with an apparatus. If there is an apparatus, on the other hand, this is mechanistic and the term 'endeavour' is out of context. The idea of homeostasis, either on the pleasure principle or the constancy principle, is troublesome to explain psychologically. If a person devoted himself to keeping excitation to as low a level as possible, he would be bored. Increasing excitation might not be experienced as unpleasure but as a relief from dullness. As Freud, in this physiological-quantity theory, reduced psychological consciousness to a mere accompaniment of bodily processes, he seemed to move back towards a scientific materialism.

It is a valid criticism of the psychoanalytic energy concept that it fluctuates between Freud's original physical cathartic quantity traversing the fibres of a nervous system and a more purely psychological, non-physiochemical entity. Freud assumed that physical energy could be transformed into psychic energy, and also that at the ontological 'gap' there would be 'surplus energy' if the psychic was transformed to the physical and a 'deficit' if physical energy was transformed to the psychic. This interactionism assumed a causal chain: a physical event (a pattern of light) causes another physical event (a neural current from retina to brain) which causes another psychological event (visual perception) which causes a further psychological event (an intention to act) which causes a physical event (a movement of the body).

Lashley and Colby argue against any evidence for such an interactionist, mind–body dualism:

Neural activity has been sufficiently well explored to rule out such broad assumptions as of the energy of the libido or of the id . . . The energy of nervous systems is that of transmitted excitations, with its implied limitations and specifications. Energy dissociated from this . . . is ruled out by definite experimental evidence . . . the derivation of psychic energy from one or a few 'instincts' finds no support in the nature of neural activity . . . Where instinctive activities have been analysed experimentally, as in studies of hunger, mating and maternal behaviour, there is nothing that suggests free or transferable energy . . . behaviour can be explained without assumption of an energy other than the interaction of specific neural elements. (1957, p. 234)

Whatever one may think about the applicability of Lashley's specific experiments to the general human psychological condition on which Freud turned his interpretative clinical insights, Freud clearly did not adopt any one or consistent stance on the mind–body problem. His doctrine of psychic energy is similar to vitalism: it is generally dualistic but not clearly so; he does not postulate a spatial order for psychical systems, only a temporal one; cathexis is called a directional energy analogous to but not identical with the energy of physics; it is intrinsically directional, as are vitalistic processes or forces. Psychoanalysis speaks of psychic energy anthropomorphically, as if it 'does things' autonomously; a mechanistic structure is postulated within which psychic energy operates. If these parallels exist between psychoanalysis and vitalism, Freud never identified cathectic energy with either 'entelechy' or '*élan vital*', nor did he ever refer in the *Standard Edition* to the two vitalists nearest to him as contemporaries, Driesch and Bergson.

If, however, psychic energy is almost functionally equivalent to a vital-force concept, does this vitalism or psychic energy hold up methodologically as a useful scientific idea? William McDougall's (1938) hormic or purposive psychology had a doctrine of energies which he linked via purpose as the central 'fact' of behaviour to free will, spontaneity and a belief in the Lamarckian inheritance of acquired characteristics. Carl Rogers (1961) has more recently supported a drive towards self-actualization in a directional sense as ' . . . the urge which is evident in all organic and human life . . . the tendency to express and activate all the capacities of the organism'.

Vitalism degenerates easily into a mere description of events under any label presumed to apply. Is a concept of vital energy useless if we do not have a 'practical' operation to define life-energy? Freudians have tended to use theoretical metaphors without rules for expanding them; hence there is a danger that 'systematic' meaning is lost. Nevertheless there is a fair amount of research devoted to measuring psychic energy (Rapaport, 1960; Schwartz and Rouse, 1961; Ostow, 1962). These experiments arouse controversy as to whether they merely serve a Freudian language in which to discuss cases or are a test of basic assumptions. Schlick (1953) defends vitalism because the adaptiveness of organisms suggests an implication of purpose. Nagel (1953, 1961), on the other hand, claims that direction (as a system without an energy concept) is a matter of structure and information only, not requiring an explanation or inclusion of force. He assumes that causal concepts of natural science are sufficient for explanation.

If vitalism is partly dead, so too is mechanism. Schneirla (1945) writes that mechanism went astray by

> endeavouring to fit all adaptive capacities directly under physico-chemical rubrics . . . and [vitalism went astray] by setting out to bring all cases under a universal supernatural causal principle. (p. 244)

Both systems have sought for an explanation of the organic event by reducing it to a 'principle' or 'category' which 'causes' it to fit. Mainx (1955) points out that psychoanalysis keeps to an energy concept that is defined as being directed. That means there is a tautological problem, since the concepts tend to be defined only by their connection with the processes they are said to cause.

Psychoanalysts today argue that psychic energy can be interpreted nondirectionally and nonexistentially as an abstract, quantitative construct with qualities and direction contributed by structures (see especially Rapaport, 1960). Structural mechanisms refer to a process in which available energy is dispersed. Energic inhibition has come to mean not just suppression or displacement of psychic energies but an elaboration of intrapsychic possibilities (for example the energy between trauma and fantasy in psychoanalysis). In physics, energy – unlike time, space and mass – is only indirectly measurable (Holt, 1965) and psychological concepts do not need to be operational in any simple sense. Freud (1914a, p. 77) argues that 'basic concepts . . . are not the foundation of science upon which everything rests; that foundation is observation alone. They are not the bottom but the top of the whole structure . . .' Holt insists that Freud's metapsychological theory could be rewritten without reference to energy and still retain explanatory power.

2. Early neo-Freudian contribution towards a self concept

a. Introduction

Harry Stack Sullivan (1953), a neo-Freudian, points out the argument against accepting scientific materialism as a basis for psychodynamic study:

> Biological and neuro-physiological terms are utterly inadequate for studying everything in life . . . I hope you will not try to build up in your thinking, correlations [. . . of 'somatic' organization with psychiatrically important phenomena] that are purely imaginary . . . an illusion born out of the failure to recognize that what we know comes to us through our experiencing of events. (p. 20)

Sullivan saw the subjectivity of experiencing, which he defined as interpersonal relations, as the concern for psychodynamic studies. This introduces a way to disentangle object relations from biology altogether. In this section the search for a self theory within psychoanalysis begins with a review of those neo-Freudians who historically can be seen as precursors in moving Freud's ego psychology towards Kohut's self theory within a neo-Freudian conceptual framework.

The work of Klein, Fairbairn and Winnicott traces ego-development back to their view of its earliest beginnings. Melanie Klein kept very little of Freud's psychophysical speculation in her psychodynamic work. She did perpetuate the terminology of Freud's instinct theory and the structural topography of id, ego and superego as well as the oral, anal, phallic and genital stage concepts. Klein saw object relations as a principle not based on biology, physiology or the machinery of personal life; she thought its essential quality was the meaningful personal experience of the individual.

In contrast, Hartmann (1964), in his system–ego theory, hoped to correlate experience with brain physiology and considered social adaptation from a biological aspect. He viewed ego-function as an organ of adaptation to be understood biologically. Adaptation as an ego-aim ends up, according to Winnicott (1965b), as a 'false self' based on conformity, whereas he sees a 'true self' as not only adaptive but creative within the environment.

Nevertheless it is astonishing how Erik Erikson (1964) went on trying to tie psychoanalysis to biological formation; this is well illustrated by his description of the id:

> The 'id' Freud considered to be the oldest province of the mind . . . he held the young baby to be 'all id' . . . the id is the deposition in us of the whole of evolutionary history. The id is everything that is left in our organization of the responses of the amoeba and the impulse of the ape . . . everything that would make us 'mere creatures'. (p. 192)

The name 'id' designates as assumption that the ego finds itself attached to this impersonal, this bestial layer, like the centaur to his equestrian underpinnings; the ego considers such a combination a danger and builds defences to prevent splitting. Here Erikson is assuming human nature to be made up of an evolutionary set of layers. He suggests that we are all split egos, like centaurs, and

therefore more or less pathological. By attaching the ego to a
'bestial' id, he reaffirms the impersonal process of Freud's
biological theory – the id-drives and the superego controls – and
neglects the personal object-relational thinking (in the sense of
self and not-self as a part of object relations) that seems ready to
break through in Freud but never quite succeeds in doing so.

Erikson has delineated ego-identities and studied their roots in
social organization but he stopped short of the whole-person ego,
which the Freudian school tends to see as a concept similar to the
self. He continues to see a strife in which self-destruction is
avoided only if the ego makes compromises between id and
superego. Underneath his ego-identities Erikson has put only an
inadequate psychic foundation: the bestial underpinnings of the
centaur.

b. Melanie Klein – an object-relative self

Melanie Klein's structural theory developed by interpretation
of the internal psychic world of ego–object relations. Unlike
Erikson, she saw these internal struggles apart from the broad
social environment. She conceived them as made up of life and
death instincts, sex and aggression. The inner drama becomes
projected on to the outer world when the baby begins to be able
to discern external objects. Klein saw a baby traumatized by his
own death instinct and therefore having difficulties in perceiving
real objects in an objective way. She believed that the death
instinct is projected on to the breast in the first instance and is
then reintrojected. This would mean that the baby's outer-world
experiences would double anxiety, as the death instinct would
colour the reintrojection of the breast. Klein then claims that envy
is an innately determined constitutional part of all infants' natures.
Between envy and the death instinct she leaves one little hope
for any friendly objectivity in personal relationships, and the
environment is left with less role of its own to play than Freud

gave it. The environment, as it engages the baby, tangles with
the baby's primary anxieties and inner conflicts.

The question one must put to the Kleinian school is this: if the
object-world is impoverished of part of its primary or intrinsic
value, can we speak of genuine initial object relationships? Klein
definitely saw the death instinct as the ultimate source of anxiety
and persecutory feelings. In working with children of two, she
claimed that their fantasy life supported this theory of innately
fundamental conflict. This fantasy world of the child contains
emotion-laden relationships within which a variety of good and
bad objects become mental images of parts or aspects of parents.
Life is viewed totally as a matter of ego–object relationships. At
primitive level, part-objects such as the breast or penis images
develop into whole-objects which the infant may experience as
good or bad. Bad experience is projected on to part-objects,
reintrojected and then projected on to parents, who become felt
as bad whole-objects.

Klein believed that instincts are object-seeking. Eros is internal
and not joined with an Eros 'outside'. The first hate-object will
create the child's anxiety; this is postulated to be its own death
instinct in projection, or Thanatos, which aims to return the
organism to an inorganic state. The breast is necessarily the 'bad
breast', as it has received the projection of Thanatos. As the baby
cannot fully control the breast containing the projected Thanatos,
he introjects the destructive/bad-sad part-object and changes
Thanatos from an instinct into a part-object and then an object,
both literally and in fantasy. External object relations give
concrete expression to Klein's theory of primary forces and their
hypothesized internal relations.

This theoretical route to object relations is probably acceptable
in this form only to the Kleinian school. Much more acceptable
to the neo-Freudians generally and also to the neo-Jungians, as
we have seen, is that there is in the baby a development of an
inner world of fantasy; this inner world is object-relational and

would be a counterpart of the ego's relation to the world of real objects, at first centred on the mother. The end results of Klein's theory is that all therapeutic work would need to centre on the patient's winning back the reality and importance of the external world which was so negatively and definitively distorted at the start of life because Eros was 'inside' only. Kleinian metapsychology rests on the domination of the death instinct.

Klein went further back than Freud into the beginning of life in tiny children. She worked with infants using play and dreams for conscious expression of the internal psychic life, interpreting symptoms of disturbed behaviour relations as clinical material to support her concepts. Klein reworked Freud's stages-of-development theories. Freud saw all libido as sexual and the oral, anal and genital zones as possessing libidinal drive for the pleasure of detensioning. He also saw the oral, anal, phallic and genital schema as a set of stages based on instinct maturation. Klein shifted interest to the quality of ego-experiences in object relations. She proposed two object-relational positions, both seen as problems to the child. These are not just transitional stages, since they are not left behind psychologically in the adult. Klein named the two positions the depressive position and the paranoid–schizoid position. Guntrip (1971) argues that the schizoid position should be considered separately from the paranoid, as the schizoid infant is withdrawn from all object relations rather than being in relationship to objects but feeling persecuted by them, as in the paranoid position.

In the depressive position, Klein postulated the baby has mostly overcome the paranoid and schizoid positions and has whole-object relations. The child then feels guilt and depression when he discovers he can hurt those whom he can also love. These schemata are totally nonbiological. The two positions may oscillate between themselves and the oral, anal and genital clinical phenomena are seen as symptomatic of conversion hysteria, with emotional problems fastening on to some body-part to find psychic discharge.

Klein did not develop ego psychology: rather, the id and the superego play an important part throughout her writing (1932, 1946, 1948, 1952), With her infantile arena of Eros and Thanatos in permanent struggle, Klein saw the ego as creative and loving, and like Freud she saw the primitive superego as hating and destructive as it contains the internalized parent as a bad object. This brings clarity to ego-splitting processes and is a fully psychodynamic clinical approach to object relations as the basis of internal development in infants. Klein realized that clinical work was in itself object-relational between the analyst and the child being analysed. Freud had developed his ideas of transference, oedipal problems and his superego concept from clinical work. Klein left the underpinning of Freud's idea of quantitative gratifications of instinctual drives, to be concerned with good and bad object relationships and the concomitant guilt, reparation, love and hate.

I wish to point out that Klein's theory in no way reflects the baby's mixed good and bad experiences of external objects in real life. Instead, even in the womb the baby is seen to have a split personality, as its constitutional nature has a love or Eros instinct permanently threatened by a death or Thanatos instinct. Thus the origins of this internal world, where the baby lives in dread of his own death instinct, exist before the baby experiences the real mother as good or bad. As the baby projects the death instinct on to the breast the mother becomes bad, as the baby thinks she carries his own innate badness. Could reparation ever heal such a disintegration as this theory claims all babies would have?

Klein argued that to counteract this the baby must internalize a 'good breast'. *But how, on Klein's theory, can the baby ever experience a good breast at all?* If bad-object experience is primary and the death instinct always precedes any projection of the love instinct on to the mother, the problem is insoluble and illogical and seems beyond the reparative clinical work which Klein actually achieved herself!

c. W. R. D. Fairbairn – a whole self

The contribution of W. R. D. Fairbairn (1954a) is particularly germinal both to psychoanalysis and to this chapter. Some of the ideas put forward here will influence the final model of the self to be proposed in Chapter VI. In positing the 'id' Freud visualized layers of the mind, id, ego and superego, in conflict with one another. The archaic layer, or id, was seen to be in conflict with the ego, or more recent cortical layers.

Fairbairn totally rejected the id concept; he saw its origins in Freud's mind as due to a conversion hysteria symptom. Freud made an intellectual attempt to project the infantile, angry, needy life-urge of an infant on to something (the 'id') outside the ego or real 'I'. Fairbairn repudiated Freud's divorce of structure from energy, seeing this as outmoded Helmholtzian-style physics. He argued against the concept of cortical layers and believed in a psychosomatic whole:

> Impulses cannot be considered apart from either object or ego-structures. Impulses are but the dynamic aspect of endopsychic structures and cannot be said to exist in the absence of such structures. Ultimately 'impulses' must be regarded simply as constituting the forms of activity in which the life of ego-structure consists. (Fairbairn, 1954a, p. 88)

Fairbairn kept to a whole-human-being concept and, like Fordham, saw the baby as a whole psychic self from the beginning. He spoke of a 'unitary dynamic ego' and rejected the idea that the ego is initially, internally split, as in Kleinian theory. He rejects Freud's idea that the baby begins as an id, or in instincts at first which seek dispersal. Fairbairn believed the baby to be a whole dynamic being with ego-potential. The baby is seen as a person from the beginning.

This brings forward a new question about what is important in the first weeks of life. It is no longer primarily a question of instinct quantification, instinct satisfaction or the reconciliation of independent psychic structures. Instead, preservation or restoration (if lost) of psychic wholeness becomes the issue of first importance. Fairbairn considered that biology studies somatic processes by methods that tell us nothing directly about subjective experiences. The opposite would be just as true: that subjective experience of a psychosomatic whole tells us nothing directly about biological processes. Fairbairn saw libido not as a biological '*per se*', which he claimed would be a reification of only one element of a more complex process. He thought that a 'libidinal ego' could libidinize any part of the body: not only mouth, anus or genitals but skin, eyes, hands and muscles are included in object relationship. Thus for Fairbairn 'the goal of the libidinal ego is the object', and the self has a libido as a basis for its object-seeking drives.

Fairbairn repudiated Klein's views in an outright manner. He saw the mother, who is a whole ego, as enabling the baby to perceive his own whole ego. There is no postulation of a death instinct in operation. Ego-development depends on initially good object relations or, if these are lacking, therapy may repair this lack. He saw the baby as internalizing a bad mother only if she is actually not good enough. There is no initial projection of death anxiety on to the mother's breast. Fairbairn thought that mothers are usually not wholly bad, so the baby splits his internalization into a 'good mother' and a 'bad mother'. The 'good mother' is projected back on to the mother to enable an idealization that permits the relationship to function for the baby. The bad internalized objects threaten the good object and guilt and depression may occur. Fairbairn hypothesized that the bad internal object is split into an exciting object and a rejecting object. Needing the exciting object sets up baby-to-mother dependencies, and to control and partly relieve this the rejecting object is identified. With this an 'anti-libidinal ego' develops through projective identification with parents when they refuse to meet the baby's needs. Fairbairn's system is complex: he saw three basic fantasized mother-types: (1) the mother who tantalizes needs but does not satisfy them (the exciting object); (2) the authoritarian mother who actively denies satisfaction (the rejecting object); (3) the neutral mother whom the child tries to please (the ideal object).

Object-splitting occurs as both the exciting and rejecting objects are repressed, while the baby projects the ideal object back into the real world. With this splitting goes an ego-splitting into three possible parts:

1. The infantile libidinal ego is always stimulated by the exciting object, needing the personal relations for ego-growth. In adults this is manifest as compulsive sexuality, need for appreciation and chronic overdependency.
2. The infantile anti-libidinal ego, which identifies with the rejecting object, results in underdeveloped conscience, hostility and self-persecution.
3. The central ego, related to the idealized parents and conforming to them after disturbing elements of both ego and objects have been split off and repressed, may become split off itself.

Splitting processes complicate every stage of later development because there is so much loss of unity between self and object. Fairbairn reinterpreted Klein and rejected the inevitability of the schizoid position, while accepting the depressive and paranoid positions. He saw the schizoid position as occurring only if sufficient fear creates a flight from object relations. This would imply a loss of ego-wholeness. Fairbairn's contribution presents an object-relations theory with great clarity and fewer assumptions than Klein's. Both Fairbairn and Klein, however, neglected the problem of the ego's origins.

d. Heinz Hartmann – an adaptive ego

I have pointed out that biology and psychodynamics have been confusedly mixed in Freudian theory. Heinz Hartmann (1964), in an essay on ego psychology, argues that Freud's theory of neurosis was built on biological concepts in that man's relationship to the environment was a study of action as its focus, not being. By relationship Hartmann means an activity-relation or the behavioural viewpoint of biology. Psychoanalysis began with a defective realization of the concept of 'person' or 'self'. Groddeck (1949) wrote: 'We should not say "I live" but "I am lived by the It".' Groddeck's 'It' is a hybrid of the 'id' concept, which Hartmann saw as the 'personality's central sphere'. He thought this included the preconscious apparatus, the autonomously developing apparatus and adaptation of the ego, which he defines as the 'organ of adaptation'. Hartmann developed his ego theory as having two functions: to solve the conflicts of the id and the superego, and to concern the ego with coming to terms with the environment. He saw the ego as adaptive: either autoplastic, altering oneself to fit the environment, or alloplastic, altering the environment to fit in with oneself.

But here we leave biology, for a human being may refuse to adapt to his environment in order to save a truth, a moral or political idea that is more valuable to him than biological survival. In this context, it becomes unsatisfactory to speak of an ego as a mere organ of adaptation. Adaptation needs to be replaced by a meaningful relationship under the ego's direction, as adaptation in itself can express only a one-sided fitting in. Personal relations demand the mutual self-fulfilment of two or more persons. Hartmann (1975) struggles to confine developing human phenomena within a straitjacket of prepersonal biological concepts: 'The crucial adaptation man has to make is to the social structure and his collaboration in building it.' We may describe the fact that the social structure determines, at least in part, the adaptive chances of a particular form of behaviour by the term 'social compliance'. This is often coined in analogy to 'somatic compliance'. Hartmann wants to see psychoanalysis as only about the organism adapting to the external structure of the world, instead of a unique development of the psyche's ego-potential in order for a person to relate to other persons.

Hartmann wants to limit object relations to a study of their relation to biological equilibrium. He does not see object relations as crucial to the maturation of the whole-person-ego. He sees the twin aspects of environmental compliance as the organism adapting to the human environment by both somatic and social compliance in a kind of parallel. But he goes beyond biology when he writes: 'By adaptation we do not mean only passive submission to the goals of society but also active collaboration on them and attempts to change them.' Guntrip points out:

> When a human being challenges or opposes his environment on principle, in defence or pursuit of positive values, seeking to promote more genuine personal relationships, then we are dealing not with biological adaptation to secure survival but with psychodynamic motivation to safeguard the intrinsic quality of personal living. (1971, p. 110)

Here the person, the quality of selfhood, is more important than survival, which is hypothesized as not worthwhile without selfhood.

3. Recent neo-Freudian contribution towards a self concept

a. D. W. Winnicott – the real self and the false self
In *The Maturational Processes and the Facilitating Environment* (Winnicott, 1965b), biology and psychodynamics are related in an essentially object-relational analysis. The biological givens are the maturational processes or innate constitutional potentialities which unfold throughout individual life. These potentialities do not exist *in vacuo*. They require an environment that supports and

permits individual growth. This releases the true or latent self. Unsatisfactory environment forces a false self to emerge in conformity with, or rebellion against, the unsatisfactory condition.

Winnicott maintains that it is the beginning of life, and particularly the quality of mothering, that facilitates the child's ability to develop his real self.

> We notice in the expectant mother an increasing identification with the infant . . . and a willingness as well as an ability on the part of the mother to drain interest from her own self on to the baby . . . This is the thing that gives the mother her special ability to do the right thing. She knows what the baby could be feeling like. No one else knows. Doctors and nurses may know a lot about psychology . . . they do not know what a baby feels like from minute to minute because they are outside this area of experience. (Winnicott, 1965a, p. 81)

The total physical and emotional dependence of the baby at first requires the mother to give him as near a perfect security as she can. Gradually she must allow the baby to gain an increasing measure of independence without basically disturbing the inbuilt sense of relationship and security. Dependence and independence should ideally be complementary. Where the person one turns to must be the person one turns away from, neurotic conflict of a schizoid nature develops. The origin of this lies in the failure of initial mothering to provide both sufficient support and freedom.

Winnicott is here proposing a fusional relationship between baby and mother that is not shadowed by the Kleinian view of bad breast introjection as the baby's world-view during breastfeeding and beyond, but is a more generalized idea of mother–baby complementarity. Although Winnicott and Klein agree that a schizoid nature may develop when the baby realizes that the mother is both the person he must turn to and yet the person he must turn away from, Winnicott believes this is mediated by 'good-enough' mothering, which may provide sufficient support and allow enough freedom for the baby to avoid the schizoid position in the sense of its being harmful or tied to Kleinian theory concerning death instinct. As I have argued above, Klein proposes an iconoclastic negativity which feels depressive as an orientation for universal theory.

Winnicott works from an environmental conditioning base conceived on a neutral spectrum, the two extremes of which are good enough or not good enough for the infant to avoid splitting the mother so acutely into good or bad. He also avoids a theory dependent on Eros/Thanatos projections on to part-objects or whole-objects as the only given in the infant's critical experience of 'Is this environment good enough?', and he is proposing the introjection of much more than breastfeeding experience as a criteria for the baby's well-enough beingness in the first days after birth. Winnicott is concerned with the totality of social facilitation around the baby as it occurs at first within and through the mother, whereas Klein is more concerned with the dispersal of sadism that is buried in her view of death instinct and its projection on to the inner/outer environment.

Winnicott (1965b) uses his term 'ego-relatedness' to describe a child's capacity to experience being alone in the presence of the mother or a representation of her, such as a cot or a pram: 'Ego-relatedness refers to the relationship between two people, one of whom at any rate is alone; perhaps both are alone yet the presence of each is important to the other.' This is the sharing of 'a solitude that is relatively free from the property that we call "withdrawal" '. Winnicott describes the building up of toleration of the mother's absence by the child in a useful formula: the baby comes to bear the mother's absence for X minutes, but then the baby feels he has lost her unless she comes back. If the mother is away X+Y minutes, she must restore her image by special spoiling and mothering. But if she is away X+Y+Z minutes, the baby sees her as a stranger because his ego has begun to disintegrate. Acute anxiety of this kind leads to the schizoid state. This Winnicott relates to adults who, if they have acute feelings of isolation, unreality and non-entity, are re-experiencing basic ego-unrelatedness caused by maternal failure in infancy. A depersonalized person is hard to reach because this schizoid core is:

> (1) withdrawn and regressed in fear, (2) repressed because the weak infant is unacceptable to consciousness, (3) disintegrated in the beginnings of its ego-structure, thus feeling unreal and not a proper person, and (4) . . . unevoked in its potentialities, never fully called to life in the unfacilitating environment. (Guntrip, 1971, p. 118)

We have already discussed Winnicott's transitional object (often the first toy), which the child experiences as standing for the reliability of the mother. As the first symbol of relationship, Winnicott sees this object as the beginning of culture. This requires us to see culture as an expanding elaboration of symbols for representing our life as persons. We have seen that this was Jung's viewpoint exactly. Ego-relatedness would be the foundation of selfhood, the feeling of 'inbeingness' as a definite self. Winnicott distinguishes between two types of experience: orgiastic – the satisfaction of tension-reducing instinct, as in Freud – and non-orgiastic, which is a reliable ego-experience. For example, he observes that a baby will stay at the breast after feeding, not for food or instinct satisfaction but for relationship. He specifically distinguishes 'this field of the bodily relationship between baby and mother' from the biological idea of 'oral eroticism with satisfaction'. In 'The location of cultural experience' (1967), Winnicott states:

> The phenomena I am describing [that is, basic, secure personal relations] have no climax. This distinguishes them from phenomena that have instinctual backing, where the orgiastic element plays an essential part, and where satisfactions are

closely linked with climax . . . Psychoanalysts who have rightly emphasized the significance of instinctual experience and reaction to frustration have failed to state with comparable clearness or conviction the tremendous intensity of these non-climactic experiences [of relating to objects] . . . We now see that it is not instinctual satisfaction that makes a baby begin to be, to feel that life is real, to find life worth living . . . *the self . . . must precede the self's use of instinct.* The rider must ride the horse, not be run away with. (pp. 369–70)

Winnicott thus creates a new and revolutionary position beyond the classical view of psychoanalysis: that instinct phenomena are to be seen as *subordinate partial experiences* relative to the whole of the person-ego growing as a result of 'good-enough' experience of personal relations. The human infant becomes a self, or person-ego, from his original state of mergence or fusion with the mother and identification with her in varying degrees in the period when he mentally separates out from her. Later, individuality will be built upon a basic self of ego-relatedness which enables an adult to experience isolation, suitable self-abnegation or self-devotion within a mature context of giving love without loss of ego-identity and an ability to defer gratification. Obviously this involves the dissolving of the earliest ego-identifications into a real object relation with a strong self-identity and capacity for self-development.

A theoretical position can now be summarized: no longer can one think that psychic life originates in purely internal physiological processes. As the fertilized cell results from two adult psychosomatic whole persons, the psyche and the soma are taken to develop together from the start. The child's first dim environment is inside the uterus. There the birth 'trauma' can cause anxiety. Good-enough mothering can allay this and help to facilitate object-relations experience. Subject and object relations probably begin with the baby's *in utero* response to noise, temperature, etc. This suggests that libido may be a basic psychophysiological drive towards the object-world. It is here that Winnicott links to Jung, who saw libido as the sum total of all drive. The ego is in control of a part of this, and develops a structural identity by organizing experience as it 'goes along'. Here we are reminded of Fordham's neo-Jungian contribution of deintegration as an ego-development theory. The self, in a Freudian setting, comes into its own with Winnicott. Aggression is seen as one part of drive that develops in the service of the libidinal ego, which in turn is part of the whole psyche-soma, whose fundamental energy is libido. Yet Winnicott's 'self', the whole psyche, does not postulate the unknowable parameters of self which Jung proposes.

b. Heinz Kohut's psychology of the self

b–1. Erotogenic zones and self

Heinz Kohut (1977) has been the greatest Freudian champion of a 'nuclear' self within a 'neo-psychoanalytical framework'. His reconsideration of orality and anality well illustrates his theoretical approach. In the Freudian school, orality was considered, if fixated at an early level of development, to be related to an ego-infantilism. Kohut believes that neither drive fixation nor ego-defects are the primary or central locus of the problem. He argues that if the child's self has not been securely established, because of disturbed empathic parental responses, the enfeebled self turns to stimulation of the erotogenic zones, and these drive aims of the self – or, in Fordham's postulation, its deintegrates – attempt to assure itself that it is alive, by over-deintegrating into fragmentation. This forces the self to turn definitely to the erotogenic zones for ego-support, secondarily bringing about oral or anal drive orientation. The ego becomes enslaved to drive aims that correlate to the stimulated body zones.

Thus two strands emerge: Kohut agrees with Winnicott that parental empathic responses must be good enough to prevent ego–disintegration within the child, but he then concentrates on a new view of the erotogenic zones, which historically Klein elaborated. Kohut reshapes oral and anal development theory within terms of influence on a 'nuclear self', in my view the first very clear and separate neo-Freudian self postulation.

In anality, Kohut maintains, it is not enough to say that because there is an anal fixation, a penuriousness develops. Rather one should look at the early stages of self-consolidation which occur during the anal period. Kohut believes that the child is seeking confirmation of his forming self through a mirroring self-object, the faecal gift. The child feels this 'faecal-gift acceptance or rejection' of his tentative and vulnerable 'creative-productive-active' self (Kohut, 1977) as confirming or nonconfirming to his self-image. If the faecal gift is rejected, pathogenic and unempathic personalities may develop or a fragmentation-producing preoccupation with faeces may occur. Kohut would go so far as to suggest that a child will abandon his joy of self-assertion and turn to the pleasure of fragments of the body-self when cohesion during the early faeces-producing period is deterred. This loss of cohesion affects the learning, controlling and maturing of the total child.

Here self-image is not determined by breast-related experience and Thanatos, as in Kleinian theory, but by the 'faecal-gift' acceptance or rejection spectrum/syndrome, so that self-objects are of early and primary importance to the child. Klein brought in negative superego ideas here, earlier in development than Kohut does; Kohut puts the faecal object as a part of superego formulation, not vice versa, with parental empathic responses determining the baby's good or bad feelings, which are introjected into the superego's formation.

In Kohut's theory anality is not merely a reference to anal fixation or retentiveness but requires a genetic reconstruction: a child who feels his self to be empty or crumbling tries to obtain reassuring pleasure from stimulating a fragment of his body-self. This introduces a more symbolic dimension to anality in

118   psychoanalysis and indicates that Kohut does not see libidinal
drive as simply attaining momentum in the child but proposes
that drive experience is subordinated to the child's experience of
the relation between the self and self-objects. Here he agrees with
Winnicott.

Obesity, for an oral example, was seen by earlier Freudians
either as a flight from castration fears or as oral indulgence. This
was believed to lead to a primary drive fixation at oral level.
Kohut believes it is not the child's wish for food that is the primal
configuration. The psychology of the self he developed asserts
that the child, from the beginning, shows a need for a food-
giving self-object. Empathically modulated food-giving is what is
needed, not food as such. If this need is unfulfilled, then the
broader experience of being a whole, or an appropriately
responded-to self, disintegrates and the child retreats to a fragment
of the larger unit, to an erotogenic zone causing depressive eating.
Kohut argues that the basis of movement towards renewed health
must be an awareness of this depressive-disintegrative reaction to
an unempathetic self-object milieu, *not* an increasing awareness
of drive (via education). Drive fixations and ego-correlations to
erotogenic zones occur when the self is enfeebled. The unre-
sponded-to self has not been able to transform its archaic grandi-
osity and its archaic wish to merge with an omnipotent self-object
into self-esteem, realistic ambition and attainable ideals.

Kohut does not see oral and anal problems as a conflict-of-
forces concept – as drives and defences, with defences that
achieve a 'secondary autonomy' from drives. He sees the problem
conceptually as a constituent of the self that has become
reconsolidated because of specific relations between self and self-
object. The decisive issue is not that functions expressing the
pattern of self are autonomous, but 'that a self that had been
threatened in its cohesion and functioning *in one sector* has managed
to survive by shifting its psychological point of gravity *towards
another one.*' A child will shift from a frustrating self-object to a

less frustrating one. Eventually, in the author's view, the less frustrating self-object might become Winnicott's 'transitional object'. The child's control of his teddy bear is less frustrating, at age one, than control of his feelings about his mother–introject.

b–2. Oedipus complex and self

Freud saw the oedipal conflict in terms of drives and defences involving compromise formations or psychoneurotic symptoms within the hypothetical space of the psychic apparatus. Kohut (1977) believes that this classical theory fails to do justice to experiences that relate to the task of building and maintaining a cohesive nuclear self. The result of this process – whether triumph or dejection – is not described by the oedipal theory.

Are oedipal neuroses and self-disturbances related? There are two theoretical possibilities:

1. An emotional retreat from oedipal conflicts may lead to a chronic defensively held narcissistic position.
2. If the self fragments, the mortification experienced by the child may lead to defensively held oedipal positions.

The classical Freudian theory states that sexual desire for the heterogenital parent occurs concomitantly with rivalrous and murderous wishes towards the homogenital parent. Although, with Fairbairn, we have considered the id concept unsatisfactory, in classical theory the id was changed by the repression of the oedipal conflict within it, and the superego was influenced by an internalized imago of the hated homogenital rival. Freud never gave any explanation as to why the superego should not contain an imago of the loved heterogenital figure as well. This walling off of the id and superego from the ego was to prevent an infantile oedipal neurosis.

There are many unsolvable aspects of such a theory. The energy required to wall off oedipal neurosis would take an enormous amount of libido away from intellectual and social learning. The ego could function independently from infantile sexuality and aggression only if the id and superego barriers were sufficiently strong, yet permeable to any intercalated helpful structures. This suggests the self as a candidate for the precondition to the Oedipus complex. The child would have to see himself as an independent centre of initiative before he could experience the object-instinctual desires that lead to conflict and secondary adaptations of the oedipal period. If the child has a cohesive, continuous self he can experience assertive-possessive, affectionate-sexual desires for the heterogenital parent along with assertive, self-confident, competitive feelings towards the parent of the same sex.

Before Kohut's contribution, parental response to the oedipal stage was neglected. Kohut points out that the parent may become counteraggressive from sexual stimulation or may respond with joy to the child's developing vigour and assertiveness. Where parental responses appropriately inhibit the child's unconscious aim, he is helped to modulate his oedipal drive expression. If a father allows an oedipal son to merge in being, he helps the child to self-consolidation and pattern-firming. Where there is no parental echo in response to an oedipal child, the oedipal nature becomes more malignant. Where joy at the child's development is clearly shown by the parents, it facilitates the child's inner awareness of a forward move to new experience from his parental self-objects. Kohut defines the oedipal complex within a self psychology as a matrix that influences the firming of the independent self, but he does not have a true theory of the self's earlier origins at birth as a nonclinical given. Kohut sees both the growth-promoting aspects of the period and its pathogenic dangers as equally important. If the end of libidinal strivings is to secure a 'self' (see Jung's individuation), then the loss of self breaks up body-mind in space, thus also breaking up the sense of continuity in time. Another danger to the self from oedipal strivings is aggression, which is a topic in itself.

b–3. Aggression and self

The classical Freudian position places aggression within drive theory. The oral-sadistic drives are tamed to using utensils to eat cooked food instead of tearing the flesh apart. Destructiveness is postulated as the primary given and the overcoming of killing is seen as a secondary aspect to tame or overcome destructiveness. What the grandiose fantasies of the self may have been when tearing apart and devouring, and how they relate to using cutlery and remaining upright as food is lifted to the mouth, is open to speculation. Although Kohut acknowledges the force of aggression, he sees it as a disintegration product related to the psychopathology of self-objects in childhood. He sees man's destructiveness as a secondary phenomenon arising from the failure of the environment to meet the child's need for optimal empathic responses. Aggression is thus considered a psychological rather than an elemental phenomenon. Like the inorganic constituents of the organic molecule, aggression is a part of tha child's assertiveness and usually remains 'alloyed to the assertiveness of the adult's mature self'.

The real danger to the cohesion of the nuclear self is inability to overcome narcissistic injury: a threat, Kohut argues, more serious than that of physical survival, male dominance or penis survival. Narcissistic injuries would be described in self theory as occurring if in childhood the self-objects' selective responses have not laid down the usual nuclear self. This leads to an acquisition of nuclear ambitions and ideals not characterized by a primacy of phallic-exhibitionistic physical survival or an active dominance. The result is a toleration of death and martyred passivity as fulfilment, seen in Buddhist self-immolations and the mass suicide of religious groups. Another variant reaction can be the appearance of a victorious survival and social dominance at the price of abandoning the core of self, with a resultant sense of despair and meaninglessness (this could, for example, have been the problem behind the suicide of Marilyn Monroe).

Aggression is incorporated into self theory as a constituent of the broader self-configuration, not as a primary instinct striving for outlet, as Freud thought. The baseline in a baby's aggressive behaviour is not the raging-destructive baby but the assertive baby whose aggressions are a part of the firmness with which he makes demands on his self-objects.

The primary configuration is assertiveness. This soon gives way to a larger configuration isolating the assertive component and transforming it secondarily to rage. *In utero*, the baby has had nine successful months of survival. The baby re-establishes his confidence, innately developed *in utero*, by healthily and assertively announcing his wants after birth. *There is no primal scream, it would be entirely secondary already at birth.* This nondestructive assertiveness serves the maintenance of the rudimentary self. Over time, more mature forms of assertiveness develop in which aggression is subordinated to the performance of tasks and can subside when goals are reached.

When the child is frustrated in his phase-appropriate need for omnipotent control over the self-object, a chronic narcissistic rage leads to Klein's 'paranoid position'. A 'conviction environment' is missing and a lifetime of disintegration products may occur. Kohut (1977) is anti-Kleinian in that he sees rage as a regressive phenomenon: a fragment isolated from a more comprehensive configuration of assertiveness, arising from a deficiency of empathy on the part of the self-object. When the child's assertiveness – as healthy merger wishes with the self-object – has remained unresponded to, the idealized self-imago breaks up into fragments and the merger needs are sexualized and directed only to the fragments. This lost merger is accompanied by a chronic narcissistic rage of sadomasochism in fantasy and action. This type of aggression may be held throughout life: for example Hitler's followers, Kleist's *Michael Kohlhaus* and Melville's *Moby Dick*. Lessening of narcissistic rage can be accomplished therapeutically by a reactivation of the original need for the self-objects' responses and the meeting of those responses to a better extent. Governments are parental self-objects; self-cohesion can be stimulated through competitive sport and increasing self-esteem within group activities.

A child's healthy exhibitionism will be affirmed by a self-object mirroring his self-assertion. Normal exhibitionism represents the whole self and the whole body. Single 'greatness symbols' take over: urinary stream, faeces or phallus. Where parental admiration fails, isolated sexualized voyeuristic preoccupations concerning adult power – penis or breast – take over. The original self-object constellation includes fragments both of the grandiose self (exhibition of one's own body) and of the fragments of the idealized object (voyeuristic interest in others' body-parts). The sadomasochistic forms of aggression develop where this constellation becomes pathological.

b–4. A self psychology in psychoanalysis
I would like now to turn to the broader thesis of Kohut's self psychology. He fully supports the position that self/self-object relations are precursors of psychological structures. This postulates that it is a transmuting internalization of the self-objects which leads gradually to a consolidation of the self.

Kohut analyses why a patient becomes angry if there is an attack on his resistances. Freud (1938) called this 'resistance against the uncovering of resistances'. Hartmann (1964) described this anger in another way: ' . . . metapsychologically speaking . . . reaggressivized energy of the countercathexes, mobilized as a consequence of our attack on the patient's resistance'. Kohut points out that Freudians have tended to think of this anger occurring because a correct interpretation by the analyst has loosened defences activating the aggressive energy bound up in them. He disagrees. He feels that the anger is a narcissistic rage caused by a repeat of the patient's early experience of faulty, nonempathic responses by the self-object. The precarious self-of-the-child as revived in the analytic situation depends for maintenance on adequate empathic responses of the self-object, so the patient projects this negativity on to the analyst as a nonempathic attacker of his self's inferiority. Any break-up of the primary self-experience, in which the child sees the merger of himself and his empathic self-object as one, is felt to be threatening.

Kohut points out that within a context of self psychology, a psychology that differentiates objects experienced as part of the self from those experienced as independent centres of initiative or true objects, there is a secure vantage point from which to control anger. Here he shifts emphasis from a mental apparatus as framework to a social psychology.

There is an important link to omnipotence, a feature of the etymology of the term 'self' as presented in the Preface, where in the Indo-European languages the self-words include 'mighty', 'master', 'I can' or 'I seize upon' as root meanings. Kohut assumes that just as the respiratory apparatus of the newborn infant may be said to 'expect' oxygen to be contained in the atmosphere so, too, psychological survival depends on a human milieu of self-objects that is responsive to his psychological 'need-wishes'. Here the deep agreement about good-enough infant environment between Winnicott and Kohut is evident.

If the child's psychological balances are disturbed by under-adequate mothering, the child will perceive and respond to this. The mother, or surrogate, as the earliest self-object, will try to remedy the child's need through action to restore the infant's homeostatic imbalance. Kohut reinterprets the child's anxiety, drive needs and rage as the child's experience of disintegration of the preceding broader and more complex psychological unit of unquestioning assertiveness. This brings about empathic resonances within the maternal self-object. The normal child moves in phase with experiences of merger with the omnipotent self-object, or mother, if she gives him appropriate vocal and tactile contact and holds, carries and talks with him. The child experiences the feeling states of the maternal self-object as if they were his own, and Kohut believes that the child-and-mother or self/self-object unit experiences these feelings in the following order:

1. mounting anxiety in the self
2. stabilized mild anxiety in the self
3. a 'signal' from self-object not to panic
4. a following calm and absence of anxiety in the self-object.

Following these stages, the rudimentary self is re-established over the disintegration products. Defects in these procedures, Kohut believes, occur mainly as a result of empathy failures – on the part of the self-objects. These would be caused by the self-object's narcissistic disturbances or a latent psychosis. If the environment is otherwise responding to the child with a full range of empathic responses, serious deprivation such as food shortage or war do not affect the possibility of a full development of the self in childhood. He does not, however, defend such a controversial statement adequately.

   Kohut's ideas may be reduced to a two-step sequence:

1. The self-object responds to the child's affect signal (not an affect spread), enabling an empathic merger of the infant's self with the more mature psychic organization of the self-object.
2. This need-satisfying action is performed by the self-object.

When deprived of this merger with the omnipotent self-object, the child cannot experience the sequence of spreading anxiety, anxiety signal and calmness. This means he is deprived of building structures capable of dealing with anxiety, which is itself a normal tension-regulating structure. On the other hand, if the self-object over-responds with hypochondriacal attitudes the child noxiously merges with this, causing himself panic or the attempt to wall himself off from panic. Then a weakness in the ability to curb affects of anxiety results. This aligns the pathogenesis of anxiety-proneness and affective disorders with the merger of the nascent self with the self-object's depressive and/or manic responses.

Kohut argues convincingly that the affective disorders were not well enough formulated by the earlier Freudians on the basis of drives and structures; for example, either depression, seen as neutralized aggression turned away from the object to the self, or as the superego sadistically attacking the ego. *Kohut restates the precursor of psychological structure to be the merger of self to the omnipotent self-object*, considering this theory to be a better and more parsimonious framework for the affective disorders than earlier Freudians achieved. In the author's view, this is the most convincing object-relations theory to date.

Problems remain for psychoanalysis and its new inclusion of a self concept. As the adult environment reacts to the baby as if it had formed a self there may be a danger of 'adultomorphic' distortion, since the baby's rudimentary self is seen to be the juncture where his innate potentialities and the self-object's expectations converge. This raises practical problems of when a mother should first see her baby: should the baby be cleaned up from the delivery first? Does a messy baby at birth occlude the baby's potential appearance as a 'perfect baby' for some mothers?

b–5. Conclusions

From this review of the major Freudian contributions to a psychology of the self we may conclude that the self-concept is needed to explain the pathology of the fragmented self (autism and personality disorder) and of the depleted self (depression). Freud's omission of a definite self concept is repudiated outright. Determinism may be adequate to explain that part of a man's psychological activities which are performed in reactive analogy to external world processes, and the law of physics may be an aid to this conception. Some phenomena, however, require for their explanation a self, or posited configuration, which is a centre of initiative – whatever its history – that as a unit tries to follow its own course.

It is generally thought that the newborn infant does not have a reflective awareness of himself as a cohesive unit in space and time. The baby is instead fused to an environment that does experience him as possessing a self and anticipates, causing a channelling of the later self-awareness of the child to occur. The mother or surrogate responds to some but not all the baby's idealized image and the different ways the baby mediates his ambitions. The baby's nuclear self is based on the responsiveness of the nuclear selves of the self-objects. The damage of the parental generation is mirrored in the baby.

Can it be surmised, by looking at these neo-Freudian theorists, that 'self' simply seems a somewhat impoverished term in their hands, whereas it may be the principal or basic theoretical contribution, in its archetypal and symbolic enlargement, as a concept in Jung's self theory and that of the neo-Jungians? There may be several explanations of the present neo-Freudian position: Kuhn has pointed out in *The Structure of Scientific Revolutions* (1962) that we do not have access to an independent real world against which theories (such as a self theory) may be tested. Instead our observations are not theory-free and, together with the puzzle-solving aspect of scientific experiment, a relativization takes place. Kuhn states this relativization to be that what we convey theoretically about the real world seems in part to depend upon the theories we have of it before we test it. This may, of course, explain both the Jungian approach and the Freudian approach, but for further understanding of the self concept in the neo-Freudian world let us look at the contribution of another neo-Freudian, Masud Khan. In *The Privacy of the Self* (1974), Khan suggests that if we examine a person analytically, within as total a field of his concrete reality as possible, a clinically important concept of self emerges: that no one can be directly related to his own self; hence the symbolic forms with which psychologists, and especially Jungians, deal with self theory emerge as essential. He points out that Winnicott's true self is known clinically mostly by its absence. Khan himself opts for the theory that a patient knows his own self only as 'notions of the self'.

From a Jungian viewpoint this seems a very tightly held view of the self's parameters; Jung's theory describes the self as the 'totality' of the person. The ego is a part, a permeable part, of the self. This concept remains mostly unconscious but is not reduced, in practice, to thinking that a patient merely has 'notions' in his/her own self-knowledge, as in Kahn's conceptual position. Jung's view is that we continue to experience archetypal images by living the historical myths onwards, but in modern dress. The living of the myth refers both to the archetypal self-images and to the possible resultant enhancement of personal self-cohesion within this enlargement of consciousness. This does not reify a self theory, since Jung repeatedly states that in the self-as-totality concept, the farther reaches of the self in its unconsciousness would remain unknowable, but what can be known in self-knowledge would not be reduced just to 'notions' of the self. I think, however, that Khan, in his 'notions' idea, is moving towards a definition of self that could be restricted to clinical descriptions within the neo-Freudian view. His concept is that in the experience of self a person is enabled to sense a psychic motility which, if it is to be glimpsed, must be shared in mutuality of trust in a private relationship to another. In this dynamic idea Khan seems to be in agreement with Kohut's idea of the self-object's self-mirroring needs as the essential basis of the nuclear self's survival requirement. Anxiety around self would be of annihilation, and the defence against this would be one of hiding or of staying dissociated. Where regression occurs to dependence on holding, the ego would need either to hold or to regress to this dangerous maladaptive self-experience.

It is interesting here to move for a moment from Kohut to Winnicott. Winnicott argues that these regressions, which are of

clinical danger to the ego but necessary, occur because environmental care has simply not been 'good enough'. Kohut agrees
here, and further elaborates the role of the erotogenic zones in
this process. Khan agrees with Winnicott that these experiences
cannot engender direct self-actualization in the patient when
an analyst interprets rationally or directly, but that symbolic
equations to this experience may actualize new psychological
beginnings in rebirth symbolism, 'born again' feelings and reassessment of self potential.

Clinicians agree widely on these clinical findings of facilitation
of self through regressions, both inside and outside clinical
situations. The ego's vulnerability in this process is seen as a need
for analysis, rather than simply an expression of persecutory
fantasies derived from instinctual conflict. In this aspect of theory
Winnicott, Kohut and Khan part company with Melanie Klein.

The death and rebirth motifs, so richly revealed in anthropological studies from all parts of the world, have led Jungians –
unlike the neo-Freudians – to dare to hope that self-images thrown
forward in dream images, as well as in simultaneous conscious
or waking realization, make their archetypal designation of an
original whole self theoretically valid as *a priori*. With this theory,
self cannot then be reduced to a clinical definition or simply
realized by its absence. Instead, symbolic image and interpretation
between the self and self-objects' relationships merge with the
teleological view that individuation of the self is man's psychological goal, however much this may at times appear to conflict
with collective needs. To contrast the neo-Freudian view and the
neo-Jungian view I would say that the neo-Freudians see the self
as rarely glimpsed except in its relative absence in ego-awareness
or by its clinical breakdown if the ego splinters. The neo-Jungian
view maintains that a Gestalt of wholeness of self-image, while
unattainable consciously except in 'peak experience' or in
symbolic image (for example the mandala), is nevertheless the
archetypal *a priori* goal of the psyche, and crucial to its dimension.

Kohut, in my view, misses this larger concept in his self conceptualization, staying within the view of a smaller self concept. This quantitative relativization does not, however, impede the clinical richness and quality of his nuclear self theory, which is an original contribution. Kohut may be the first profound bridge between Freud and Jung. Freud's and Jung's contributions are not separated by forces at the roots of the philosophy of science or of world-view, or even by differences of personal individuation, but by the intuitive largesse of Jung's self-as-totality theory, which transcends dependence on the tighter clinical definition preferred by Freud and the neo-Freudians.

Jung's self theory also brings into question whether testable theory can be the parameter of speculation about psyche in science (see Chapter V). It is now time to turn to the neo-Jungian work and build up a bridge to my own theoretical conjecture. Chapter III now begins my view as a Jungian analyst; therefore the term 'self' will henceforth be used to indicate totality of the psyche, retaining a central archetypal significance of self-ordering in the experiencer-of-self as its basis, but never its parameter, which is unknowable.

Autism: the childhood self in disorder

Who in the world am I? Ah, that's the great puzzle!
Lewis Carroll, *Alice's Adventures in Wonderland,* Chapter II

1. Introduction to autism as a clinical concept

We have now seen a theory of the self as put forward by Jung and the neo-Jungians. The self theory can be substantiated by looking at a failure of the self-function in childhood: infantile autism. The ground on which to consider autism theoretically needs to be laid. Because autism distorts the development of the self (as a disordered state of integration), it fits with Fordham's deintegration theory: that is, if the self fails to deintegrate normally, the disorder that results is autism (see section 4 below). In normal development the deintegration/reintegration of self would build the ego-development that is missing in the autistic child, as we shall see in the description of integrative failure characterizing infantile autism.

The general pioneer work on the syndromes of infantile autism which particularly relates to this study of the self has been done be Bender (1953, 1959), Despert (1938, 1951), Kanner (1948, 1954) and Rimland (1964). The psychological structure and origins of autism have been studied by Freudian and Kleinian analysts: Bettelheim (1956, 1967), Isaacs (1948), Klein (1932), Mahler (1955, 1969, 1975) Tustin (1972) and Meltzer (1975). Chapter II has indicated that a Freudian and Kleinian foundation can now be extended and modified to include a neo-Jungian concept of the self.

Despert, in summing up his early work with autistic children in 1938, described twenty-nine children, studied over a period of seven years. In all cases he noticed a failure to achieve emotional relatedness to reality. One symptom of this was their use of words echoically as signs, but never as direct communication with others. The autistic language had too little ongoing function or external feedback to engender its normal development. Bender (1959) has pointed out that this lagging maturation occurs in all patterned behaviour of austistic children, be it autonomic, perceptual, motor, intellectual, emotional or social. Rimland (1964) agrees with this and describes autism as a 'total integrative failure'.

Anthony (1958) has grouped the various syndromes of infantile autism into a workable schema (see opposite).

To grasp an overview of the field it is necessary to define primary and secondary autism in dynamic terms, and then to define primary and secondary narcissism. This classification relates primary and secondary autism to primary and secondary narcissism. In considering primary autism it is useful to remember that in general the primal cavity in the infant's early experience is his mouth, and that he interprets his mother's significant caring parts through his own most significant body-zone. That is, hands, breasts or face can be experienced in autistic affect as a mouth. In primary autism these 'mouth' feelings prolong into a mouth-experienced 'hole' type of depression. Bowlby (1969) has emphasized that infants need more than available food. They require 'bearable sensory stimulation from without, and the relief and excitements arising from stimulation from both internal and external sources' (Tustin, 1972). Clinical material from Spitz (1955) and Shevrin and Toussieng (1965) has brought clear evidence that too little or too much tactile stimulation in institutionalized infants prevented them from diverting their attention from sensations in their own bodies (either unrelieved irritation at deprivation or excessive reactive stimulation to overhandling),

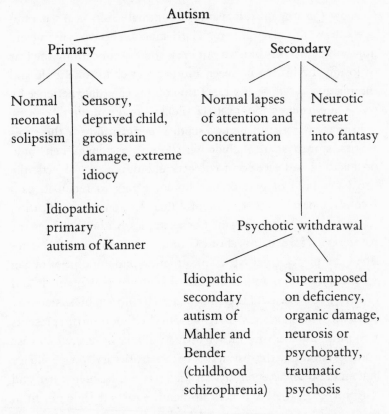

and this often led to marasmic states and death before the age of three.

Secondary autism develops where waiting for the nurturing person becomes intolerable to the child. This overreaction is made comfortable by the autistic process, which produces a pseudo self-satisfaction. Clinical material (Tustin, 1972) indicates that the beating of a child's heart may sustain him when the mother is absent. It is not known if this is because the nipple in the mouth is associated with the beating of the heart or whether the infant has an inborn awareness of the mother's heart and may think that if his own heart beats, mother must be present. The heartbeat is predictable, whereas the mother's presence is not.

The defence against the panic of unbearable physical separateness causes secondary autism. The distinction between living and nonliving objects is blotted out in an anxiety concerning the fear of losing the bridge between mother and child, or nipple and mouth, and avoiding any repetition of this painful experience by repressing feelings about the (tactile) loss of the mother.

Primary narcissism is the Freudian designation for the ego's original store or share of libido with the unconscious. When libido begins to be cathected on to objects and ideas about objects, the ego takes hold of part of this libido, trying to retain it, as a secondary narcissism. It is helpful that Anthony's classification relates autism to narcissism. For example, Anthony relates the pathological form of 'psychotic withdrawal' both to normal states (for example 'normal lapses of attention and concentration' in secondary autism) and to abnormal states such as neurosis and organic brain disease. He claims that each entity in his system can combine with another, so that a case of childhood autism presents a continuous spectrum rather than a number of discrete disease entities. Although the distinction between primary and secondary autism has been accepted by Fordham (1976), Mahler (1969) and Tustin (1972), these workers all mention cases that do not fit in easily to either type of autistic disorder, primary or secondary.

In the 'idiopathic primary autism' of Kanner (1948) the differential diagnoses are between brain damage and mental defect. Kanner maintains that the less serious secondary autism is different from obsessional disorders, although Bion (1955) and Meltzer (1975) see obsessional states as more like autism. Kanner's (1954) overall criteria for autism, however, retains the 'obsessive maintenance of sameness' as a major aspect of the syndrome.

Prognosis in autism is poorest when there is mutism. Children who never speak or who never do so beyond a few words are less likely to recover than those who have started to speak but regress in response to a traumatic event such as the birth of a sibling.

Mutism as a symptom suggests that the core of the disorder stems from the very early life of the infant (Fordham, 1976).

Autism tends to interfere with normal language development because processes of identification with speaking objects are stunted. Identification through the autistic child's narcissism encourages him to deal with the bodily features of objects rather than the mental function required in interrelationship with them. Meltzer (1975) claims that even where there is some speech, these language events occur within the autistic state and are essentially meaningless (as in equivalent epileptic states). Gestures and signals are sufficient to control objects, which – as they are dehumanized through poor identifications – is all the autistic child desires to do.

In general the inner mental activity of verbalization and its manifestation outwards, vocalization, is not so clearly conceptualized by science that clinicians can know how to frame it theoretically when severe disturbances occur. Clinical research is heavily based on an analytical approach to speech. The clinical way psychologists generally consider language seems to be based on the content of Wittgenstein's 'deep' language (1945) and Chomsky's 'deep grammar' (1966) and can refer to Langer's ideas on a musical basis of language (1942), which is interpreted to apply to 'deep' rather than 'surface' structure.

The child obviously requires a deep grammar, in Chomsky's structural sense (1968), to represent states of mind and to order thoughts in a way suitable for communication by some means, rather than, as in Bion's view (1955), just to evacuate thoughts easily or blindly in a constant projective identification. Presumably, inner speech 'must find an object in the outside world which has sufficient psychic reality and adequate differentiation from the self, to require the vocalization of this inner process in order for communication to take place' (Meltzer, 1975). Desire for communication with others at this level must be sufficiently maintained, or autism develops. (I shall be developing my ideas

136   about normal infant speech under the section in Chapter VI on the speech con-integrate.)

Donald Meltzer has tied the problem of a deficit in object-awareness in the autistic child to the mutism or near mutism evident in autism, and sees this as a 'dismantling of self' (1975). He argues that the autistic child maintains a ruminative preoccupation with the way objects are linked together. This relates to obsession-ality, as in the autistic child there is an oscillation between omnipotent control of the object and a separation of any mental linking of objects, to gain a better obsessional control of them individually. Meltzer describes this oscillation as essentially leading to a suspension of mental life, a self-induced stupor. This leads to an internal sense of spacelessness of self, which continues in the post-autistic child.

The constant monitoring of the object when the stupor is not present is an effort to keep the object split so that the oscillation of obsessionality described above can continue. Otherwise the split would tend to reunite, since its good/bad qualities would tend to move to a whole-object as self-object. In this theory, Meltzer agrees with Melanie Klein that in a child part-objects normally move to whole-object comprehension.

The dismantling of self described by Meltzer leaves the autistic child in a passive state that allows for any exciting object of the moment to gain his somewhat suspended attention. Since some autistic children cannot distinguish between the inside or the outside of objects, the object falls into bits and has a paper-thin aspect. The child then serves this dilapidating object with some attention. He splits the object and then idealizes it. Meltzer compares this double aspect to the tendency of a primitive permeability in the autistic child to the emotions of others, especially those of the mother, as well as an insatiable sensuousness which causes a compulsion towards repetitive possessiveness of mother. It is possible that the primitive permeability moves to attacking any linkage between objects (in the cognitive sense of relatedness) so that the ego cannot hold normal mental comprehension of objects' relatedness and 'allows' objects to fall into bits and then spring back together again as if by magic. This impairment of ego-function harms both introjective and projective processes, as the ego reintegrates only objects that become 'exciting' after the long periods of induced stupor, with its obsessive splitting and ego-pathology, which Meltzer views as a dismantling of self in the child.

This abnormality of mental life in the autistic infant can damage at least five aspects of mental life that are essential for language development. Meltzer considers that there is a deficit in mutism suggesting severe damage in the autistic self/ego in:

1. the desire to communicate states of mind and information;
2. the need for objects to have a psychic reality;
3. the normal identification and attention to speaking objects;
4. the building of a vocabulary for dream thoughts;
5. a thinking sufficient for elaborating dream thoughts to processes of thinking and memory.

Even if mutism improves and the child is diagnosed as post-autistic, Meltzer suspects that a pregenital oedipal jealousy interferes with a 'verbal coition of internal objects', so that the introjective and projective damage in the ego may remain in some impairment, and symptoms of the obsessional and ritualistic attempt to control the dehumanized aspects that objects assume for the post-autistic child continue to be present. This leaves little psychic energy for a normal desire for communication:

> Because the identification processes are so interfered with and the adhesive mode fails to delineate the particularly human, let alone animate, aspects of the objects but rather their sensual and mechanical qualities, the distinction between animate and inanimate, human and nonhuman, does not develop or lead to

the evolution of internal objects which are a suitable object for speech. (Meltzer, 1975, p. 205)

I want to turn now to the influence of the mother on the infant, which is another important aspect in the literature on autism. Both Anthony (1958) and Mahler (1969) argue that the mother is less significant in the primary group than in the secondary group, and they would not find the mother's influence absolutely decisive in either. The designation of 'idiopathic' infantile autism is thus justified. On the other hand, Winnicott (1955, 1958, 1965b, 1971a) definitely considers that there has been an environmental defect which must include the mother's role, and Bettelheim (1967) contends that autism occurs because the children so afflicted came into the world only to confront mothers who wished for their death. Tustin (1972) sees the mother–infant interaction as the basis and fulcrum of the therapeutic repair necessary in the treatment of autism, implying that the aetiology of autism includes a defect in the baby's relationship to its mother.

2. *The genetic hypothesis of autism*

For the development of the thesis of autism as a disorder of the self, we shall confine ourselves to a study of characteristic features of idiopathic autism – that is, the full-blown clinical-pathological disease. There are two types of hypothesis postulating a 'barrier' between the child and the external world.

Anthony (1958) presupposes that an autistic child is born with a 'constitutional stimulus barrier' which may be insufficiently reliable or grossly defective through insufficient maternal care, or may be both strong and sensitive and yet become pathological as a defence against defective mothering.

The majority of workers – Mahler (1969), Winnicott (1955), Bettelheim (1967), Tustin (1972), Rimland (1964), Bender (1953) – do not presuppose a barrier from the beginning, although it may become established later on. Mahler, for example, believes that autism arises from two stages of infant development which may not have been outgrown. Each stage lies at the root of two kinds of psychosis she distinguishes. In primary autistic psychosis, or the first stage, the infant has no awareness of his self as distinct from the inanimate. 'Symbiotic psychosis', or the second stage presupposes a separate mother and baby who fuse into a unity 'which is characterized by delusional, omnipotent symbiotic fusion with the need-satisfying object' (Mahler, 1969). Since an insecure boundary between mother and baby is assumed in symbiotic psychosis, a rigid and separate classification other than primary autism (where no self-object boundaries exist at all) may be difficult to sustain without resorting to a barrier concept where both types of illness can be included, the barrier postulated as variable.

How a barrier comes into existence has different explanations among workers in the field. Rimland (1964) speaks of organic failure of the arousal mechanism in the centrencephalic system; Bender (1953) places the origin in some disorder of intrauterine life; Tustin (1972) argues that the barrier develops out of very early psychotic depression; Bettelheim (1967) ascribes it to a death wish on the part of the mother; and Winnicott (1965b) thinks it is wholly due to environmental failure. In the present state of knowledge, it would appear that any one of these explanations, alone or in combination, could describe most aspects of the global integrative failure, with its arrests and regression, which autism contains, but that no sufficient definitive explanation or proof of a barrier has been empirically put forward by any of these experts.

3. Object relations in autism

The child's relation to the 'external' object is arguably the most elementary of all characteristics of autism in that mothers are quoted who detect the disorder as originating during breastfeeding (Fordham, 1976). With a hypothesis of such an early origin, the core of the disorder is unlikely to be completely understood merely in terms of a child's retreat to an 'inner world'. The literature agrees that autistic children manipulate any object that engages them and that the child's interest in the object is not exploratory but complies in advance with what he has already obsessively decided he wants to do with this object, be it a toy or a hand or arm of a person. Failing this, the autistic child will rage or panic, treat the object as nonexistent or cease to be interested. Fordham (1976), Kanner (1948) and Diatkine (1960) have separately argued against a lack of perception of objects on the part of the autistic child, and they maintain that there is a close inspection of reality. Diatkine says of one child: 'He lived in a perfectly perceived world, but one devoid of meaning as an abstract painting composed without inspiration.' The child, because of the world's apparent meaninglessness to him, does not investigate what he perceives. Autistic children exhibit a passive compliance when adult intervention changes their activity. This curious detachment apparently affects the child's own choices as well. Tustin (1972) maintains that the autistic child will omnipotently try to control human objects, but will do so as if they were inanimate.

These descriptions of autistic behaviour suggest that if autistic children live in an 'inner world' it may well not feel so to them; rather, they live with an object-world that may be precise and organized, but not in terms of what is inner and outer. We have noted that a firm distinction between what is internal and what is external requires a child to reach a stage where the ego is strong enough to distinguish between inner and outer after the state of fusion with the object has been lived through and superseded. If this has not happened a barrier is set up, not against parents as external objects or to protect an inner object of the child, but against *any not-self-object*.

There is, however, a type of autism where secondary fantasy systems may work as unreal world-systems. Symbolic representation occurs in these less ill children and they develop object-relation systems, but observation of real objects is not precise and is exaggeratedly determined by affective processes. With such children the adult must enter the child's world-system so that the child's self can fuse with him and continue in maturational development.

Meltzer (1975) points out that the obsessional quality of the autistic child can lead to total withdrawal of attention in an effort to manage massive depressive anxiety. Containment of the object is not possible and mental life disappears. Objects seem to be 'paper-thin', lacking three-dimensional quality:

> Only isolated motor and sensory modalities remain, so that the child presents the pattern of a ruin which the therapist can handle like an archaeologist who confines his activities to observing bits and pieces which he can grow to recognize as isolated bits of a structure that is no more. (1975, p. 223)

It must, however, be said that the dismantling and reoperation of single sensory motor modalities and the surface nature of object relations may express an attempt of the self, albeit a distorted one, to arrive at a simple operational unit so as to begin development and correct the fault.

The obsessionality which characterizes autism arises from two factors in self–object relations: it depends on omnipotent control by the self over the objects and it relies on attacks by the self to the linking of objects to separate them so that they may be better controlled. This attack on the linkage of sensory modalities seems to be an essential operation for the autistic state proper, as has been pointed out above in considering Meltzer's work. It is directed against the ego's attention to sensory modalities in a passive and nonsadistic mode: 'The ego-function of attention is manipulated in a way that simply allows the experience of objects to fall into bits and to spring back together' (Meltzer). There is, therefore, a spectrum of sadism. At one end of this spectrum would be the cruel pleasure with which objects are held in a state of suspended animation. At the other end would be the nonsadistic dismantling of the self which Fordham sees as an attempt to reconstruct a healthy self from one simple sensory modality upwards. Interference with emotional responsiveness in the autistic child seems to refer to a 'cerebral' oversimplification when obsessive thought obtrudes upon distorted object-experience.

This may relate to Winnicott's 'transitional object' (discussed in Chapter I, section 3) in that the dismantling mechanism so evident in autism could be the basis (in normal development) of the formation of transitional objects. Normally a transitional object is the infant's first 'not-me', but also 'not-mother' object which moves to a self or 'myself' as separate from, yet related to or potentially in relationship to, all other objects. If external objects are not correctly or normally perceived, a strong narcissistic organization, a factor in autism, may develop an essentially perverse or fetishistic tendency and the transitional object is then focused upon to reinforce narcissistic isolation. If so-called transitional objects are strictly adhered to or substituted in lieu of human relationships, this can be a first reliable sign of pathology (Mahler, 1969). Winnicott (1953) agrees with the overall psychological claims that autistic children have severely abnormal object relations and describes the breakdown in perception in autism as the breakdown of 'the perceptual human task of keeping inner and outer realities separate and yet interrelated'.

Rodrigue (1955) sees the idealized first object – the breast – as an object stimulating defensive observation, because any alteration of it would be terrifying. This is theoretically argued because the breast, as an idealized 'internal' object possessing characteristics of omnipotence, is invulnerable to destructive drives ejected into the external world. Thus the infant erects autistic defences against a potentially 'terrifying world'. Preserving the 'good-object' projection can reinforce defences. Rodrigue proposes that a 'bad object' is dealt with by negative hallucination. It is actively removed from relation to the ego by denial. This would suggest a triple process in the autistic system: (1) projection, (2) a negative hallucination to eliminate the projection, and (3) idealization of the 'internal' object. Freud (1924, 1938) originated this idea of eliminating projection and argued that the object is made nonexistent by affective processes which prevent it from having any effect on the ego. Freud considers the ego's alienation from reality to be the pivotal disturbance in adult and adolescent psychoses. In infantile psychosis the fact is that the baby has to become acquainted with reality gradually via the mother. The psychotic child is unable to use his mother to arrive at a primitive or core-sense of her as a need-satisfying object. In this case a solid sense of external reality is never attained.

Rodrigue's theory suggests that the autistic child's acute observation of reality should be interpreted as a continuous scrutiny of the object (the breast-mother) in case defences should fail at any point. He sees this as a primary feature of autism.

4. The self and autism

Fordham (1976) has attempted to bring together the ideas presented above into one theory resting on his concept of deintegration. This neo-Jungian theory, drawing on the Freudian and Kleinian studies already discussed, is based on the idea that a healthy baby is a psychosomatic unity or self and that the self will contribute, by deintegration, to the differentiation of all psychic structures in the course of growth. Deintegration differs from the release mechanism of the ethologists in being conceived of as a psychic as well as a physiological process. Deintegrates derive from the primal self and carry the attribute of wholeness, treating the 'external object' as a part of this wholeness. In breastfeeding, 'if the child's mother does not match the infant's need closely, she, or any part of her not provided, is deemed by the infant not to exist' (Fordham, 1976).

Empirical evidence of the mother's and baby's interactions is hard to obtain in the earliest period. Feeding schedules are useful, for too great an ease in feeding may lead later on to the compliance symptoms of autism. In idiopathic autism, deintegration seems to have become split off in the autistic baby from the normal psychological correlation to the body by the time breastfeeding begins. The baby shows no effort to relate to the mother – no smiles, friendly looks or play during feeding. If this pathology of integration is formed, the organism will be damaged whether before or at birth, or the mother may unknowingly damage the baby through her unconscious wish for his psychic or even physical death.

Whatever the degree of integrative pathology in various autistic children (and personal behaviour patterns are reported to vary enormously), it is postulated that none of their behaviour patterns is built into the 'main body of the self' (Fordham, 1976). If, for example, in breastfeeding the neurophysiological apparatus operates without its normally available psychic counterparts, reintegration is too rigid, negative and dehumanized. This prevents a coherent ego–self relation, which in turn prevents a continuing self-identity and self-esteem. A system develops which makes 'external' objects conform and be treated, along with parts of the body-image, as the primal self, or the autistic child may annihilate them altogether. Apparently deintegration/reintegration either does not operate at all or only partially.

Before ego-development, the infant cannot distinguish 'not-self'. In autistic children, where no capacity for symbolization exists, the postulation of a basic catastrophe in the relation between baby and 'breast-mother' is useful. Bettelheim believes that the baby despairs when the feeding experience provides no communication, because he cannot participate in it and becomes defensive.

5. A defensive barrier theory

For autism to be a problem of damaged or overpermeable barriers between self and not-self, defence systems would need to exist in the self to respond to impingement. Stein (1967) has postulated that the self has defence systems which preserve identity and establish and maintain the difference between self and not-self. He points out that immunological research suggests a theory that immunological reaction is aimed at rejecting or annihilating not-self objects such as bacteria and alien tissues. Biochemical processes are furthered in a healthy way only by objects that can be assimilated to the self (see Chapter IV for a full discussion of this theory). A barrier in autism may be constructed if the baby has pathogenic noxious stimuli *in utero*, during and after birth. A persistent reaction of the defence system would take place which, through the baby's projective identification, would become compounded to parts of the self. Not-self-objects would hold a great danger and would be felt to be the principal focus of attention so that no inner world would develop, deintegration would not proceed normally and the primal-self integrate would persist against maturational pressures. This would lead to disintegration and the defence system would build up to violence and hostility, split off from the natural libidinal communication with the object.

Autism suggests that an infant cannot shut out or organize the continual flood of perceptual stimuli received into the self. The autistic child does not relate as a whole either to internal or external objects. This obstructs his growth. The component parts of the self in relation to the whole organism cannot develop.

The several models for autism to which I have referred above might be summarily expressed as follows: they indicate (a) an extreme vulnerability to stimuli; (b) a dissociation of behaviour from the self/ego integrates; and (c) a defensive barrier. The field remains wide open for further research; it is too soon to attempt a full integration of the kinds of symptoms turning up in the literature to construct one theoretical model for autism.

The best overall statement in terms of the author's *a priori* assumptions of self theory is that of Fordham (1976), who states his resultant general approach to the theory of idiopathic autism (as a disorder of the self in infancy) in this way:

> It is assumed that the essential core of autism represents in distorted form the primary integrate of infancy, and that idiopathic autism is a disordered state of integration, owing its persistence to failure of the self to deintegrate. (1976, p. 88)

The autism theory strongly supports Fordham's general theory of deintegration within a theory of the self in early childhood. It is parsimonious in combining aspects of Freudian, Kleinian and Jungian concepts into an integrated self theory which can explain what is now known about self and infantile autism. The fact that autism does so distort the development of the infant self provides evidence that there is a self that can be distorted and that this self is an essential concept in the theory of very early human life.

Chapter IV

Self and physiology

He that is giddy thinks the world turns round.
Shakespeare, *The Taming of the Shrew*, V. iii

1. The infant self and physiology

In this chapter I shall argue that there is a basis for assuming a clear physiological self in the theory of infancy, and I shall defend analogical arguments from that basis as an approach to a further convergence of depth psychology and experimental psychology. The reader will begin to see the results of pairing the two disciplines towards a greater union of thought in the physiological studies that relate to self theory.

The known facts regarding the physiology and maturation of the brain provide a basis for the claim that the infant has a considerable brain-function at term and that the correlation of physical state with self/not-self is a justified study.

Cortical brain-function (Herrick, 1963) is arguably different in kind from subcortical brain-function. Qualitative differences in morphological organization show up, especially in reflex responses:

> Reflex responses usually follow immediately upon presentation of their adequate stimuli and their central adjusting mechanisms are elaborated within the relatively direct lines of conduction employed (medulla oblongata, midbrain, thalamus, corpus striatum, etc.) . . . cortical functions are in larger measure

delayed reactions and individually acquired controls redirecting and recombining the innate reflex . . . (Herrick, 1963)

The introduction of large masses of higher correlation tissue concerned with delayed reactions within the innate reflex apparatus would tend to distort the reflex patterns and interfere with their prompt and efficient independent action when this is desirable. (Herrick, 1926; reprinted 1963)

The neurophysiology of attention-mediating systems in mammals involves feedback networks between nuclei of the thalamic reticular system and the neocortex. The reticular formation consists of a network of interconnected neurons. Magoun (1952) has shown that excitation spreads over this in a gradual change of its level and that some of the fibres run upwards from the reticular formation to the structures of the neocortex. Descending fibres from the neocortex create a 'reflex ring' principle, capable of changing cortex tone but also under cortical influence that subordinates lower structures right down to the brain stem.

Bronson (1965) contrasts the global-alerting capacity that takes place if brain-stem activation of the neocortex occurs with the rapid and focal alerting mechanisms of the thalamic reticular system, which allow for an attention either to specific sensory modes or to particular input patterns within these modes. He firmly believes that thalamic nuclei activate parietal, occipital and temporal areas just adjacent to primary sensory-reception areas. The control which the neocortex has over the thalamic reticular system would enable the neocortex to modulate its excitation level, enabling selective attention to 'significant' aspects of immediate input. This allows the infant a chance for 'exploratory behaviour' if other dominant motivational systems are not turning attention to 'needs-relevant' objects only.

The option to delay responses by an inhibitory process is important for learning from experience. If several immediate possible responses are not made, there is additional time to consider the nature of the stimulus and select a response appropriate to the context of previous similar responses held in memory. Brain lesions that interfere with the option to delay responses (subfrontal, temporal, anterior limbic or hippocampal) usually impair recent memory-functions.

A selected behavioural response could involve a symbolic withdrawal from the stimulus, with or without a physical withdrawal. On the other hand, if responses are made without regard to internal state and the impingement of painful external stimuli, a sufficient condition exists for the development of a dual consciousness or 'unreal self'. The human cortex allows a very young child to respond to environmental stimuli with a lower threshold than the normal response to visceral stimuli. Cortical function is sufficient to mediate responses with a relative disregard of visceral imperatives. Thus young children

> have the sufficient neurological capacity to eat when they are not hungry, to 'potty' when there is no need, to use a spoon at mealtimes when fingers are preferred, to 'shush' when they would otherwise cry or scream . . . *ad infinitum.* (Janov and Holden, 1975, p. 61)

When external stimuli are very intense, the disregard of visceral imperative may occur to extreme degrees – for example primary anorexia, extreme obesity, drug abuse, alcoholism. These clinical illnesses suggest that human cortical ability to symbolize the relation to external stimuli may mediate responses with no observable relevance to the personal, visceral need. It should be pointed out that 'the organization of the human cortex does not present a necessary organization for this dual consciousness, only a sufficient one' (Janov and Holden, 1975).

The study of body-memory has led to the development of a new logic or dialectic regarding the adequacy of specific parts of the brain at a given time of early development, and what portion of the body and brain might code early preverbal memory. An example would be the memory of a painful stimulus in a three-month-old child. The infant would not represent a painful reaction by an overcontraction of his lumbosacral muscles or facial frowning because the muscles of the face and body-wall – the sacrospinal, truncal and proximal limb muscles – are mediated by a portion of the brain not yet adequate in either afferent or efferent function to allow this. One would look to the median zone, where trauma could be represented: in stomach pain, oversecretion of hydrochloric acid, spasm of the colon, anaemia or cardiac arrhythmia.

Myelination is the process whereby nerves obtain the white fatty covering named myelin which enables the nerves to conduct impulses more rapidly. Myelination of the brain, even in adults, is sparse in the median zone, so the paucity of myelin in this zone in infancy cannot be a basis for rejecting functional adequacy of a newborn's brain. Neurological function is not all-or-nothing. It represents degrees of reactivity. The median zone is made up of multisynaptic nerves interconnected ablaterally like a three-dimensional spider's web. Median-zone nerves are not connected serially or in parallel. Little is known about all that such a median system can do at three months. What is known is that with increasing age the mediation of the stimulus–response relationship increases functionally. The difficulty in precise statements about this is that – using our capacity to move the fingers as an example – simple finger movement is represented at spinal cord level, rerepresented in the medulla, pons, the relay systems in the mesencephalon and with extensive elaboration by the basal ganglia. It is known that further modification, fragmentation and selective inhibition occur at the level of the cortex.

The relationship between the development of myelination and the onset of functioning in nerve pathways is now documented with some accuracy (Yakovlev, 1962). This is important, because adequacy of the brain system in the visual and vestibular systems

correlates behaviourally in an almost one-to-one manner with
the thickness and distance of myelination in a given pathway.
Yakovlev shows that body and limb posture extension occurs at
five to eight months, when the requisite vestibular pathways are
myelinated, and underlies the adequate relationship to gravity,
helping to mediate the ability to roll over, sit up and finally to
stand.

The brain has three concentric layers: an inner matrix zone,
which is never well myelinated but starts to become so first; a
middle mantle zone, which is next to myelinate; and an outer
marginal zone, which myelinates last.

> The progressive myelination of the neuraxis is the most readily
> observable morphological criterion of maturation . . . In the
> central nervous system, myelination until term is confined
> almost exclusively to the fibre systems of the mantle zone in
> the wall of the neuraxis . . . It spreads from within out, towards
> the marginal zone, but the fibre systems which develop in this
> outermost or cortical zone of the neuraxis, or are derived from
> this zone, do not begin to myelinate until the end of gestation
> is reached and the infant is about to face extrauterine life.
> (Yakovlev, 1962, p. 29)

In the normal infant, at term, the observed facts support the
argument that the inner brain is mature enough to mediate visceral
responses and the central nervous system is myelinated in the
mantle zone. For concepts of a self/not-self awareness it would
be important to find out if the mantle zone of the brain could
contain a system of fibres which can register pain as protection of
the self from anti-self. French *et al.* (1953) argue for two pain
systems in the brain: a lateral one and a medial or middle one in
the reticular core of the neuraxis. The latter system is most
susceptible to general anaesthetics, which suggests a dominant
quality or capacity. Hilgard (1973) and Leibeskind *et al.* (1973)
corroborate that in cats, electrical stimulation of cells surrounding

the middle of the midbrain abolishes pain reaction for the duration of the stimulus. This supports the idea that there may be a gate to pain from the periphery in the middle of the midbrain. Critchley *et al.* (1972) and Janov and Holden (1975) also support this thesis.

From this work it can be argued that the brain of a newborn child is mature enough to register and transmit pain along the course of a medial reticular pain system and that depth psychology, in its concern with early experience, is supported by these findings. This is fundamental to the idea that the self is functionally whole enough at birth to be subject to attack (pain) from not-self, or that which is outside itself via environmental stimuli. The midline pain experiments also support the idea that the quality of early handling by the mother or caretaker is important to infant pain relief. It also supports psychosomatic indications that adults when stressed will, if they have had pain-filled infancies, emit visceral dysfunction which reflects an obligatory learning of maladaptive visceromotor reactivity in relation to this early pain.

The neurophysiology of attention supports the idea of a sensory gating function residing in the rostral pons and midbrain. Hernández-Peón (1969) argues for a gating contribution not only from the neuraxis below this site but to all cerebral sensory analysis. This would include early body-memory. The principle upon which this argument is based is that the midbrain reticular formation, via reciprocal relationships with the neocortex and the limbic system, is serving a 'strategic' function of directing attention to particular sensory inputs rather than to all, thereby diminishing attention to 'irrelevant' or less important input. This is documented by Hernández-Peón in electrophysiological data supporting selective enhancement/inhibition of neuronal activity as the basis for directed attention. Different biochemical neuro-transmitter substances are claimed for general vigilance as opposed to focused attention. According to Hernández-Peón, a midbrain gating function can be electrophysiologically demonstrated during REM sleep.

If one views neurosis as a disorder which limits one's consciousness, gating operations to pain stimuli and selective impulse occlusion in the brain-stem reticular formation provide pertinent support that traumatic early painful experience establishes patterns of neuronal interaction which may partially occlude awareness of the entire visceral and extrapersonal environment. Where perception and response bear an obligatory relationship to earlier pain or trauma, there is a limitation of options and an impoverishment of consciousness. All levels of the neuraxis may be affected: at the level of visceral function it is a consciousness of feeling state; at the functional level of the body-wall, outward expression of the internal state is postulated; beyond the body-wall, relation to ideas, sensory environment and interpersonal relationship may be affected. These discrete levels of consciousness, if gated, would become 'unconscious', but not biologically so. Long-lasting changes in the central nervous system would produce neurosis. Gate theory (Janov and Holden, 1975) proposes that pain may be biased upwards or downwards within the levels of the neuraxis for long periods of time. The pain system is seen as dualistic, with a lateral component mediating knowledge and a medial component mediating the suffering of pain. Holden proposes the orbitofrontal hypothalamic projection as the locus of a third gate. This locus is based on evidence, from studies of hypnotic analgesia and the coconsciousness in some temporal-lobe epileptic patients, that gating is occurring in the telencephalon as well as in the brain-stem reticular formation and the spinal cord.

These gating systems represent three protective control systems which the self would experience as both facilitating and as warning devices, and also as pain controls. The interfaces between the environment and gate one, as well as between gates one and two, are believed to exist in the dorsolateral grey of the spinal cord and brain stem, in the medial rostral mesencephalon and in the

154   orbitofrontal cortex. The orbitofrontal-hypothalamic projection is seen as the highest third gate.

Although the work cited supports a thesis of a three-level gating system, more empirical proof must be found for certainty in this area of theory. Putting the gating system aside as a proposition needing further proof, there is sufficient empirical evidence of myelination and medial brain development to support the hypothesis of the existence of a self/not-self at or very soon after birth.

2. Self, immunology and psychosomatics

A self/not-self awareness may in the first place be concerned with or about defence. If one accepts Jung's archetypal theory and considers the archetypes as interrelated constituents of the self which would have a teleological aspect of serving the individual as a whole, then the self would have a defensive or protective role towards itself at a more basic level, and definitely so in the infant in advance of full ego-development. A weak ego would be overwhelmed both by powerful archetypal unconscious material and by the impinging outer world of objects.

To recognize not-self the self would need to possess a great number of items of information, referred to in biology as 'the message'. The message, on present knowledge, is encoded in the structure of genes made up of desoxyribonucleic acid (DNA) in a folded double spiral shape. The message-carriers are believed to be a type of ribonucleic acid (RNA) in a chain shape determined by the pattern of DNA. Psychologists and biologists tend to agree that these messengers may be in the form of templates, enzymes, hormones, genes, catalysts or pheromones.

These diverse messengers are described in theories relevant to them by appropriate or acceptable terminology:

The psychological message concerns: (1) a diversity of specific responses to stimuli from what is not-self; (2) it must be all-

pervasive so as to reach all defence outposts; (3) it enables the
individual to recognize what is imposed not-self even if the self
shares with the not-self certain features; (4) . . . it prohibits the
wrecking of elements of the system as if they were extraneous.
(Stein, 1967, p. 104)

In biology the defence system is a somatic system with four
analogous characteristics to the four psychological aspects of
messages described above (Burch and Burwell, 1965): (1) the
somatic defence system shows a wide range of specificity; (2) its
agents are ubiquitous or pervasively present; (3) this system
recognizes the not-self; (4) in predisposed persons, the agents can
attack self-tissue in a 'misguided' way which is presumed to be at
the root of autoimmune disease.

   As neither the nervous nor the endocrine system is able to fulfil
all these functions, Burch and Burwell assume that the biological
analogue of the self would be the lymphoid stem cells and/or
the undifferentiated mesenchyme cells of the reticuloendothelial
system (Gell, 1957). There are data consistent with such a postulation of some psychosomatic equivalence between stem cells and
self without any intention of indicating that there is a lateral
psychophysical parallelism between the self-archetypes and the
endothelial system, which is autonomous and free from total
nerve control (as the self is also thought to be in terms of its
superordinate function). Neither hormonal nor nervous systems
store or carry information that allows a secondary response: for
example, antibody production can go on months or even years
after the first immunization. Stein (1967) points out that this
reminds one of belated psychological reactions to trauma in early
childhood. However, even if deposited patterns in the nervous
and endocrine systems are not thought to be paralleled by those
borne by the self, this would not prevent functions like conscious
acts or symbolization from being delegated to the former systems.

   Anatomically, the lymphatic system is described by Burch and

156   Burwell (1965) as correctly qualified to serve as a defence against not-self. Random disordering, due to the enormous complexity of the genetic message, could be found in the stem cells. Medawar (1957) points out that evidence supports the theory that the antigenic substance which stimulates antibody formation is DNA, from which chromosomes are made. If inoculated, DNA can bring about genetic transformation and behave as if it were a gene.

This idea of immunological mistakes is important to these general considerations. For example, in mammals the unborn offspring obtains necessary nutriment by sharing the mother's blood circulation in the womb. But if cells from the embryo's blood pass the barrier of placenta and enter the mother's bloodstream, antibody function can be induced. If these re-enter the baby's blood, haemolytic disease or damaged red blood corpuscles can result. Another example would be chronic inflammation of the thyroid gland where autoimmune disease sets in, a condition where the organism erroneously or to its detriment destroys a needed constituent as if it were not needed. In thyroid inflammation as described by Burnett (1962) the gland has been invaded by lymphocytes which release antibodies and ultimately render the thyroid useless.

The distinction which enables the organism to recognize self and distinguish it from not-self may depend on the stereochemical fit of the 'mirror-image' with which the organism is confronted. Steric shape refers to the different positions in space which atoms occupy within molecules of the same chemical constitution. Differences of steric shape are characteristic of amino acids on which life depends (Libby, 1965). An identity of stereochemical fit could be schematically assumed when an object characterized by troughs and peaks is turned to its mirror-image, so that its troughs and peaks correspond. Complementarity would reverse the object and mirror-image so that peaks face troughs and vice versa.

This idea of two types of fit would account schematically for the maintenance of biological identity when either the self-archetype or the lymphocyte encounters a not-self pattern of either type of fit in mirror-image. In the identity-type fit Fordham's deintegration theory, involving quick reintegration of an object when there is a good fit, would be the archetypal self theory in analogy; psychosomatically, the process whereby the original whole or self becomes structured into interrelated elements (or messengers) occupying certain postulated preferred stations (statistically) would be an identity-type fit.

Fordham describes the second or complementarity type of steric fit, when the correspondence between object and deintegrate of self is not exact. At first the object will not be perceived at all, but a tolerance develops so that the object is later perceived even when it does not fit the deintegrate (Fordham, 1957). In view of the examples given in autoimmune disease, with their disastrous consequences, it must be said that in immunity theory the nonfitting object is an antigen or toxin. A toxin is toxic because its structure is in some sense a complementary fit to a genetically predetermined one.

Burnett (1962) assumes that the function of the antigen is to stimulate a pre-existent pattern into activity. In Fordham's theory of deintegration this is precisely what the object does to the self as a pre-existent structure at birth. Just as at first a foreign substance may be accepted by the organism, the repeated injection stimulates an antibody into action, and when injected, antibodies provoke an immunological response. It is not surprising that the steric fit necessary for genetic stability can become pathological if changes develop from an identity to a complementary relation. This happens if an immature organism (the infant) is presented with a foreign substance as if it were a part of the self. When the self knows that the object stands in a relation of complementarity to the archetypal image, the host will not tolerate the object.

An example of complementary opposites and their possible

incompatibility is Parrish's (1966) work on sperms and ovum in infertile women. In four out of forty-eight infertile women, destructive antibodies specific to the plasma coating of their husbands' sperm was produced. Biologically, complementarity can lead to a violent reaction.

An important example of this is reported by Turnbull and Hawk (1966) in the study of regional ileitis in the colon. Unlike chronic ulcerative colitis, in colonic ileitis the mucous membrane is not primarily involved. Rather, the self appears to be destroying the colon as not-self via the lymphatic and reticuloendothelial systems. Acheson and Truelove (1961) found that the disease often attacked patients suffering from a conflict between the need for dependence and the family's ideal of independence. A period of immaturity unduly shortens the time for digested (or introjected) not-self material to be accepted, and psychoimmunological tolerance is not developed. Twice as many of the patients they studied who had destructive diseases of the digestive tract were weaned from the breast during the first month of life as in the control group, who had later weaning.

In viewing the principle of self/non-self recognition, the essential problem is that when tolerance of self-antigens breaks down, autoimmune deficiency syndrome may develop. Inappropriate responses to innocuous antigens such as pollen may give rise to allergic hypersensitivity. In some infections, immune reaction to resistant micro-organisms may damage tissue as much as the infection itself does. Advantageous immune reactions may shift to hypersensitivity, as both mechanisms have an underlying similarity.

Whether an antigen is eventually accepted as self or rejected as not-self is partly dependent on timing: antigens are accepted as self if they persist long enough. In the embryo, it may be that any antigen that is present through the immune system's maturation will be accepted as self. If lymphocytes are tolerated at an immature stage they may only later develop a capacity to be

immunized. But in the adult, even with mature lymphocytes
present, tolerance can be induced with some antigens, such as
foreign immunoglobulins, when no adjuvant stimulus is also
present. The tolerance/immunity decision is vitally influenced by
adjuvanticity of stimuli; most antigens will produce a primary
response but these will produce tolerance if injected in many large
doses over time. When lesser doses are given over the same time,
this often potentiates the immune response instead. The operation
of immunological circuits, as to triggers and adjuvanticity of
timing, is so complex that as this book goes to press AIDS
(autoimmune deficiency syndrome) is on the increase without a
vaccine antidote.

From the layman's point of view the difficulties in compre-
hending the most basic immunological aspects of the prevention
of viral disease, and particularly of AIDS, is formidable. In the
first phase of the immune system's response to viral attack there
is a non-antigen-specific response of interferons and natural killer
cells, but at the same time the virus-infected cells are susceptible
to a lysis of the natural killer cells. As the virus replicates, the
production of humoral antibodies begins and there is an activation
of T-cells that can have a positive or negative effect on the function
of immunity. Cytotoxic T-cells may lyse with virus-infected cells
or may induce a delayed type of hypersensitivity.

T-cells develop under activation from the thymus when they
are induced to become T-lymphocytes. Upon maturation the T-
lymphocytes recognize differences between foreign cells and
foreign antigens and self-cells and self-antigens. T-lymphocytes
are mobile, and after circulating through the blood and lymph
pass into body tissues, where they detect foreign substances such
as bacteria, fungi, protozoa and virus-infected cells. They attack
foreign substances by producing chemical messengers, the
lymphokines, which increase the function of phagocytic defence
cells and fight foreign substance in many ways.

B-cells are the other major system of the immune response.

They appear first in foetal liver, then in adult bone marrow and are precursors of plasma cells, where production of antibodies and immunoglobin occurs. T-lymphocytes' products influence the antibodies produced by B-lymphocytes, which interact in a sequence with special proteins, named 'complement proteins'. The proteins are precursors of enzymes that can initiate inflammation, lyse foreign cells, facilitate phagocytosis and neutralize or destroy viruses.

These two systems, T and B, influence each other both positively and negatively. This is highly regulated by the lymphoid cells (suggested above as self/not-self determinants) as well as by external influences from the brain or the endocrine glands. A new population of lymphoid cells, the natural killer cells, circulate in blood, lymph nodes, spleen and other lymphoid tissues and attack tumour cells, virus-infected cells and embryonic cells which are out of place.

In the immunological abnormality of AIDS patients, the absolute numbers of lymphocytes are low; T-4 (helper cells) are low and T-5,4 (helper/inducer cells) are both low and inverted in ratio (Good, 1984). It is not clear what happens to the natural killer cells, as amounts present in AIDS victims vary enormously. The interaction of lymphoid cells is extremely disturbed in AIDS patients; medicine refers to this as the depression of autologous mixed lymphocyte reaction and allogenic mixed lymphocyte reaction. There are also B-cell disturbances, resulting in a near chaos of unresolved scientific problems. I have presented just a few of the facts about AIDS to the lay reader in an attempt to show the complexity and confusion within the immune system in this disease.

In view of this complicated and dangerous set of cross-triggers and unknown response confusion in the immune system, the World Health Organization (WHO Workshop, 1987) has proposed that an AIDS vaccine would need long-term B-cell memory and memory for T-helper cells and cytotoxic cells. T-lymphocytes do not usually require viral antigenic determinants for the induction of neutralizing antibodies; however, as mentioned above, the virus-infected cells are susceptible to lysis with natural killer cells. This has created an insurmountable problem for the immune system so far.

In the psychological world, is there any less confusion about what is self and what is not-self? The analogy still holds through between psychological self/not-self and immunological biochemical self/not-self theories, but the difficulties are well beyond present knowledge and one approaches these analogies with caution. It is interesting that with no answer at this time in the self/not-self immunological research work, attention is turning to stress factors and studies are showing that stress alone can alter the immune system. For example, recent evidence from Sweden (Arnetz *et al.*, 1987) has proved that socioeconomic stress factors alone changed the immune system of unemployed women. Women in southern Sweden who had lost their jobs were shown to exhibit a significant alteration in their immune system response after nine months out of work, compared to working women matched in a tightly controlled study. For the unemployed women there was a decrease in the phytohaemaglu-tinin (PHA) reactivity of lymphocytes and a decrease also in reactivity to purified protein derivative. Both these reactivities are considered to stimulate the helper T-cells in immune response. Although the emotional, cognitive and behavioural reactions to unemployment are widely known, the fact that certain functions in the immune system decrease under socioeconomic stress has wide implications for self/not-self functions within the imposed loss of self-confidence, self-esteem and self-support in prolonged unemployment.

Physiological, pathological and experimental findings in the field of immunity and autoimmunity have been presented as analogous to unconscious processes concerned with recognition of self and not-self in Jungian theory and the related processes of self-defence and self-destruction described. Types of psychosomatic illnesses as well as viral illnesses have been used as illustrations.

3. A defence of the analogical act

Analogy, if presented in rigorous scientific and theoretical discussion, is heuristically useful. In the *New Oxford Dictionary*, one definition describes analogy as 'the resemblance of form or function between organs which are essentially different'. Where analogy is noticed, especially in medicine and biology, it is rarely carried through by logical argument in the step-by-step fashion of the philosopher. Much of the philosophy of science comprises theoretical situations that rarely happen in the real life of the laboratory or the clinic, and the term 'analogical act' is considered more germane to my argument. Analogical acts are an aid to discovery because they suggest clues and hypotheses. They concern resemblances between the relationship of things, rather than between the things themselves. The value of even erroneously described analogues can be profitable, as it was with Malpighi: encountering insuperable difficulties in his anatomical studies of animals, he looked instead at their analogues, the plants, and founded the science of plant anatomy.

In biology and medicine, the examples of how analogies have helped new discoveries are legion. In neurophysiology these would include nervous transmission and electric current; the brain and the electronic calculating machine; the eye and the photographic plate; and the study of memory, which employs many analogies in its understanding. The Ancient Greeks (fifth century BC), who did not allow autopsies, used analogy in their attempts to understand the movement of body fluids, conception, respiration, nutrition, congestion and the formation of bladder stones. Descartes was concerned with the analogy between mechanical and physiological action, and analogy became the cornerstone of comparative anatomy.

Since analogies have a long history in generating hypotheses to inspire further investigation and development, it is scientifically justifiable to include the carefully argued analogues between the self-archetype and certain aspects of immunology. The analogical act never proves; it may, however, bring revolutionary advances if scientists detect certain analogies not seen by others, and thus giving a new basis for further progress.

Throughout this chapter we have seen how the notion of self and any failure of self/not-self discrimination in the psychosomatic totality of psyche has growing evidence from the neurophysiological and immunological spheres, which are totally outside the former boundaries and procedures of depth psychology. More and more, however, they have come to be seen as linked into it; similarly, the empirical observation of the depth psychologists is now vital in, for example, the AIDS epidemic, where medicine has not yet reached any cure or partial cure. Greater perception of what is self or not-self may be at the frontiers of the psychological knowledge needed to cure what at present seems incurable by laboratory or physiological knowledge alone.

Chapter V

Theory in psychology

Without theory, practice is but routine born of habit. Theory alone can bring forth and develop the spirit of invention.
Louis Pasteur, on taking up his professorship at Lille, 1854

1. Introduction

The map for this chapter is not an easy one for the reader to visualize, as I wish to bring together far-reaching aspects of scientific/philosophical argument to support the self theory which will be extended in the next chapter. Thus far it can be seen that a self concept is heuristically essential in analytical psychology (Chapter I) and central in the neo-Freudian contribution of Kohut (Chapter II). Autism, as a pathological distortion of self, makes the idea of consciousness as needing self-consciousness (for a structural basis of developmental psychological health) seem important clinically to many workers in the field (Chapter III). Analogues of the self are proving valuable to physiological theory concerning the immune system and its possible psychosomatic base in the study and elaboration of self/not-self dichotomy in immunological theory and research (Chapter IV).

I now turn to areas needing clarification to defend broadly the form of self theory I shall present in Chapter VI. First, however, we need to look at the role of observation in theory construction and look at some self concepts in relation to Kant's, Sartre's and Popper's philosphically related arguments, to Mischel's cognitive models and to other dynamic construct models such as that of Rychlak. By moving through or across these areas of self-related theory and its field of investigation we shall gain some view of the terrain shared by self theories. This maps a broad spectrum of allied, but partly separate, areas of contribution in the philosophy of psychology, depth psychology and experimental psychology.

This chapter is not a synthesis but a consideration of essential information to complete an amplification of that further material which the reader will need as *a priori* to understanding the infant self/ego theory to come. It is now time to lay down the philosophic preconditions for a self theory. Without establishing these prerequisites, I cannot define and share my position as to the choice of what empirical evidence is to be included. Without such an exposition, empirical material would be used omnipotently by psychologists. Philosophically ungrounded ideas can lead to wrong expectations in psychology. A misconceived self theory would be one with incorrect conceptions about how theories and observations actually build and grow up.

In reconsidering behaviourism, for example, I shall show that Pavlov was unaware of major discrepancies between his theory, description and methodology. I shall be demonstrating how Popper's view of scientific progress and his reliance on falsifiability of theory as an essential ingredient of scientific law has been outgrown in the series-of-theories concept Lakatos has described as the way science advances. This reconstruing of what is most essential to scientific advance detects selfhood in a conceptual space that neither behaviourism *per se* nor Popperian philosophy *per se* can achieve. To begin to discover what this conceptual space can be, we need first to consider how the identity of self has been seen by various workers in the field.

The identity of self is a basic awareness of sameness across time and space. Through breaks in this self-awareness during sleep or when unconscious, we are made aware of self as a continuity in its personal distinctness from other selves and objects. Hume argued in his *Treatise* (see 1896 edition) that we cannot have an idea of self, since we know nothing but sense impression. In Book II, however, he wrote: "'Tis evident that . . . we are at all times intimately conscious of ourselves, our sentiments and passions . . .' He saw self as merely the sum total of experiences, but if the self is linked to what is commonly named the individual differentiated personality, it itself must change, since it is both partially dependent on physical and intellectual development and partially independent via its inventive initiative.

The polarity between self and environment is the subject of most self studies. Knowledge, including culturally acquired knowledge, may affect interpretation of this polarity. As Ryle (1949) suggests, it may be almost impossible to observe oneself as one is at a given instant, but one can reflect on oneself an instant later. We can develop theories about ourselves through posing problems and testing our conjectures. This is an ongoing learning process.

Fantz's experiments (1963) with five-day-old babies show that they fixate for longer periods on a schematic drawing of a face than on a similar non-face pictorial arrangement. Dependence on caretakers makes persons very important within the objects of a baby's environment. Through others' interest in him and through body-discovery the baby learns that he also is a person. To be a self, expectancy over time of one's self extending to past and future involves a theory of expectation. However many ways of acting that being a self may include for the baby, social experience will add to the sum of self-awareness. What can be said to be individual about an organism that is an open system or group of systems with atoms frequently joining and leaving these systems? The material particles and energy are in constant exchange through metabolism with the environment. To the extent that this is self-controlling, the organism is a centre of control. A baby is a developing organism as a body before it becomes a person in the sense of a consciously perceived unity of body and mind, or psyche-soma. The baby's knowledge of his mother or principal caretaker leads on to his need to learn what is part of his body and what is not. In time the baby distinguishes between persons and things. This knowledge is needed prior to his discovery that he is a separate self.

Underlying this idea is a principle of social cognition: that any knowledge gained about the other must also be gained about the self. Bannister and Agnew (1976), in a chapter on the child's construction of self, maintain: 'The ways in which we elaborate our construing of self must be essentially those ways in which we elaborate our construing of others, for we have not a concept of self but a bipolar construct of self/not-self or self-others.'

Lewis and Brooks-Gunn (1979) observed the first two years of development in the baby and propose a division of this development into four periods:

1. Birth to three months: Infants are particularly interested in other babies as social objects. Single action-outcome pairings are seen regularly enough to postulate these primary circular reactions to be differentiated.
2. Three months to eight months: Means and ends relationships are established. The baby and his own mirror-contingency becomes of interest to the baby within an action-outcome behaviour unit of experimentation. The self–other distinction is not consolidated prior to the notion of permanence.
3. Eight to twelve months: The critical development is the permanent establishment of the permanence notion that enables the infant to have a self–other distinction. Plans, intentionality, self-recognition, independence from some contingencies all appear.
4. Twelve to twenty-four months: The representational behaviour-of-self begins and self-recognition is more dependent on feature analysis than on contingency in experimentation. (The child can recognize self in pictures as well as in mirrors.) A categorical self-knowledge begins with gender and age.

In his language the child uses complex means–ends and symbolic representation occurs. For example, there are sentences we use once and never construct again. Understanding such a sentence is more than understanding the sequence of words, at which one might initially fail. A unique experience is suggested, not a learned response to a former stimulus, which probably has a brain-process that is also necessarily unique. Brown (1965), in describing processes involved with the child's acquisition of syntax, mentions the induction of latent structure as the most complex and finds this more reminiscent of the biological development of an embryo than of the acquisition of a conditioned response.

In general the self seems both to observe and to take action at the same time:

> It [the self] is acting and suffering, recalling the past and planning and programming the future; expecting and disposing. It contains . . . a vivid consciousness of being an acting self, a centre of action. (Popper and Eccles, 1977, p. 108)

Adaptation to the external world may be inherited and learned. Both forms of knowledge can have complex informative capacity. Inherited knowledge, in the unconscious and found in the genes (the genome of the organism), provides the background from which to acquire new knowledge. The idea that sense-data are the only entrance to the intellect ignores the selection of evolution: ten thousand million neurons live together in the cerebral cortex. Eccles (1964) estimates that some of these neurons may have ten thousand synaptic links, which suggests a huge potential including genetic read-out in the inherited background of the baby. Critical ability, in the sense of knowledge as the object of knowing or that 'which is known or made known' (*Oxford English Dictionary*), leads to hypothesis and conjectural knowledge. Looking at an object causes an experience of sensation, but one then queries the problem of what it is. Man is constantly required to infer that other higher vertebrates have achieved conscious awareness in their decisions about interpersonal behaviour towards himself. Husserl (1948) argues that the one indubitable fact in human psychology is that of consciousness. Knowing demands a knower. Just as there is no consciousness without an object, so is there also none without a subject. 'All knowing is consciousness of knowing' (Sartre, 1956).

Sartre proposes three knowings, to which I will add a fourth. He describes these as the normal extent of regressive comprehension; for example, 'I knew that I knew that I knew!' The first knowing is the phenomenological knowing of whatever the object is (realization). The second follows in the knowing of the first knowing (memory via recovery and recall). The third knowing is a reflexive consciousness of consciousness, or knowing that one knows the first knowing. This third level of knowing is no longer a summation process. But as Sartre argues: 'Consciousness of self is not dual. If we wish to avoid an infinite regress, there must be an immediate, non-cognitive relation of the self to itself.'

In my view there is a fourth knowing, or a consciousness in which knowing is not known or transformed to cognitive knowing. If behaviour does not become an object of another behaviour by the same actor it is less than conscious or unconscious, but one can none the less speak of it as a knowing, or at least as a ground of knowing. This fourth level, a ground of knowing or being, is not a higher level of cognitive judgement but may relate to a ground of self-experience that intuitively includes unconscious and conscious self-integrates in its psychological resonance. Both Jung and Fordham have clinnically elaborated a possible psychotic core of experiential influence of the self, thought of not only empirically but experientially as 'beyond experience', that is, in the totality-of-self.

My theory of a fourth level of knowing that is not dual or cognitive clarifies the sense that every experience is a partial experience of mind's total nature and activity, or totality-of-self.

This fourth level senses that mind has attended to only a part of the whole of the ground of knowing and therefore recognizes totality, which is known to be greater than the fullest active attention. This can be compared to Fordham's sense of the ego at its fullest awareness as remaining only a part of the self, never equalling it. This is sensed non-cognitively in the manner of my fourth level of knowing. When Sartre stopped at three levels of knowing he remained unaware of the further resonance that part-knowing indicates as a further parameter at the threshold level of that which is beyond the apprehension of the partial.

Instead of a hypothesis that our mind is a stream of experiences and the self only a summation of these as a functionally unified system of responses (Skinner, 1953) I would argue that our minds focus active attention incorporating a selection programme which is adjusted to the repertoire of behavioural responses available but is not based on a mere summation of these. Rather, the adjustment of behavioural response is based on an experiential 'validity' of knowing that has been apprehended by levels three (Sartre) and four (Ryce-Menuhin) indicated above. For example, if we look at Penfield's (1958) stimulation of the cortex in his patients, this stimulation enabled them to relive past experience while they retained full awareness of their body localization as they lay on an operating table. The patients reported that they maintained a conscious awareness of self while the perceptual experience of the past was restimulated. The central nervous system apparently steers the organism in an attempt both to relate to biologically relevant environmental aspects and to devolve some tasks to a hierarchically lower unconscious integration.

The individual organism, unique genetically and experientially with a long evolution of the central nervous system contained within it, must, in a unified or self-conscious and self-reflective way, use its own germ plasm linked to its own brain's connections to conscious/unconscious processes in its own descriptive function of language. This is the uniqueness or self of individuals, built up through the long evolution of human individuation.

Self includes both dispositions and expectations. Dispositions to recall to consciousness give continuity to the self via memory, and dispositions to behave unconsciously contain inbuilt expectations (Jung's archetypal theory) as well as inborn reactions and responses such as the newborn baby's expectation of being fed. Psychologically and genetically this knowledge is *a priori:* prior to all observational experience. Observation tends to be selective and presupposes similarity or its opposite. It also tends towards classification. This leads to an adoption of a frame of reference, to expectations and to formulations within theory.

I question the idea that science proceeds from observation to theory, rather than testing theory against observation, because although it is true that a particular hypothesis is designed to explain some preceding observations, the need for explanation invents new hypotheses and, expecting to find regularities, imposes them on to experience. Theoretical framework needs constant reassessment. Conjecture and refutation, rather than the preservation of current dogma, can be traced back as a method to Hellenic tradition and to Thales. A principle that emerges in Popper's work (1959, 1963, 1966, 1977) is that the criteria of demarcation for scientific theories are testability and falsifiability.

The logical validity in repetition based upon similarity, or the inductive method, has been successfully refuted by Hume: instances of which we have no experience cannot logically be claimed to have to resemble those of which we have had experience. This questions reliance on statistical probability as an all-inclusive proof of any behavioural tendency. Habit does not originate in repetition: walking or speaking begin independently of repetition, before it can play any part.

Repetition is not perfect sameness for several interpreters: each is repetition-for-us if it is based on similarity-for-us. A giraffe and I might not experience a repetition as the same sameness because the giraffe and I would each have a certain point of view! If, logically, a point of view (such as a system of interests, assumptions, anticipations and expectations) must precede the decision that a repetition has been made, then the point of view is not merely the result of repetition, because it existed independently before the repetition. So induction, or a passive waiting for repetitions to impose regularities on us, is replaced by a theory of trial and error and the search for 'similarities-for-us'. Scientific theories are therefore inventions rather than a digest of observations, put forward for trial to learn if they oppose observations in a decisive way. This would presuppose a self rather than support an idea of building a self through regularities. Such a critical attitude enables the survival-of-the-fittest theory at a given period in scientific history and, if an inadequate hypothesis is eliminated, the survival of science as such, as it can classify all theory as conjecture or tentative hypothesis. Empirical test and evidence can falsify by deductive inference but not by inductive interference, since no observation or experiment can give more than a finite number of repetitions. Statements of laws – for example B depends on A – always transcend possible empirical evidence. In general science accepts a theory as long as it stands up to the severest test that has yet been designed to refute it.

2. Behaviourism: a reconsideration

In this section I shall argue that behaviourism is incompatible with self theory and an inappropriate instrument for the 'self-field' in psychology. If the theory of conditioned and unconditioned reflexes can be seen to be incompatible with self/ego psychology, it would clear some of the historical confusion about whether a concept of ego within self, or consciousness, is needed to explain the study of acquired behaviour. This is essential, as by 1927 Pavlov had claimed that every action of an organism is a reflex arc, which put into question the idea of voluntarily initiated

action or ego-choice in behaviour and reduced all behaviour to 173
physical forces (physics and chemistry). In this brief but vital
reconsideration of the reflex arc as Pavlov presented it, I hope to
put aside one of the last blocks to an understanding that voluntary,
goal-orientated ego-behaviour does not have to be dependent
on conditioning or involuntary response to prior conditioning,
although it may sometimes be influenced by either or both. I can
then move on to look for the self concept in its ongoing perceptual
field.

Can the theory of unconditioned and conditioned reflexes survive
severe test?

Behaviourism, based on the reflex theory of behaviour and the
association theory connected with it, has used the concept of the
'conditioned reflex'. It is historically associated with Descartes,
Locke, Hume, Loeb, Bechterev, Pavlov, Watson and initially
Sherrington, although he repudiated the reflex theory in the
preface to the second edition (1906) of his *Integrative Action of the
Nervous System*.

Epistemological problems arose concerning the concept of
the 'conditioned reflex'. Within the suppositions of mechanistic
materialism which later found biologists refraining from admit-
ting concepts of consciousness or volition to science, Descartes
(see Haldane and Ross translation, 1911) defined the concept of
'reflex' in 1649. He thought animal nerves were comparable to
statues that were plumbed for water. Sensory nerve stimuli gave
rise to inborn automatic involuntary reactions. This idea has
persisted. Pavlov (1927) wrote that ' . . . psychologists . . . are
studying at the present time these . . . inevitable reactions of the
organism . . . due . . . to the inherent organization of the nervous
system.' Neural connections between receptor and effector organs
were seen in contrast to conscious action or volition. Reflexes are
automatic and a consequence of stimulation of a sensory receptor
initiating a nervous impluse transmitted along a specific neuro-

174 anatomical pathway to an effector organ. This is the conceptual 'reflex arc'.

The use of 'automatic' and the implication of 'involuntary' action in this definition, and the notion of a sensory trigger for a type of response, imply the existence of a class of nonautomatic actions. There are also actions which, although fully automatic and involuntary, are not due to the mechanisms of the reflex arc, or its specific naming would be superfluous. Efron (1966) gives examples: the 'reticulocyte response to chronic anaemia, the contraction of a muscle following a mechanical blow, and the movements of muscles during convulsive seizures'. Chemical action in the effector link of a response to afferent stimulation is illustrated by milk ejection in lactating animals. The stimulation of the nipple, giving an afferent neural release of pituitary hormone, is followed by an effector response of the hormone's chemical influence on the mammary gland.

Voluntary movement, on the other hand, presupposes a concept of consciousness. Its purpose, initiation and regulation to ensure its goal are consciously established. Here we are moving away from the reflex arc to voluntary goal-action. This could include walking, for example. In walking stretch receptors, if stimulated, will activate the alpha motor neurons, causing muscles to contract. Stretch receptors are initiated by mental action – the desire to move to a goal – so the automatic mechanisms involved would not by themselves lead to a classification of walking as nonvoluntary action in its inception. Stretch receptors are under efferent response – i.e. under the control of the central nervous system – when walking becomes a habit.

As there has never been a purely anatomical-physiological definition of a reflex mechanism, physiologists have instead asked if all involuntary actions are reflexes. Sherrington (1951) thought the reflex innate and inherited, but Pavlov argued for habits based on training, education and discipline as a chain of conditioned reflexes. By 1927, Pavlov used the concept of the reflex as encompassing every action of the organism mediated by the central nervous system. Sherrington held out for a definition which excluded any behaviour dependent on a faculty of consciousness. By 1931, Skinner declared the concept of reflex free of any differentiae and called it any 'observed correlation of stimulus and response'. Sherrington argued that a 'simple' reflex did not actually exist, as any motor neuron in the anterior horn received too many connections from neurons elsewhere in the spinal cord to be considered as having only one input. All parts of the nervous system's concurrent input to the motor neuron would be present, not just the input from a particular afferent pathway.

If the pure reflex is neither a physiologically definable mechanism nor a definably exact anatomical structure, it can be defined only by reference to the concept of voluntarily initiated action in which an ego/self would participate. Skinner (1931) recognizes this problem by stating:

> We have been proceeding . . . upon an unnecessary assumption . . . that there is a flexion reflex . . . such an assumption is wholly gratuitous . . . our knowledge of . . . the arc is . . . derived wholly from the observation of a correlation . . . (pp. 449–50)

In general the epistemological chaos surrounding the reflex concept was caused by the underlying premise of mechanistic materialism, which claims that one day all phenomena will be reduced to physics and chemistry. A problem arises, since all the laws of physics and chemistry are not yet known. Reductionists, if failing to 'reduce' all consciousness to physics and chemistry, point out the inadequate state of present knowledge, but rarely include themselves in this condition when claiming that reductionism will succeed. Skinner maintains that any differentiae that isolate reflex activity from all other activity as responses – for example the reflex as unlearned, unconscious, involuntary or restricted to special neural paths – are 'negative' and 'unscientific'. If reflex means nothing but a response, the term need not be retained if it is no longer synonymous with involuntary behaviour. The materialists seemed to hope that consciousness might be biologically irrelevant and that all behaviour is determined by physical forces beyond one's conscious control. If all behaviour is a chain of reflexes, the mechanistic thesis would be maintained. But the complexity of the central nervous system indicates that one cannot isolate a reflex arc, so the theory is not testable or refutable.

Acquired responses to stimuli, in Pavlov's view, needed 'new reflex mechanisms' or 'temporary connections' as innate motor and glandular responses to stimuli. But this does not sufficiently explain acquired responses. No anatomical or physiological evidence has been found to support the postulate of temporary connections. No histological or physiological discoveries have brought forward any facts to prove any altered state between neurons as a consequence of previous experience. Eccles (1964) discounts known changes in synaptic efficiency, such as in tetanus or following prolonged disuse of monosynaptic transmission, by pointing out that ' . . . the demonstrated changes in synaptic efficiency are that long periods of excess use or disuse are required in order to produce detectable synaptic change.' Thus the concept of an acquired reflex or a conditioned reflex may be meaningless in normal health or in organisms without synaptic trauma.

None of the physiological responses described by Pavlov as 'conditioned reflexes' or responses (striate muscles or glands) is found in unconscious animals. This observation demonstrates that the concept of consciousness (ego-within-self) is needed to explain both the study of the reflex and the study of acquired behaviour. But Pavlov maintained that he could scientifically 'ignore the mental state of the animal'; this violates the logical assertion that the facts of consciousness cannot be ignored. Pavlov did in fact consider the mental state of his animals by (1) referring to 'alertness', 'irritability', 'somnolence'; (2) choosing to work on conscious animals; (3) showing that conditioned reflexes disappear during sleep, but unconditioned responses do not; (4) choosing an experimental chamber without 'distractions' for the animals. He was apparently unaware of this discrepancy between theory, description and methodology.

The reflex concept is an abstraction. It is tenable only if it is looked at in an out-of-system way. As a ground for the study of the self-as-total-field, therefore, it is inappropriate and reduced to an isolation that is no longer relevant as a theoretical base for self study. Where can self theory more appropriately find its analogues?

Both materialism and depth psychology have tended to lean on the classical Newtonian conceptualization in which persons and objects move through a Euclidean space, maintaining substance as they go. Historically, observation may have been contaminated by such conventions. If the world is not as atomistic as supposed but more 'continuous', it will be of interest to psychologists to become aware of the emerging 'field theories' in physics, where any absolute distinction between matter and void is increasingly questioned. Weyl (1949), in discussing electrons as waves rather than as substance, maintains:

> . . . a material particle is merely a small domain of the electrical field within which the field strength assumes enormously high values . . . an energy knot, by no means clearly delineated against the remaining field, [which] propagates through empty space like a water wave across the surface of a lake; there is no such thing as one and the same substance of which the electrons consist at all times. (p. 184)

Learned tendencies to perceive in an atomistic fashion, supported by the sharpening properties of the central nervous system in interesting visual gradients, have been reviewed (Marr, 1976). Campbell and Robson (1968), for example, suggest that the visual system's *modus operandi* analyses contours and objects in continuous components (sine waves) by Fourier analysis. Perception of the environment is seen both to imply and to be implied by a nervous system. Following Einstein, the most recent theories in physics indicate that all properties of any parts of matter reflect their interaction with other parts.

Field theory illustrates a possible analogy between emerging physical concepts and Jung's self theory. The whole field (self plus environment) is held to contain perturbations (ego's reception of outer and inner environment) which propagate through the field (see Fordham's deintegration theory in Chapter 1, section 3 as the self/ego deintegrates and makes matches to archetypal form-tendencies of the unconscious) to gain conscious interpretation. Structures in field theory are the interacting and interfering of the perturbations, or the self's assimilation of the self/ego's integrates plus other inner and outer input. As the whole structure needs accounting for (the self theory of the person), not only the description of the interaction as 'continuous' (the ego continuously analysing inner/outer input), the analogy between field theory in physics and aspects of Jungian self theory can be helpful. If a person 'adopts' stable patterns of process, he is taking 'properties of the field' that are *relatively localized in space and time*. This is the self's psychological role.

I think that a structural-process theory of self, reappraised and combining elements of Jung's and Freud's conceptual theories, enables a parsimonious, holistic psychological hypothesis of this 'field' or experience of self in consciousness. The self is the totality of one's relative being (unique consciousness), in a localization of space and time and within the continuous 'universal mind' or 'perceptual field'. This suggestive metaphor is too open with huge concepts like self/environment as metaphorical agents. I shall now begin to prepare to bring this field down to partially testable empirical material, which I will be presenting to the reader in the chapter to come.

Before presenting my new theory of the self/ego, I wish to point out the scientific problems in using depth psychology as its perspective. Behaviourism as a possible mode of presentation has been negated on logical and empirical grounds. However, specific experimental studies are vital to learning about the self, provided they are not based on inductive reasoning only and are not so 'subatomic' in nature as to be too hierarchically removed from a holistic view of the 'self-field'. Psychology's advance requires that a body of workers think in terms large enough to see a self as a part of all the environment in continuous relation to one's own 'energy knot'. This is the psychophysical sense of self-unity in individual mind-beingness.

3. Assessing falsifiability in depth psychology

Popper (1965) speculates:

clinical observations . . . are interpretations in the light of theories . . . criteria of refutation have to be laid down beforehand . . . but what kind of clinical responses would refute, to the satisfaction of the analyst, not merely a particular diagnosis but psychoanalysis itself? (p. 38, n. 3)

This question can be misleading. Suppose a critic of psychoanalysis were to produce incontestable evidence that all psychological conclusions based on psychoanalytic theory were false. Would this invalidate psychoanalysis? Many hypotheses would have been refuted and would need rewriting, but the vast amount of psychological data needing explanation would remain and the general hypothesis that the unconscious influences conscious behaviour and can be linked by a series of interconnected psychoanalytical postulates would not be falsified as an approach.

Psychoanalysis itself would not be refuted. Disciplines involving systematic research cannot be refuted: only hypotheses can be refuted, and then only very carefully constructed hypotheses accessible to well-bounded experimental testing. Even if

180   hypotheses are inadequate in psychoanalysis, the discoveries made about behaviour in special conditions would remain and need explanation. Revision of a discipline does not demolish the fresh observations it continues to make. Revision of psychoanalysis would itself be psychoanalysis. The questions it asks would remain.

Another problem in falsifying theories and scientific statements has arisen through experimental work in physics. Work with individual paths of photons has shown that a precisely identical series of experiments will give differing results. When solitary photons are shot consecutively at the same point of a half-silvered mirror, half the photons will pass through the mirror and half will not, but no detectable variations in experimental conditions can determine which individual photon will pass through and which will not. Like events may not produce like effects. Some scientists are therefore abandoning the principle of the uniformity of nature. Jeans, sums up the combined theories of Heisenberg, de Broglie and Schrödinger in discussing Dirac's theory, which states that

> . . . events in the phenomenal world are not uniquely associated with events in the substratum (subatomic physics, etc.); different events in the substratum may result in phenomena which are precisely similar, at least to our observation. (Jeans, 1942, p. 173)

This view of physics is described by Johnson (1948) as 'pattern without demand to know of what thing we discover the structure,'

Scientific criticism may be said to be moving away from the need for models in the mechanical sense, while retaining form or structure for expressing functional dependence and keeping measurement, abstraction and transformation as methods of description. Patterns are not falsifiable, but statements are. In Einstein's (1933) relativity theory, electric and magnetic forces are not real. They are, rather, mental constructs resulting from an effort to understand the motion of particles. Gravity is a similar concept in this respect. These concepts are revisable rather than refutable when terms like 'energy' or 'momentum' in the Newtonian theory of gravitation have been used.

Einstein's mass–energy equation $E = mc^2$ is not falsifiable in the sense that a prediction from the equation could be falsified, for example, 'Star J will appear to Observer E at space-time s-t'. If this imaginary prediction were falsified the mass–energy equation is not false, as it is still applicable to the general class of phenomena from which it has been abstracted. When Newton's 'myth' is rewritten in terms of Einstein's relativity theory, there is a temptation – since relativity theory claims to fit the 'facts' – to suppose that relativity theory will never be revised enough for its original form to be considered a 'myth'. Facts are not independent of the form of theoretical statement subsumed, and statements based on observations are not independent of prevailing theory and chosen paradigm. Factual aspects of theory are its observation statements and specific lawlike hypotheses, which at a given time are thought to be factual. Reports about the scope of a law and its applications to particular cases are falsifiable, or at least revisable. When reports and applications are confirmed, however, the question remains whether the methods of representation and technique from which inferences are drawn are sound.

Most laymen will think that fitting data to the theory is the fundamental problem in science; however, unless a theory is testable, or partially testable, it cannot be used in this way. In science theory which is wrong may prove as valuable as theory which, when tested, remains 'right'. This is because theory tends to be updated and built upon through continual correction of its error. Correct interpretation is dependent on successive correction of inaccuracy and relies on some testability to advance accuracy. But testability does not have to be immediate. It must be potential or partial and Seaborn-Jones (1968) has shown that

182   this applies to psychoanalysis. Argument for this will be presented at length below. Although it will be contended that psychoanalysis is partially falsifiable through testing, it will be seen to have other ramifications when a self theory is included, as in analytical psychology. But these considerations need further preparation (in the next section) before they can be added into my argument's further elucidation about the ground of self in theory.

Popper has put forward falsifiability as a necessary requisite for scientific theory/hypothesis formation. Before questioning this view more critically, I wish to discuss whether psychoanalytic hypotheses and those of Jung's analytical psychology are falsifiable. Jeans (1942) has pointed out that in physics every observation in quanta theory involves 'the passage of a complete quantum from the observed object to the observing subject, and a complete quantum constitutes a not negligible coupling between observer and the observed.' The sharp division between observer and observed is thus questioned, and the relation between subject and object rather than the object of the subject–object relationship is what is perceived.

In psychoanalysis, agreement between trained observers using tape-recorded sessions of an analysis – about interpretative effectiveness and the falsification of specific predictions – is an objective forward step within depth psychology concerning subject–object relation as a psychological interaction. It is the relationship of subject–object itself with which psychoanalysis deals. Prediction hypotheses about an analyst's interpretations and their effects can be verified or falsified by several observers. Lawlike hypotheses drawn from predictions are not conclusively falsifiable but may be updated and made more heuristic by superseding earlier hypotheses. These hypotheses about the psychic development of individuals (or of groups) are stated in the form: 'Xs, if assumed to be 'Y' are more intelligible to the patient', not in the form, 'all Xs are Y'.

Derivative assumptions, prevalent across psychology, need to be considered closely. Is it scientifically important for them to be falsifiable in Popper's sense? Seaborn-Jones (1968), in analysing this problem, asserts that scientific judgement should deal with sound but untestable derivative assumptions because

> hypotheses and unformulated assumptions which are derived from, and not formally deducible from, theories and high-level hypotheses play a very important part in determining attitudes and expectations. (p. 100)

Seaborn-Jones has divided psychoanalytic hypotheses into a large number of classes. Nine will be considered here.

First, he finds that retrospective hypotheses about interpretations are falsifiable, as they can be confirmed or not by a number of observers. Predictive hypotheses, if specified so that 'interpretations p,q,r . . . will be followed within twenty-four hours by changes a,b,c . . . in the analysand's behaviour', are conclusively falsifiable. There is a second group of hypotheses which, although not conclusively falsifiable, are directly or indirectly testable and are of theoretical and practical importance: these would be anomaly hypotheses (p is inconsistent with q), and observer agreement would at least be a starting point for their consideration. Interpretative or focusing hypotheses are frequently confirmed and are modifiable (they are influential to the patient's behaviour). Ahistorical hypotheses about the subject's unconscious fears are not directly falsifiable, but the analyst revises his hypothesis when interpretations based on ahistorical hypotheses fail and thus modifies such a hypothesis; psychodynamic laws, like any scientific laws, are indirectly testable by testing predictions taken from them, for example:

> If . . . the hypothesis 'Obsessional symptoms are a defence against phobias' yields the prediction 'As the obsessional symptoms disappear during analysis the phobias will appear', the

appearance or non-appearance of the phobias constitutes a test of both hypotheses: a direct test of the second, an indirect test of the first. (Seaborn-Jones, 1968, p. 101)

Historical hypotheses such as 'he probably suffered from phobias m,n,o . . . in his second and third years' are more speculative than decisively testable. Hypotheses about communities as a unit of psychoanalytic behaviour are not conclusively falsifiable or testable, but the pragmatic value of *prima facie* statistical or experimental confirmation could be considerable.

Finally, heuristic hypotheses within analytical techniques are not privately conclusively falsifiable, as they are often based on the analyst's unspoken and therefore unprovable interpretations during analytic sessions. Carl Rogers (1967) has pioneered the making of private therapy public through recording and filming techniques. Obviously, if the analyst wrote down his unspoken hypotheses during the session being filmed, this would be timed to the spoken word as it is taped and would supply independent observers with predictive material that is falsifiable.

Ideas spread across science from hypotheses and often make inadequate the criterion that science should be reduced to a collection of hypotheses. Freud's idea concerning the unconscious need for punishment has updated views about delinquency and crime; ideas about connections between breastfeeding, sphincter training and its conceptualization and the character and mythology of primitive tribes has affected approaches in anthropological, sociological and psychological investigation. Of course, it is unscientific to produce sweeping social hypotheses from these scientific ideas.

There is a problem for all psychologists concerning their own freedom from the enactive element in choosing various modes of theory presentation. Where there are conscious and unconscious motives for distorting or distrusting a theory, the psychologist's own psychology is being projected into the discussions. Demarcation applied to people as scientists may be heuristically as important for the formulation of scientific hypotheses as Popper's falsifiability criteria. Seaborn-Jones defines this theory of demarcation as applied to people in this way:

> A person is scientific to the extent that (1) he is prepared to modify, reformulate or abandon his beliefs, either in the light of new evidence or in the light of philosophical criticism; (2) he uses deductive methods to form his hypotheses; (3) his predictions are not enactive in such a way that they change the situation they describe or predict; and (4) he is free from motives for distortion. (1968, p. 118)

It would follow that to revise a theory using the above demarcation, one necessarily needs a detailed knowledge of the theorist's purpose and method. As my self theory is a revision and conjunction of elements in Jung's and Freud's formulations, using Fordham's extension of Jung's theory, their work and the work of the Freudian and Jungian schools (to the extent that these can be clearly defined) has been extensively reviewed and considered where relevant to our subject: the self in childhood.

4. Falsifiability in projective techniques within Jung's analytical psychology

Symbol and myth as they appear in dreams have been a tool of interpretation in all of depth psychology, as has the use of projective techniques in analysis such as spontaneous painting, building sand-pictures, active imagination (a specific Jungian technique), clay modelling, etc. Classically, projective techniques have been criticized for being on so broad a level that the material is not classifiable in any narrow sense. Many responses may arise from recent or past experiences at a superficial level as well as at deeper motivational levels connected to unconscious contents. Because analysts are trained to analyse on these various levels, shifting quickly from and between them, it is extremely difficult to quantify these procedures into standardized tests. The layman or the unanalysed psychologist may think there is too much danger of the analyst projecting his own projections on to the projected material of the patient! Attempts to make published projective tests valid have partially failed, although the success of the individual therapist's use of projective techniques, where patients often express great appreciation and benefit from the analysis of projective material, is well known.

Especially with children (but also with adults) difficulties with questionnaires and oral interviews are avoided and play-like projective techniques are in wide use. Where psychologists draw on depth constructs in designing their hypotheses and testing procedures or activities, an enrichment from analysts' insights is widely reported. Fantasy, as a release of overt and covert levels, is widely accepted by Jungian and Freudian analysts, but a sufficiently objective description of this work is still lacking. Incremental validity – in that these tests add to other diagnostic techniques to round out a fuller clinical picture of a patient – is an important contribution from the use of projective methods. Experienced givers of the Rorschach test, provided their theoretical orientation is acceptable (Freudians use this widely, but Rorschach was a Jungian), claim very effective interpretative and diagnostic results. As each projective technique has its own language and orientation, judgement by the untrained observer leads to confusion and misunderstanding. The information yielded from covert levels is distinctively useful in the clinical setting as long as a team of workers understand the language being used and the techniques themselves, whether the setting is more public psychiatry or more private analysis.

The hypotheses derived from Jungian projective techniques (for example Kalff's sand-play or Jung's use of 'active imagination') would lead to the same classes of hypotheses as for the main body of psychoanalysis and analytical psychology. It is assumed that theoretical validity would have the same problems and stimulus value for scientific advance from Jung's work as it would from the work of Freud and his followers.

Kant's (1788) decision concerning synthetic *a priori* judgements, so often claimed to be a fallacy in the interpretation of projective techniques, is that synthetic *a priori* knowledge is possible because the mind, in constructing the world of appearances, always reads certain things into it. Kant held that *a priori* concepts were read into experience both by the mind as well as by intuition (which Jung defined as largely an unconscious function). Where these genuinely belong to the construction, they are empirical and force themselves on us through the forms of judgement in which our thought is expressed. Interpretation, or knowledge, is held to be a kind of synthesis: there is an active interpretation of sense-data received (such as that produced in projective techniques) and one finds new connections not always initially obvious, such as the different representations of a single changing object.

Alternative theories in various projective interpretations might serve too, but if a method works and gives results it is heuristic to retain it where it is at least indirectly testable, observable (the advantage of creative painting, sand and clay techniques) and even falsifiable. In building 'world pictures' in sand-trays the patient is projecting and constructing an objective picture, using in the sand topographical objects from life such as people, buildings, vegetation, symbolic figures, animals, vehicles, water, landscape, etc. He is using the world of appearances and constructing his own best guess of the real world or of the world of his immediate inner experience. There can be no certain test that his projection is accurate to his inner world, but what right have we to suppose that it is definitely not accurate?

The only way we can, as selves, conceive of others' selves is by drawing an analogy to our own self introspectively and by using empathy to the other's self. There is more to oneself than the appearance of one as object, or there would be nothing for one's self to appear to inwardly. One's consciousness must exist in order to carry out this phenomenological construction: 'I am myself'. The possibility of such experience depends on the self knowing itself as an object of experience. If one were only an item in the phenomenal world there would be no subject for experiencing. But self as subject need not be an enduring and independent substance; the self is continuously synthesizing through reflective, adjusting, insightful learning.

Psychodynamics develops from theory based on many classes of hypothesis. These may have testable or indirectly testable assumptions, many of which have predictive value. Both psycho-analysis and analytical psychology need a more formal scientific grounding, in both theory and technique. The essential dimensions of depth psychology are its historical discovery and study of the theory of symbol. Other aspects are its study of intersubjective logic and the temporality of the subject, mythology, the psychology of religion and a specific and unique use of language in the 'interpretation of resistances and transferences or even to differentiate the affects proper to repression and the structure of the individual myth in obsessional neuroses' (Lacan, 1966). The problem of intersubjective time has been further secured in depth psychology through the theory of games.

5. Falsifiability in series of theories

Experimental results giving counterinstances to a theory may not kill it. An auxiliary hypothesis or a suitable reinterpretation of its terms may save it. Falsification at any price can be modified by setting standards to demarcate scientific from pseudoscientific changes within theory. Since the thorough appraisal of a theory must include an assessment of its auxiliary hypotheses, its initial conditions and its preceding theories to ascertain what change brought it about in the first place, a methodological falsificationism needs to consider series of theories. If problem shifts are theoretically progressive, they are scientific. If new empirical content is corroborated with a new theory, the emerging fact makes it empirically progressive. Thus a series of theories must produce new facts, not just be in agreement with the observed facts.

Lakatos (1970) believes that this shifts the ground of what falsification is. In dealing with one theory, scientists have tended to lean on the results of experiments: if they confirm the theory it is acceptable; if they contradict the theory it is rejected. In the context of a series of theories falsification 'depends on the emergence of better theories, on the invention of theories which anticipate new facts . . .'

The relation of falsification is not simply between theory and the empirical basis but becomes a multiple relation between competing theories, the empirical basis and the empirical growth resulting from the competition between theories. Here the urgency is upon replacing any hypothesis by a better one. There is no falsification before the emergence of a better theory. 'Refutation without an alternative shows nothing but the poverty of our imagination in providing a rescue hypothesis'. A theory is acceptably scientific, according to the argument, only if it has corroborated excess empirical content over its rival and leads to the discovery of novel facts. This then gives theory explanatory power, since it represents growth. It is empirical and takes the activist approach from Kant. Lakatos calls this approach that of the 'sophisticated falsificationalist', and it implies that learning about a theory is learning new facts which it anticipated. Leibnitz (1717) prefigured these theoretical concepts when he wrote to Conring: 'It is the greatest commendation of an hypothesis (next to proven truth) if by its help predictions can be made even about phenomena or experiments not tried.'

Falsifiability in general suggests that one has implicit expectations about what 'should' happen and from this reductive view (like behaviourism) assumes that facts, as simple observations, can be accepted or refuted. If, however, facts are endowed with meaning-premises, as a self theory requires for its continual building up of self by deintegration–reintegration, such a theory cannot stand or fall simply by either simplistic validation or refutation. No scientific community exists simply on a yes/no basis, but endeavours to establish meaningful premises from its scientific activity as a paradigm for its empirical and theoretical development. A self theory, by establishing a field of observations which are described, can bring a parameter for meaningful premises. In these meaningful descriptions *a detection of establishing, in a series of theories, a related field of observations* can be achieved. This field in self theory has a self which not only registers this detection, but then can register that it registers (Sartre's 'third level') and then *senses the field of registration* (my own fourth level proposition of self-knowing, adding one regress more than Sartre proposed). This fourfold sensing of the field of registration, or of detection, would be the self-as-totality, the self theory as conscious and unconscious, as in Jungian formulation.

I want to move now to further confirmation in cognitive psychology and in philosophy, to continue this explanation about the theoretical *a priori* in self theory and what it construes for its own ground of *registration*-into-scientific-theory.

In his philosophy of science, Popper doees not describe as such. Instead he holds to abstract argument for falsifiability as essential to theoretical construction and advance. To register a view of self as sociologically registered by others as well as by oneself, it is necessary to modify or reconstrue Popper's reductionism to a view that some falsification in testability helps theory; but it needs a reformulation which allows us to think about self as a totality-of-field which includes other selves. Inclusive to this community-of-selves view would be the Kuhnian contention (1963) that paradigm shifts indicate what communities believe in or accept as meaningful. Our organism brings us to patterns of theory via our belief, or meaning-premises that self-and-others construe as the ground of being – or self.

6. *Cognitive experimental psychology, a neo-Kantian humanism and the self theory*

Experimental science is perhaps defined more by bringing measurement into the reality than by what quantity it approaches. William Mischel, a cognitive psychologist, has retained a self concept. In so doing he opposes Skinner (1975), who attributes control of behaviour to the individual's environmental and genetic history alone. Mischel (1973) thinks that Skinner ignores the individual's capacity to process information selectively in terms of the person's own psychological state and his constructs. He emphasizes continuous interaction between person and conditions. In the analysis of the covariations between behaviour and conditions the problem of environmental contingencies arises, for often these are partly determined by human beings in society. Environmental contingencies also cannot be divorced in their effects from the varying interpretations and psychological transformations imposed by persons perceiving these contingencies. Reciprocity between self and complete social environment suggests a complexity where both the personal and environmental variables are so very numerous that one wonders if, in the name of clarity or parsimony, it is possible to make heuristic hypotheses amidst this multiplicity of person–situation interactions. The manipulation of such variables suggests an oversimplification of actual human situations. Life is not lived under control for a third-person observer's data. The person as 'self' comes at life with the ability to align premises, just as the experimenter does (by his judgements of 'order' made on the evidence 'order' his statistical assumptions and his experimental design).

'Variable', as a term in science, is used as a methodological construct. Theory defines variables to see if they hold up to testing. Person variables and situation variables suggest an impossible dichotomy, as any situation demands that a self would additionally put meaning into the equation. If self-directed purpose comes into the events under experimental observation, can it be non-parsimonious to include it as a cause? Control and prediction of an 'independent' variable, or the experimenter's own teleological framework, suggest what theory is actually being supported in advance.

Classical mediation theory and self theory run into problems: the ideas of Tolman and the sign Gestaltists, as well as Woodworth's S–O–R (subject-organism-response) theories are built on the premise that mediators (signs, rules, models) are input and 'past' responses rather than simultaneously 'present' responses of the self within the organism. This eliminates the effect of possible arbitrariness in behaviour. An exclusive demonstrative explanation for behavioural description results. In early mediation theory no place is allowed for dialectical reasoning. Miller, Galanter and Pribram (1960), in applying the concept of the feedback loop as a fundamental building block which they called the TOTE (test-operate-test-exit), imply a simultaneous comparison, using feedback, of what stage a plan or intention has reached. The operational stage of the organism's response to that comparison could be new, not only repeated responses of the organism.

Mischel (1973), however, updated these traditional mediational views and claims that his objective is a

theoretical framework that recognizes the constructive (generative) nature of information processing, the active cognitive operations through which stimulus meanings may be transformed, the goal-directed, self-regulation and planning through which the individual may avoid 'stimulus control', and the anticipatory quality of human expectations . . . Each person is potentially his or her own best assessor, engaged in evaluation and interpretation of behaviour as well as its enactment. (pp. 255ff.)

Thus such a cognitive social learning theory seems more concerned with self theory, which has primarily been the province of humanists and Jung's analytical psychology until the last decades of cognitive experimental work. The newer view of self moves from a concept of 'change' to a concept of 'identity'.

Phenomenological empiricism increasingly attests that the term 'self' should be a fixed or unchanging (theoretical) contribution (as dynamic structure) made by the reasoning organism to the sequence of events within which it behaves. This self premise changes over time, but is giving a fixed contribution of 'self' to an isolated behavioural event (assuming that one could be isolated 'exactly for now'). This implies a stable framework within a given event. Kelly's (1955) personal construct theory and Kuhn's (1963) paradigms suggest a 'self' operating either via self-regulated assumptions within statistics or the fixing of parameters in paradigms to lend a series of events 'order'. Where the self takes a premise, this beginning or fixed point is named by Rychlak (1976) the 'protopoint'. Rychlak's definition of self is as a construct:

> . . . a construct enabling the theorist to conceptualize the contribution made to behaviour by an organism which brings meaningful premises to bear from a protopoint. The term 'self' captures the impact or 'logical weight' of a precedent meaning (premise) conveying sequacious implications for the sake of which behaviour to follow is at least partially determined. (p. 131)

This is an introspective formulation. It does not deny a contribution from the unconscious as well as from the conscious, and reflects that sense of orientation and identity in behaviour everywhere 'for this unit of time'. Premises can be several or changed as the organism 'comes at' any one life-situation. The multiplicity of premises possible to the self at a given moment is an area psychology has yet to peruse and study. Unconfirmed premises do not 'go away' but, as Jung (1954) discussed, these 'shadow' or repressed premises come back through dreams and into complexes where self-definition is functioning poorly and is not under the individual's fuller self-control. The psychological uncomfortableness of multiplicity of premises gives cognitive, phenomenological and depth psychologists much to think about.

Rychlak insists that until a child knows the meaning of 'left' he will not know the meaning of 'right'. This is a conceptualization around which perceived or phenomenal reality becomes a meaningful dimension for comprehension; for example long–short, unity–plurality, possibility–impossibility, etc. Meanings, if bipolar, give meaning to the 'other'. The idea waits on experience:

> Kant was not saying that individuals were born with the meaning of words put into them by the environment but with innate 'formal causes' like bipolar comprehension around which meaning can become organized by the self. Affective assessment of dialectical judgements along bipolar spectrums are idiographic assessments. (Rychlak, 1976, p. 136)

Reinforcement, on this view, is not only from the environment or tissue needs of the body but is also positive or negative through the affectively assessing human being contributing as he 'comes at life' with his self. These affective states depend on our unique judgements. The self as a continuing 'actor', constantly evaluating, is described everywhere in the literature of the world. This is the neo-Kantian concept of self as having premises which may bring sequence to behaviour but which the self alters constantly through continuing assessment/reassessment of all contributing factors in its individual moment-to-moment ego-evaluations.

But we must not reify the self. In the self model proposed it will be claimed only that a reappraised self concept is sufficiently instructive and not inconsistent with general psychological experimental data (see Chapter VI); that it is heuristically essential in analytical psychology (Chapter I), in the neo-Freudian framework of Kohut (Chapter II), to the theory of autism (Chapter III), valuable to physiological analogues of the self (Chapter IV) and centrally important to neo-Kantian humanism, to Mischel's cognitive models and to several of the dynamic construct models (Chapter V).

A new model of the self/ego in infancy

You can't make an omelette without breaking eggs.
Attributed to Robespierre, the French Revolutionary leader

I now come to my theory of the early self and my model of the initial ego-process. The emphasis of the theory concerns the developmental relationship between ego and self: that is, that as the self deintegrates bits of self reintegrate as ego, if a match occurs to archetypal objects and/or other recognizable self-objects. This reintegration takes the deintegrated self-bits back into the ego and forms its structure. To clarify this ego-formation we have taken a long journey through the work of Fairbairn, Winnicott and Kohut and reviewed Michael Fordham's refinement of Jungian theory. To proceed further, the proper conceptual and scientific framework has been reassessed and the field established for further research in self theory (Chapter V). This has given us boundaries in which to place a further self framework in not looking at ego as one entity but discovering its cluster of separate areas or unit-of-ego in empirical and experimental work with babies and young children. Thus, instead of speaking of ego as a mostly indefinable complex of some sort, I am attempting positively to describe and give evidence concerning my discovery of the con-integrates, a cluster of ego subparts or subsections that build up in infant children's early ego-development.

In section 3 of Chapter I, I have suggested that the con-integrates – a term I have originated – can be thought of as huge, unifying, Gestalt-like complexes of deintegrates, conjoined to ensure survival through effective performance and perception. I argued that the con-integrates help to clarify a group of very large deintegrated aggregates which reintegrate in special systems of great biological significance. These con-integrates are like storage bins for increasingly recognizable areas of psychological experience which the ego develops as it separates out partially from the self. I suggested in the Preface that it is endemic to the ego's deintegration/reintegration pattern that a great range of ego-material is accepted by the self/ego system for use and storage. Below, I will describe my theoretical approach to the memory stores and its systems which the infant ego develops.

The con-integrate self/ego system attempts to make clear how the ego-match to archetypal images and recognizable self-objects develops the personality from infancy. I would argue that after early childhood definite expression of development becomes more dependent on the nature of the environmental stimulation to the ego-integrates I will be describing in this chapter than to exact IQ levels in infants. I have suggested earlier that one could say that intelligence levels may largely depend on the initial experiences of self, mediated by the ego, its con-integrates and the multi-integrates (to be described), and the general fortunes of health, both genetic and maturational. Self-integrates help to define maturational intelligence.

I have also maintained in the Preface that as all activities, functions and structures of the psyche are subject to development, a theoretical requirement has been a clearer differentiation between ego and self and a more detailed developmental concept of the ego during the first years of life. The con-integrate theory modifies ego/self theory by suggesting that the ego-conglomerates are vital support systems for ego-processes. The seven con-integrates to be introduced and described fully in the later part of this chapter are speech, the ego-shadow, the ego-ideal, the aesthetic, play, the persona and defence-of-the-self.

It is now essential to become technical and schematic as this chapter unfolds. I hope the reader will bear with me because we come to the core-concepts of ego-development which break new ground in Jungian theory. After presenting the theory of the con-integrates I will describe and defend their existence with a full description of each separate con-integrate postulated here. It will then be possible, in Chapter VII, to present a vivid clinical portrayal of how these con-integrates come into the everyday ongoing world of the child by describing a sand-play therapy undertaken with me by a three-and-a-half-year-old boy. This case study will bring a human dimension back after the discourse needed to describe the theory and its model.

1. *The theory of con-integrates*

I now feel that appropriate ground has been laid to propose a new contribution to the theory of self in early childhood. I wish to underpin Fordham's theory of the deintegrates, which states that as the self deintegrates outwards to the object, reintegration gives a tendency towards unity, since reintegrates are a derivative of a wholeness or an original self. This presents a global theory without any hierarchical postulates or more testable lower levels to consider. In proposing seven con-integrates which develop early, during the first two or three years of life, I am clarifying further what happens when deintegration is reintegrated back after the first ego-differentiation from self begins. It is my contention that the seven con-integrates not only support overall psychic wholeness but specifically serve the ego's most urgent developmental needs.

Why seven con-integrates? I believe the seven discussed below give the best illustration of what a con-integrate is and what purpose or aim it serves. The number to be considered is restricted to the most essential for an introduction to the theory. There may be more, and other theorists may wish to bring arguments forward for these, or to extend the hierarchical levels of theory further than I shall. The con-integrates are closely allied in dynamics and structure to ego-development; seven psychological areas which I have observed very early in childhood are designated as con-integrates. They grow out of self, as Fordham has shown. Con-integrates are present in all children; they take precedence over lesser complexes as a linking and supporting part of ego-orientation.

The boundaries of con-integrates are permeable to the ego as it reintegrates its deintegrates back for placement within psychological structure. These boundaries are not permeable to one another. There is no reason to assume that over time brain-cellular patterns cannot develop upon these conglomerates provided they develop normally, but it is postulated that the con-integrates are basically *a priori* within the structure and process I shall postulate for the self/ego.

Looking at each con-integrate separately, they vary as to whether they involve only conscious and/or unconscious levels. Let this explanation develop gradually as its further implications emerge; here I must ask the reader to be patient, as the complex aspects of the con-integrate theory need to be approached in a step-by-step manner if their function is to be comprehended.

The ego-shadow, the ego-ideal and aspects of speech involve structurally unconscious components at all stages of life. The other con-integrates are conceived in description as conscious, although obviously they have unconscious aspects in terms of total self-totality. Where a con-integrate has unconscious structure it has permeable boundaries both to ego-consciousness and to the personal unconscious; the shadow, technically, also reaches to the collective unconscious (see Diagram 3). The brief study of this preliminary drawing will prepare the reader for the binary ego-process model to be studied further in a flow diagram. Diagram 3 is only a rough preparatory sketch of the fuller model to come.

Multi-integrates are cognitive developments exclusively dependent on adaptation and reaction, including physiological motility, and are thought to be consciously built up. In the self-

Diagram 3: Self/ego con-integrates

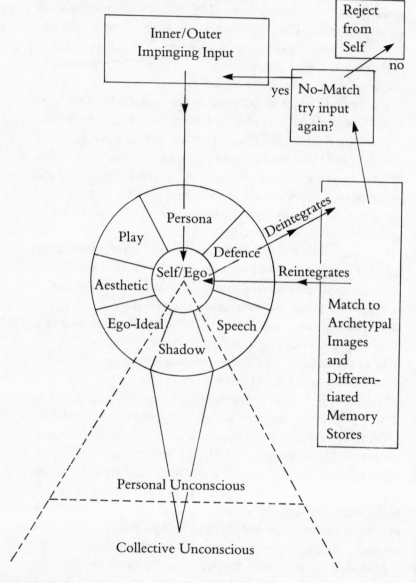

hierarchy multi-integrates stand underneath the con-integrates and are less ego-dependent and ego-related, although all the integrates rely to some relative extent upon the ego for their function.

Non-integrates are fragmented bits of cognitive material which the self stores in case a match to later input may require their use. If this seems unlikely, non-integrates are pushed out of the self entirely. Thus I believe there is some material processed through the self that is not retained in memory.

Two kinds of memory store are proposed: the first directly related to the acceptance of material by the ego as it deintegrates out to find a match either in archetypal images from the collective unconscious or in a highly differentiated memory store, available to recall and to recognition. The second memory store is a non-differentiated storage of non-integrate material which may be available upon recognition of related bits or aspects of its material. This is not available to immediate recall, at least in the first months of life, but is more easily available to recognition.

The psychological areas put forward as con-integrates represent differing structural types in existing theory. They may be arche-types themselves, complexes or functions in existing Jungian theory. But in view of the self/ego reintegrating back distinctive and definite deintegrates, it is maintained theoretically that it is not a sufficient explanation *to allow no further differentiation than Fordham's theory does* as to possible systems developing around the gradually differentiating ego and essential to its dynamic structure.

In seventeen years of study and consideration of Jung's psychology I have never comprehended how ego-function has been so little considered by Jungian analysts other than Fordham, or why the process of ego (as opposed just to a structural distinction) is almost unwritten about in Jungian literature. This surprise about omission of interest in ego stimulated my decision to write this book, which asks the reader to make a first step beyond the existing Jungian theoretical situation. It is a reification of ego *not* to bring further theoretical postulation to its subsystems, and I have asked myself why this reification has occurred among the very psychologists who claim to have the most advanced self theory in their theoretical formulation. The further delineation of self theory is, in my view, dependent on a more differentiated study of ego, not vice versa. It is time to differentiate the ego's primal process at hierarchical levels in Jungian theory. Before proceeding further, the ego–self relationship should be reviewed and redefined.

The term ego is used here as the seat of consciousness. This concept is based on the theory of the ego's original state as being unconscious at birth, or contained within the self as the original totality. Neumann (1954) symbolically describes the original psychic state before the birth of ego-consciousness as the Uroborus, or circular image of the tail-eating serpent, as a representation of the self or totality out of which the individual ego is born. During the first stages of life the separation of ego from self and their constant reunion shows in the form of an emerging ego which retains its primary identity with the self or self-system. The ego-processes all input as the free centre of the psyche which can differentiate, store or reject incoming perception either out of the self entirely or into the personal unconscious as repressed material.

As the presiding seat of consciousness the ego orders and focuses capacities of awareness. This process, illustrated in a flow diagram at the end of the book, enlarges its own structure as it develops. In elaborating the ego's surrounding structures into a new model, an attempt is made to clarify theoretically the process-structure of the ego itself, as it separates out from the self. Because the ego can split or be destroyed, it must have a protective system around it; con-integrates are postulated to separate out and unite incoming stimuli received by the ego into at least seven categories. Where stimuli do not fit these con-integrates, a lower hierarchical level of multi-integrates is proposed (this is discussed further below). Beyond these postulations one could propose that incoming stimuli not interpreted as con-integrates or multi-integrates would simply reintegrate to the less differentiated portion of the self, named as a less differentiated store of non-integrates.

Operationally, the con-integrate has permeable boundaries to the ego but not to other con-integrates, except via the ego. This aspect of dynamic boundaries is important as the basis of my claim that the con-integrates are separate subsystems of the ego process-structure. Where ego-development is noticeably weak or undifferentiated in the child, it is postulated that part of the problem is a too-slow development of con-integrates which defend, delineate and strengthen the ego and clarify areas of awareness necessary to performance and perception. Con-integrates are both adaptive and interpretative. They coagulate or bring together, via their boundaries permeable to the ego, the reintegrates of their specific area which are fundamental to the early growth of ego and its participation in infancy and childhood. It is proposed that with the exception of the play con-integrate, which merges into a play-work content over time, the other con-integrates remain throughout life in their original focus and have in this regard the closest access to ego-material and ego-process.

2. The flow diagram of the self/ego system

Now it is time for the reader to pull out the special flow-diagram map at the end of the book. Leaving this pull-page opened out in full view while reading on will greatly facilitate understanding of the theory process being described.

In the flow diagram a basic conceptual sketch of the con-integrate system within the self, including the multi-integrate and non-integrate levels, is attempted. The diagram gives a binary and conjectural formulation of how input material may be processed through the archives of the self and its integrates' system of allocation.

The self/ego system has an Input Control Centre (A) in which initial registration of outer and inner input occurs. Since the ego's task is to focus the capacities of consciousness, the facts and data of the outer ectophysic environment are processed through the same system as the inner endophysic input from the matrix of inner psychic life: for example memories and recollections, affective emotions and the subjective components of conscious functions (thinking, feeling, sensations and intuition) and invasions from the unconscious. All incoming material passes the Threatening-to-Ego Test Centre (B), where contents which are threatening to the function of the self/ego system may be taken from processing into the personal unconscious for enforced storage in the Personal Unconscious Repression Storage (B').

a. Repression

Repression makes inoperative contents which threaten the ego at a given moment in time. This rejection of threatening input implies that ego-development must be sufficiently conscious to resist that which is dangerous to itself and to keep it out of consciousness by relegating it to the personal unconscious: ' . . . [ego] is the mental agency which supervises all its own constituent process . . .' (Freud, 1914a). As the ego begins to deintegrate and reintegrate, the conscious begins to emerge: ' . . . repression is not a defence mechanism present from the very beginning . . . it cannot occur until a sharp distinction has been established between what is conscious and what is unconscious' (Freud, 1925b). The ego, which is in direct contact with the external world during deintegration/reintegration, is adapted to the reception and exclusion of stimuli and is governed by considerations of self-preservation and safety. It must also defend itself against overwhelming demands of the internal input, such as threatening instinctual contents of great power from the collective unconscious. The weak and immature ego of the child is particularly vulnerable to external dangers: parents ideally create a security for the child's ego, but the child pays for this security by a fear of the loss of love from caretakers which would render him helpless to some of the dangers of the external world.

Repression of these security fears involving childrens' parents often occurs and if ego-development lags behind libidinal development generally there is a precondition for neurosis. The phylogenetic influences also act on the ego; if very intensified these can become intolerably painful and repression is attempted. It is assumed that associative material to the repressed will also be repressed, but the present state of knowledge is less than clear about this. Unpleasant mental content probably covers a wide field, but repression itself is initiated by anxiety arising from interference with conscience or other means of preserving the parents' love, or interference with the maintenance of self-esteem. Internalization of the primitive threat from parents influences the repression sequence. Culture influences parents' opinions as to what behaviour in the child should be punished. Ideas or memories relating to motives that are punished would be what Freud considered unpleasant content that might be repressed.

Early experiments have been full of methodological defects (Sears, 1942) but Kline (1972) argues that there are some significant exceptions to this tendency. Wilkinson and Carghill (1955) studied the recall of two stories from dream sequences, one neutral and one containing symbolic oedipal material. Recall for the oedipal story was significantly worse. Levinger and Clark (1961) took reaction times and galvanic skin responses to emotive words and to neutral words. Further rotated factor analysis of all variables gives this experiment the quality of irrefutable evidence for repression theory. The multivariate statistical check ruled out competition between responses as the determining factor of the results, although its influence must be estimated, and failure to recall was shown to be related to the emotionality of words.

Jung's word-association studies (1918) give impressive clinical evidence for the return of the repressed. Subjects when asked to repeat a list of word associations sometimes responded with difficulty, were reduced to silence, changed responses or were unable to associate again to certain words. Galvanic skin responses were higher for disturbed response than for undisturbed response. These indicators of emotionality can be regarded as evidence for the return of the repressed.

Problems with testing repression lie in what the criteria for normal can be; an apparently neutral stimulus might be related, for some people, to repressed material. Anxiety, as studied in experiments, has not been related to Freud's concept of the specific areas (discussed above) which constitute unpleasant content for the ego in relation to repression thresholds. Virtually no repression experiments have been devised for very young children, nor does it appear likely that the laboratory can concoct oedipal or castration wishes or other profound anxieties.

b. Deintegrates and archetype

Remember to pull out and keep the flow diagram to study for facilitation of your comprehension as we continue.

If the Input (A) is not sent to Repression (B') it moves to the Deintegration Matches (C and D). Deintegrates are like islands of consciousness in the sea of the self; they are archetypal predispositions for objects and experiences that activate bits of ego-consciousness which meet and link up. The deintegration process refers to cognitive and conative aptitudes and applies to the entire development of infant, child and adult. Through the self/ego-process system, deintegration and reintegration continually take place and the reintegrated parts of the self/ego become more realized 'in terms of flesh and blood, space and time and also have more consciousness attached to them' (Lambert, 1981). The ego emerges, through the coming together of the initial pieces of ego-consciousness, into a whole ego-capacity. The ego can link the archetypal potentialities tested in the model by a match of the archetypal image (C) to a conscious reality; and this forms the internal archetypal self-objects spontaneously:

> If we were to ask what the difference is between the original self-integrate and the reintegrated self, after an appropriate series of deintegrations, at the level of maturity suitable for the stage of life that has been reached, we could describe it in terms of content. (Lambert, 1981, p. 19)

At birth, the infant's primary self-integrate is a conglomerate restricted to archetypal potentiality and nothing else. But at later developmental stages the ego-centre makes coherent not only archetypal potential but archetypal images not yet fully experienced as well as archetypal internal objects fully identified by the ego. These cluster in ego con-integrates.

Reintegration begins to occur if an archetypal match is made at (C) and the content moves to (E), the Reintegration Locus of Control, for further processing. Where a direct archetypal match is not made, the Differentiated Memory Store (D) is searched in case associated differentiated material is stored there and indicates that integration to the ego-integrates is possible. If the content is less than ready for the integrates, it remains stored (D'); otherwise the differentiated material is sent for reintegration (E). If the content does not find any match in (D) at all it is sent to a secondary memory store, the Undifferentiated Memory Store (H'), where it is matched to any fragmented ego-bits it may contain or include. It is stored there or sent back through the whole system for rechecking if at (I) the identified ego-bits demand reprocessing. If no ego-bits are identified the content is pushed out of the self/ego system (J). Before discussing the integrate system (E,F,G,G',H,H') further, I wish to elucidate the difference between the two memory stores of the system, the differentiated (D') and the undifferentiated (H').

c. Memory stores

In this section I shall be discussing the memory stores in relation to my con-integrate theory.

The critical difference between the differentiated memory store and the undifferentiated memory store is that the latter stores only non-integral ego-bits of information, not yet in a form suitable for recall but readily available to recognition where and if the original stimulus is present. In the absence of the original stimulus, recall involves an ego-orientated process in order to generate reconstruction within the ego system's memory search and its verbal correlates. Recall develops much later in infants than recognition, which Friedman (1972) tested in babies only a few days old. As quite substantial development is required for the ego's role in recall and the differentiated memory storage, it comes as a support for the self/ego model that recall is present only after one year of age (Piaget and Inhelder, 1973). It is only then that the ego-orientated differentiated memory store can develop as a function and as a growing structure. Here I lean on Gottlieb's (1970) model for recall, which assumes that there are 'reciprocal effects in the relationship between structure and function whereby function can significantly modify the development of the structures that are involved in the events'. Gottlieb admits that structural development is probabilistic against a norm, but argues that it is unique to each child's endogenous and exogenous stimulation. For fostering and channelling prenatal physio-anatomical growth, the stimulative events that determine the sequence and outcome of prenatal behaviour are: (1) pre-sensory mechanical agitation, (2) interoceptive stimulation, (3) proprioceptive stimulation, (4) exteroceptive stimulation, (5) neurochemical stimulation, and (6) musculoskeletal effects of use or exercise.

Gottlieb reports supporting experimental evidence for his theory about prenatal stimulation from chick and duck embryo studies and from experiments on unborn kittens and guinea pigs.

In chicks, movements are required from the embryo's own skeletal muscles to create articulated internal cavity formation and the sculpturing of cartilaginous surfaces. In duck embryos, prenatal responses to strong flickering light enhances electrical responses at the retina, telencephalon and the optic lobe. Hormones injected prenatally can alter the sex direction of male chicks and guinea pigs. If the structure were unidirectional it would continue to determine function blindly and simply throw off these manipulative exogenous stimulations. Gottlieb's bidirectional structure-function hypothesis assumes reciprocal effects: that function can modify development of both peripheral and central structures.

Ego-development may well not be an invariant course; it may be continually reactive to stimulational factors at all its stages. This tallies with the integrate theory in that recall would be available as ego-growth permits a wider scope of differentiated storage to occur and be accessible. Both recognition and recall depend on acquisition and retention of information and both involve a match-decision process. (Recall needs additional processing such as complex encoding skills, linking stimulus items, elaboration, generative representation, verbalizations, etc.) These processes are facilitated in the self/ego model in that the check with the differentiated memory store comes first before integrate-matches and the secondary non-integrate store are reached. Of course, the process remains slower in recall than recognition because of its complexity and later partly because of the huge storage in the differentiated store.

In the self/ego model recognition would take perceptual input directly to each memory store; with recall it is assumed that self-generated representations requiring an independent ego-integration are matched with memory representation and that under normal circumstances this is principally linked to the differentiated store.

In psychopathology the undifferentiated store of non-ego

material may flood verbalization, as in the 'word-salad' of full-blown schizophrenia. The differentiated store where recall may evoke a full impression – in the absence of a model – that an object or event has been experienced or perceived at a prior moment in time requires symbolic representation. Such internalized images are dependent on a healthy ego for the correct mnemonic process of recall involving figurative knowledge under a mnemonic referent. Obviously ego-damage seriously impairs the control of mental imagery and language, so here too in psychopathology a 'word-salad' may develop from the differentiated store.

The original healthy ego reintegrates a sufficiently whole image or clear mnemonic referent to differentiate integrate-memory back into language in the process of recall. I would argue that it is the role of the ego and its memory storage as an integrate (differentiated store) or a non-integrate (undifferentiated store) that is the initial criterion for the structure and function of storage.

Perlmutter and Lange (1978) report that two-year-olds are sometimes better than adults at recognizing old items presented again. Recognition involves, on the self/ego model, the quick scan of both memory stores. In the two-year-olds the differentiated store is still rather empty; this could explain their speed in recognition scan. Later the differentiated store is very full, but improvement in encoding strategy via rehearsal would enable test results almost to equal out up to middle age. Recognition rarely improves much with age; that points significantly to the early availability in the first year of non-integrate memory-bits which the self/ego system scans as strategy and practice during the gradual tuning in of the ego-integrate differentiated storage, which becomes active at about one year. (This postulation of memory stores within the self/ego model can assimilate the theoretical dual-process information models [see Kintsch, 1970, Klatzky, 1975] and Piaget's intelligence-dependent developmental memory model.)

d. Reintegrates and the integrates

Remember to consult the flow diagram at the end of the book to aid understanding as you continue. When a deintegrate reaches the reintegration (E) centre it is first matched to the con-integrate prototypes (discussed at length in the next section). The seven con-integrates are closest to ego-identity and process and they have first choice of assimilating the material which the self/ego deintegrate accepts into reintegration. The con-integrates build up residues and implications from ego's controlling direction as it balances, directs and processes the inner and outer impingements which reintegrate into the con-integrates' function. All con-integrates are intrinsic to the infant's need to interpret experience, and they incorporate the infant's most ego-related needs.

Ego-reintegrates that do not belong to the con-integrates move to the Multi-Integrate Match (G). These are conscious bits of self which fall outside the con-integrates but which the self/ego can use progressively and developmentally. They cohere in the principal sensory, perceptual and motility systems. Multi-integrates might be the very complex cognitively and conatively developed areas, like the learning of a second language and other skills requiring combinations of integrates secondary to the con-integrates and beneath them hierarchically. Examples would be learning to play the piano, creating computer programs or interpreting Egyptian hieroglyphics. It is outside the task of theory at the level of the con-integrates to comment further on multi-integrates. They deserve separate empirical study.

Where no multi-integrate match is made, content is matched to the Undifferentiated Memory Store (H). It remains there should it contain sufficient ego-bits for retention. If not it is checked at (I) for a repeat processing through the self/ego system if any ego-bits are identified in the content at this last checkpoint; if not sent back for reprocessing, the content is pushed out of the self/ego system altogether (J).

The binary-process scheme is an efficient descriptive method for imaging these processes and was introduced to clarify my model of the self/ego and its integrate system. The entire system is dependent on the ego as a growing locus of control within and relative to a self that integrates its *a priori* archetypal configurations against the endophysic and ectophysic real ties of the infant's psychic life. This model has the advantage of being suitable for all developmental stages in the life of the self/ego and its emerging consciousness through its match-storage system. It has parsimony in its model construction of great economy, and I could not discover a simpler conceptual framework that would integrate the extraordinarily complex data: that is, everything a person can relate to and integrate into himself at any stage of life.

3. Description of the con-integrates

The seven con-integrates will be defined and described with reference to the self–ego relationship that begins in infancy.

a. Speech

With the influx of tape-recording and videotaping the analysis of linguistics and acoustics has assumed vast proportions. Details of the infant's approach to speech have never before been so fully documented. Much of this work is reported for its own sake; some of it is related to theory. The overall quality of experimental work in the last two decades emphasizes the sense of utterances as more important to the infant child than their form. Work has often centred on distinguishing speech sounds in terms of phones, phonemes, distinctive features, phonological rules and intonation. These are the elements usually classified in the scores of recent publications on language development in children.

Some of the valuable discoveries in this literature relate to the development of speech perception in the very young baby. Eimas *et al.* (1971) discovered that one-month-olds have categorical perception of phonemes. This is well before the infant begins to approximate speech sounds in babbling, usually at three to four months. By ten to fifteen months some words are intelligible, and after the age of two there is more evidence – reported by the de Villiers (1978) – that the correct reproduction of distinctive features on their own as a learning device becomes important. Studies of deletion and substitution based on later babbling suggest that in its last stages babbling is already partially governed by restrictions similar to those of the phonological development in early words. Between two and four the child learns a rather limited scope of grammatical rules using agent, possessive and locative. Simple two- or three-term propositions are first mastered and then shades of meaning, signalled by grammatical morphemes, are added in a relatively stable order.

The relationship between a child's world-knowledge, intentions to communicate and early word-strings is a difficult study. The boundary line between the sense in which the child may have an idiosyncratic linguistic category in his head and its similarity/dissimilarity to the generally accepted system of the category is difficult to judge or delineate. Experts argue over early semantics in child language. Bloom (1973) believes the child's correct use of words like 'this,' 'more' and 'all-gone' means that children understand the semantic relations involved (nomination or existence, recurrence and nonexistence). On the other hand, Braine (1976) believes the semantic status of such terms is narrower in a child's grammar than in an adult's. He points to the groping patterns of early speech and suggests that children express a meaning before they learn word position in linguistic strings.

Both Nelson (1976) and Rosch (1973) point out that the exemplars of nouns such as 'cat' or 'chair' may share some physical features, but a search for common features among all proper exemplars fails and leads to null sets. This suggests that the child searches for semantic meanings, not physical elements of syntax, and that core-meanings, feeling, function and experience combine into prototypically organized experiences in which core-meaning is lodged. Further experience then elaborates this. Language enables the child to demand, to question, to blame and to deny. The de Villiers believe that the child comprehends more information than he can at first express in language and that he uses conceptions of events based on stored information as to what is likely in a situation and what is expected of him.

Condon and Sander (1974) report the results of a decade of films of neonate and caretaker taken during the first hours of life. Their interest is the connection between linguistics and kinesics. Condon hypothesizes that the neonate moves synchronously with adult speech as early as the second day of life. Body motility is seen as partly growing out of sound patterns around the child as well as from its well-documented relation to touch. Film was analysed in sixth-of-a-second 'units' and self-synchronous rhythm hierarchy was discovered in babies' motility, character-istic of human speech behaviour. The unit is a segment in which several body-parts will sustain their direction or speed of movement for brief duration.

This reveals a behavioural 'mode' that contrasts with previous and following 'bundles' of speech-movement. This may be characteristic of all nervous systems. A listener moves synchron-ously with a speaker in an 'entrainment'. In videotaping infants from twelve hours to two weeks old, the stimuli used were an adult speaker and audiotapes of English, Chinese, vowel sounds and tapping sounds. Precise synchrony of infant movement with the articulatory structure of adult speech was discovered.

By moving into the organization of his cultural speech structure the infant gains a huge number of repetitions of linguistic forms before he uses them in speech. The neonate participates in communication from the first day of life through entrainment of body movement to environmental speech patterns. This behavi-oural evidence suggests that entrainment to speech may be innate and that a con-integrate is developing within the self/ego from the first or second day of life. It can become delineated only with the ego's own development.

The use of continuity in early child language suggests the early participation of the ego. 'She came it over there' was a sample from a child's use of 'come' while watching a dog take a piece of food into the next room (Bowerman, 1974). This child had always used 'come' with the meaning 'move'. She thought it could also mean 'cause to move' by hypothesizing that it might operate as 'walk', in 'the dog walked' and 'the man walked the dog'. Children tend to build on what they already know. Early objects are usually named only after they noticed, picked up and studied. This choice of objects suggests that the ego is involved in naming objects and that language has the formation of a con-integrate in close relation to ego–object delineation from the first weeks of life.

Clark (1978) has traced the use of continuity and hypotheses in the development of deictic terms, which in person deixis involves 'I', 'we', 'you' or 'they'. Deixis relates to objects with locatives or demonstratives like 'here' or 'that'. The study of deixis also includes place, movement and cause. Gestures start off and are built into directives in language by children in a series of developmental stages. The learning of 'here' or 'there' is dependent on the ego's separation from the outer object or speaker in order to comprehend where the point of view originates. This is essential within deictic language.

Personal interaction and the shyness of a child dynamically affect the way linguistic ability develops. Language is closely related in its idiosyncratic development to the complexity of ego-needs and the way these are linguistically met in the child. The speech con-integrate develops in the early weeks of life and continues throughout life as a principal mode of expression. The speech con-integrate is postulated as indispensable, important to ego–object separation and as taking to itself all available linguistic signals for cognitive development. The large area of the left hemisphere usually used for much of speech development shows its great biological significance. For the self to utilize its complete sphere of ego-consciousness, speech becomes enormously important to the expression of ideas as information and as theory.

b. Ego-shadow

Jung designated the shadow generally as a principal archetype in the collective unconscious and also as the repressed material in the personal unconscious. To avoid confusion, my term ego-shadow relates not to all repressed material but to repression intimately connected to the ego itself, particularly to its birth. On the flow-diagram model, this material would be automatically repressed by the Threatening-to-Ego repression centre and then that material most closely related to the stage which ego-development had reached would be filtered into the ego-shadow con-integrate for unconscious storage of ego-material. This process, which is unconscious, is not shown in the model diagram itself. I insinuate it here. The ego would control release of ego-shadow material in projection as it becomes tolerable to the ego from its conscious standpoint.

I put the ego-shadow into self theory as a con-integrate because repression is present in the baby as he deintegrates out from the self to incoming phenomena, tries a match to the archetypal level to achieve reintegration into the ego and may quite early on begin to reproject outwardly again the repressed material of both the personal and collective unconscious. This is specifically relegated by the ego-shadow con-integrate on to his growing conscious ability to tolerate a mismatch between ego/self and deintegrates. This toleration prevents disintegration, and I believe all babies would experience disintegration without a repression system for ego-protection.

For example, we can consider that at the moment the mother stops a breastfeed the infant may cry in rage, having no cognition that he will get another feed later. Eventually he may be able to repress the anxious feeling as the nipple is withdrawn, or as he spits it out, and this repression into the ego-shadow con-integrate may enable him to tolerate the wait between feeds *prior to a cognition* that he is in a secure feeding schedule. In this way the ego-shadow would be serving the need of ego-development and preventing disintegration from the first days of life.

Repression can initially serve a positive role to increase the child's toleration of delay in meeting immediate ego-needs and to help delineate the curious or deintegrating 'I' from a fearful and anxiously repressed nature. The shadow as an overall term contains all the nonconscious aspects of personality over time, from both collective and personal levels of the unconscious, and can be measured only in its projections. When a child begins to play he can project good and bad repressions on to toys or the play situation, enabling child therapists to catch glimpses of unconscious material.

Where there is a birth trauma through late or difficult delivery, oxygen problems or surgery directly after parturition, the shadow itself as a whole and the ego-shadow as a prefiguration in the con-integrate system can protect the birth of the ego out of the self by repressing and containing birth traumata so that something like normal ego-development can begin. There may be a birth-archetype which would co-ordinate other elements of the fight for life outside the womb in the body. Birth traumata bear a relationship to psychic life, whether they remain unconscious or are later raised to consciousness.

The ego separates out gradually from the self until the child begins saying 'I', drawing himself as 'me' or acting out himself as 'myself' in play. However difficult a problem the shadow may be in the personality of adult life, the ego-shadow as a con-integrate is indispensably helpful to the initial survival of the ego system in infancy as it begins to separate out from its initial fusion with the self. As the child's ego gains in stability and range, the ego-shadow con-integrate functions when inhibitions and repressions, especially close to the ego, occur.

c. Ego-ideal

The ego-ideal con-integrate is conceptually based on Freud's superego but, it is argued, takes effect earlier in the child's ego-development than Freud postulated. Freud believed the superego to be the residues of the earliest object-choices of the unconscious; it did not form until the resolution of the Oedipus complex in the child. It was derived from a transformation of the child's earliest object-cathexis by identification with and introjection of the object. Freud may not have realized, in his early writings, that it could be formed before the resolution of the Oedipus complex, because he conceived of the superego as partly linked up to a reaction formation in relation to it. Chasseguet-Smirgel (1985) points out that in Freud the ego-ideal of 1914 and the superego of 1923 belong to different topographies, which adds to the difficulties of the original description of both. The ego-ideal appeared well before the superego and is heir to primary narcissism in that the superego comes to substitute for narcissistic perfection when the baby was his own ideal ego. The superego in Freud, according to Chasseguet-Smirgel, is heir to the Oedipus complex.

I believe the two need to be separated out; that the superego begins to form earlier than Freud or Chasseguet-Smirgel believe. In *Inhibitions, Symptoms and Anxiety* Freud wrote:

> The biological factor is the long period of time during which the young of the human species is in a condition of helplessness and dependence. . . As a result, the influence of the real external world upon it is intensified and an early differentiation between the ego and the id is promoted. Moreover, the dangers of the external world have a greater importance for it, so that the value of the object which can alone protect it against them and take the place of its former intrauterine life is enormously enhanced . . . (1926, pp. 68–9)

From the pressures of this anxiety, I would argue that the Oepidus complex contains many derivatives of incestuous desire and is a *general condition of the psyche* that can recur again and again throughout life and whose conception is separate from and, in my view, entirely different theoretically from the ego-ideal. The ego-ideal develops as a resolution of primary narcissism *in spite of*, not as heir to, the ongoing Oedipus complex, which can be only *partially* outgrown. I see no empirical evidence in adult patients that the Oedipus complex ever stops affecting adult psychology repeatedly at different ages and stages.

An earlier formation of ego-ideals in infancy is in no way dependent on a reaction formation to oedipal or Elektra complexes. The existence of narcissism in infants before the ego is differentiated enough to risk non-narcissism suggests an early identification with the lengthy childhood helplessness and dependence of self/ego (as Freud states) upon parents or caretaker and the beginning of a permanent expression to the influence of the parents. The ego-ideal, even if it does begin with the mother and her nutritive role, normally includes the father at a very early stage. There is no reason to assume that the feminine and masculine sides of environmental influence on the infant do not begin almost at once, from the atmosphere of the caring situation forward. This is particularly true now that fathers are tending to take a more active role with babies from their birth (Parke, 1979). I would argue this parental introjection builds the ego-ideal independently of the phase of oedipal conflict also being experienced by the infant from its archetypal sources, which are: (1) deintegration matches to the feminine and masculine archetypal preconfigurations, and (2) the reintegration back to ego-awareness linking archetypal images to the child's gradually developing parent-imago.

Eventually an expression of the influence of siblings and older relatives and friends of the household would be included within the ego-ideal along with the influence of the parents. Whatever personal evocation of the parents archetypal development enables

220   a child to have, much happens psychologically as this influence moves into the development of external personality traits:

> We know that the loss of the mother (without adequate substitute) during the first year of the child's life can lead to death, severe psychological deterioration and psychotic disturbances, whereas if the loss occurs after a normal primary relationship in the earliest developmental period the chances of the child's healthy development are much more promising even if he becomes ill. (Neumann, 1959, p. 129)

Jung maintained that the real mother evokes the mother-archetype in the psychic structure of the child: this can function independently of the mother's reality as a compensating psychic reality. The same would be true for the instigation of a father-archetype. Both archetypes would make secure the ego–self relationship achieved in a successful primary relationship (usually to the mother, but possibly to a maternal father). If the primary relationship is the basis for security, nourishment and containment in the long dependency of the baby on its caretaker, then the ego-ideal has ample time to develop as a con-integrate. It would influence the regulation of development within the child's psyche, between him and other individuals and later between him and society. In childhood, the overall intrapsychic development can be described as an initial

> . . . interdependence of ego and self, conflict between ego and self, growth of ego and consciousness out of the unconscious and conflict between ego consciousness and the unconscious as a result of increasing independence. (Neumann, 1959, p. 133)

At every stage the ego-ideal con-integrate must be developing in its hierarchical, conservative and authoritative influence on the ego. Freud was very defensive in his arguments about the oedipal situation and the superego and he overlooked the realization that ego-ideals were developing much earlier and that this influences the child's ego in the first year of life.

It is proposed that the con-integrate of the ego-ideal begins its long development early in the infant's development through the discipline and learned strictures of behaviour from the parents or caretakers and continues to operate, with modification, throughout life.

d. The aesthetic

Aesthetic appreciation has been documented by C. W. Valentine in *The Experimental Psychology of Beauty* (1962). The bulk of the statistical summaries referred to children over the age of four and is just outside the age range considered here, although the individual case material from Valentine's children is very helpful. It is a part of common experience to hear children of two, three and four years old frequently use the word 'pretty' when referring to flowers and pictures. This showed up in Valentine's child 'Y' who took Binet's Faces Test (see Burt, 1921) and always showed preference for 'pretty' faces. When using the Binet test Burt found that 33 per cent of three-year-olds chose the 'pretty' face in each of three pair-choices presented, 67 per cent of four-year-olds did so and 91 per cent of five-year-olds. The criteria for 'prettiness' would be widely debated today. Was Binet simply measuring 'average' types of faces against 'non-average', to which the children responded as 'like' or 'unlike' their normal daily environment? Was he measuring evenness of photogenic facial features as against unevenness?

Spontaneous verbal description showing feeling for aspects of the beautiful may be a truer indication of the aesthetic in the very young. In his *Psychology of Early Childhood* (1924) Wilhelm Stern reports that his daughter 'L.E.', at four years and four months, said: 'Who has made the dish so beautiful – just like a picture? How nice it looks – apples and vine leaves, you see yellow below and green above.'

In arguing that the development of aesthetic discernment should be a con-integrate it is important to establish that the aesthetic dynamic is closely related to the growth of ego-consciousness. Arrival at the stage where the child can abstract himself from his needs and experience pure will and self-control while making aesthetic choices involves previous developmental processes (Abenheimer, 1968). In the early oral phase of development – related to needs for being fed, protected, touched, comforted and brought into some sort of dialogue with caretakers (in vision, sound, holding and playing) – the less good responses the baby experiences make him exhibit defences. Self-awareness begins as the need for survival and help. In the anal phase that follows, the Freudian school believes that in the conscious expulsion of faeces the infant becomes aware of his own power. The omnipotence that results is neurotic. It becomes non-neurotic when the infant can show aggressive power without needing to feel omnipotent and achieves another development of flexible self-awareness. A third level of self-awareness, essential to aesthetic experience develops during the oral and anal phases. It occurs when a child can abstract himself under pressure of needs and dangers with self-control, in an authentic self, as the agent of controlled will.

An ultimate essence of all aesthetic experience has been described by Worringer (1908) as the need for self-alienation. He means this in the sense that the contemplation of the aesthetic takes the self away for a time from the problems and dangers of existence. At the same time, there is a bi-polar quality in aesthetic experience. As well as requiring the capacity of self-alienation it requires empathy, which can objectify self-enjoyment and is a self-affirmation. In empathizing our will into another object (art, music, nature, etc.) we absorb ourself into the outer object with our urge to know it and accept, momentarily, its fixed boundaries. These boundaries limit the usual ongoing differentiation of individual needs, and a self-alienation occurs. 'In empathy . . . I am

not the real I, but am inwardly liberated from the latter . . .'
(Lipps, 1903).

As the ego builds itself through the deintegration – reintegration process it reaches a level of function where it can afford to fuse temporarily with an object of aesthetic pleasure and thereby gain distance, through alienation, not only from the ego but from the self-defences. In what is felt as an empathetic ego-fusion to the object, we are witnessing an ego-choice which is a self-affirmation in terms of need or taste, but a technical self-alienation in terms of the intensity with which the ego merges 'into' the chosen aesthetic object. In the development of ego-consciousness the child seems to experience two directions simultaneously:

> On the conscious level he goes on developing even finer differentiations among the appearances of the real things around him, while in his unconscious fantasy life he undoes even the most fundamental differentiation of commonsense reality and so creates images that cannot have any possible correlate in rational thought. (Ehrenzweig, 1967, p. 266)

Both these developmental aspects, conscious and unconscious, play into the aesthetic experience, which involves a fine conscious choice and differentiation as well as the projection of unconscious image.

Aesthetic experience is paradoxical in its combination of object-ified self-enjoyment and a temporary self-alienation in the urge to abstraction and fusion outside the self and its normally fixed ego-boundaries. The aesthetic experience is a con-integrate because of the accumulation of these experiences, which begin in early childhood, and because of the particular relationship the aesthetic has to ego-development and temporary separation from total control of the self. The feedback of the aesthetic, when it enables a temporary release from some self-defences, helps one reflect more clearly upon the significance of the self and facilitates its authentic realization. The aesthetic builds ego-consciousness,

224 which contains ' . . . its enabling awareness and consciousness, its focus of perception and its factor of mediation between itself and the environment within and without' (Lambert, 1981).

e. Play

Play is a universal element of childhood. Play is a concept on its own, not reducible to any one sociopsychological view of the universe or to any one stage of civilization. The play element has existed in all cultures and in all known historical periods. It may be described as a suprabiological form through which society expresses its interpretation of life and the world (Luria, 1966).

Why is play civilizing? The play element introduces into civilization certain rules and the concept of fair play. This enables civilization to presuppose limitation and some mastery of the self, which gives people the ability to understand that personal conduct within any civilization must remain within certain freely accepted bounds.

A general characteristic of play is tension and uncertainty. 'Will we win? Will it come off?' are uncertainty conditions fulfilled in card games or football, in crosswords or archery, in shaking a rattle or reaching for one's toes. In the play world, if the rules are transgressed, the whole world collapses. In the same way, nations go to war if the currently accepted lawful rights of national sovereignty are overstepped.

Play has been considered both as a physiological phenomenon and as a psychological response. These approaches overlook an aspect of 'at-playness' in play that imparts meaning to action. The fun of playing is rarely measured when experimenters view play as quantitative. In some types of play, biological functions may be seen. A biological approach assumes that play must serve something which is not play. Theories about this mention the need for abreaction, for outlets of harmful impulses, for wish-fulfilment and for a means to bolster the feeling of personal value.

This may involve the release of extra energy through imitation, experimentation, assimilation and competition.

The contrast between play and seriousness is a fluid one. Vygotsky (1962) thought that for the very young child serious play meant the child was not separating the imaginary situation from the real one. In this way aspects of play are irrational. A game can represent a contest, or it may become a contest for the best representation of something. Both Luria (1966) and Piaget (1951) agree that play is the leading source of development during preschool years.

In viewing play as a con-integrate it is important to note how useful it is to early ego-strengthening. The child both pretends and tries to master adult situations through accommodation to external conditions and assimilation of experience into meaning. Play is an activity occurring before a behaviour is fully organized, suggesting that aspects of ego-development are underdeveloped. Play can be a preparation for life via the realization of the environment that it can demonstrate, as a repetition of experience and as the communication of symbolic fantasy. Symbolic play is assimilative in that it organizes thinking in terms of symbols and images already partly mastered. The child's egocentric position during symbolic play enables him to make a transition, over time, to a more and more accurate representation of reality. As the child is more adapted, play becomes constructive and eventually the child very gradually plays less by himself after he enters the arena of school life (Millar, 1968).

The idea that play may be an antidote to understimulation or boredom suggests that the building of more ego-experience is needed within an optimal àmount of stimulation. But the concept of optimal stimulation has a wide application, given the great variation in individual babies' metabolic and environmental stimulation levels. Both in its inner and outer reality for the child, play constantly challenges the ego through its directedness, concentration and release of another form of play or non-play activity. Play is very much the child's own private ego-directed world and is therefore a strong conglomerate, integrated around the ego very early.

As the child grows, he learns through play's zone of proximal development: the imaginary is often near to the memory of the real, and voluntary intentions may combine with the formation of real-life plans and volitional motives. In creating imaginary situations, abstract thought develops. These abstractions, when expressed as rules, lead to the understanding of rules and the later division between work and play at school age. Play is a preamble to work.

In the young child there are many unrealizable tendencies and desires. Under age three, the infant wants immediate gratification. Play can be said to be invented at the point when the unrealizable tendencies appear in development. What interested the infant no longer interests the toddler. Piaget describes the transitional nature of play as an intermediary between the situational constraints of early childhood and play ideas free of an actual situation. In game rules, the child can set the rules by himself free of the one-sided influence of an adult or make rules he jointly establishes with his parents. Freely chosen game rules include both self-restraint and self-determination. The ego is being relativized and has a close developmental relationship to the play con-integrate.

f. Persona

Jung defines the persona as

> . . . a function-complex which has come into existence for reasons of adaptation or necessary convenience, but by no means is it identical with the individuality. The persona is exclusively concerned with the relation to the object. . . (Jung, 1921, p. 465).

Throughout the stages of life one adapts one's persona constantly to pressures of the environment and of one's own evolving value system. Persona is

> a psycho-physical attitude that mediates between the inner and outer worlds, a kind of mask we develop to maintain a relatively constant or consistent front to the outside world, through which those we meet may relate to us fittingly. (Jacobi, 1976, p. 36)

Where in early childhood do we see signs of adaptation that are reflected in external behaviour? The infant's early persona is immediately involved with smiling. Ende and Harrison (1972) measured this to be at a rate of eleven times in every 100 minutes. They related this to an internal arousal state or change of state and to recognizable EEG patterns. The social smile appears in the third week, when a mechanical noise no longer elicits a smile as well as a human voice does and as eye-to-eye contact begins to alter smiling patterns further (A. Macfarlane, 1975).

I would argue that the first almost embryonic appearance of a persona in the baby begins with his use of the social smile, at first unconsciously and later very consciously and manipulatively. Schaffer (1971) argues that reciprocal behaviour, which would involve the baby's use of cognition and a conscious persona, begins at the very end of the first year of life. Reciprocal intentional signalling to the mother requires comprehension of the difference between self behaviour and the behaviour of the other and some awareness of feedback from self-produced behaviour. Feedback also requires the ability to anticipate the outcome of behaviour from past memory and to regulate responses in relation to this feedback.

The close connection with ego-development is obvious if the persona helps the signalling processes and enables the child to begin to test details of his behaviour against the feedback he receives from his caretakers. Although the persona is very gradually socially developed during early childhood, it becomes such

228   an important aspect of adult behaviour as to give it sufficient force
to be a con-integrate from the beginning of infancy.

Behavioural studies have tended to quantify measures of
smiling, crying, eye movements and the like without picking up
the idiosyncratic differences within these modes in individual
children as their persona develops and acts to alter their manner
of appearing and doing. Families mould persona so individually
that by the time the child enters school he will need to undergo a
major persona adaptation towards the group. The persona's
adaptive function deals with incoming stimulation in a principal
way from very early life and is, I believe, a con-integrate in its
great influence upon the ego's role in behaviour and style of
response throughout life.

g. Defence-of-self

Self-defence as a con-integrate refers to the ways the infant can
defend the self-constellation psychologically. This is particularly
dependent on the early sources of security and competence and
of ego-defence. A study of how personal relationships begin in
childhood suggests that they depend on elements of security and
competence between child and caretaker. Whether the child is
socially advantaged or disadvantaged does not give us a probability statement about what damage may occur to the self at
psychiatric levels of disorder. Often children from stable homes
do show disorders of the self and children from disadvantaged
homes may come through unfortunate experiences and still
develop competence and psychological security.

In earliest social development, in the first months of life, infants
respond in much the same way both to familiar adults and to
strangers. At about seven months infants usually attach to a
specific person, although this can happen at any time from three-
and-a-half months to fifteen months (Ainsworth, 1967). Neither
feeding nor caretaking is the essential feature. The intensity of
interaction seems to have the greatest effect in bonding (Stayton

and Ainsworth, 1973). Increased anxiety and fear expressing an ego needing defence, or illness when the self is attacked, increases the baby's attachment-seeking (Bowlby, 1969). There is a persisting hierarchy among attachments (Schaffer and Emerson, 1964).

The reduction of anxiety in a strange situation if a familiar person is present proves how important bonding is (Cohen and Campos, 1974). Bonding is differentiated from attachment by the selectivity in relationships in which the infant persists over time and place. It is associated with toddlers at the age of one or two, who use the ego in this lasting selection of relationships more apparently than in infant attachment, where ego-competence is still not ripe.

Newborn infants react in a specific and individual way to frustration since deintegrates do not yet reintegrate easily. A similar reaction is present in surprise, when the ego must try cognitive appraisal. Fraiberg (1968) points out that every baby defends or protects himself in very specific ways. Anxiety can become attached to ideas where previous experience produced pain, frustration, instinctive denial (hunger, cold, pain and general somatic distress), loneliness or the need to be autonomous. J. W. Macfarlane *et al.* (1954) studied 100 twenty-one-month-old infants and found that 30 per cent had fears. At three, 70 per cent were affected by specific fears.

By the third week the normal baby is using smiles to ensure that adults will interact with him. This is a primary defence of the self. The grasping reflex in the first two days enables a baby to hold on to a hand or finger and gain stability and contact at once. At six weeks, amidst the gurgles and babbling and crying, some syllables can be heard. There is a rapid read-out of defences for the self as the ego deintegrates out to objects to assimilate them and reintegrate those which match his self/ego development. Self-defence, like the other con-integrates, is a very early vital reservoir of experience and capacity to cope with attacks to

230   security, competence and survival. It would occupy a central position of control among the con-integrates, filtering incoming stimuli from the ego to see if defence of the self were needed. Then the incoming stimulus would filter into other con-integrates or, if more general in nature and further down the hierarchy of self, it might be designated to a multi-integrate level and find its way to the more general store of integrative aspects.

4. Further con-integrate theory research

What kind of empirical research is applicable to the study of the con-integrates? It could be said initially that wherever an organization of a behavioural element can be postulated as present in the child's psyche from three months forward (e.g. Spitz *et al.*, 1970; see Preface), this is the developing ego and its integration system visibly functioning; this begins and delineates the con-integrate research area for study. After speech occurs, its patterns should reveal some of the con-integrates as they develop further in function, provided the observer is equipped to study the projection of archetypal images from the collective unconscious as it projects outwards from the child's ego-shadow con-integrate, affecting his speech interactively on an ongoing basis as he grows older. The ego-shadow aspect has not yet been included in the study of infant speech.

Depth psychologists are needed to help interpret play in the infant. Often activities are reported with little understanding of their symbolic significance, and hence of the play con-integrate's true relation to ego-process. The ego-ideal con-integrate can be measured by finding differences in behaviour which parents' behaviour style elicits from the child, and studying the child's projections of archetypal material as he interacts with parents. Sand-plays, drawing and painting made by children are useful projective tools. They symbolically present unknown and re-pressed aspects of con-integrates and their photographic record can be correlated with longitudinal behaviour studies concerning the child's ego-relations within family dynamics and early experience at school.

The aesthetic con-integrate cannot be measured quantitatively early on, but careful observational records of developmental signs of the earliest aesthetic awareness could lead one to its origins and its process, which have never been clearly defined in psychology. I hope the description of the aesthetic con-integrate has been a step towards remedying this.

The persona con-integrate and its development – metaphorically likened to the mask as used in Greek drama to hide the actor's face, but needing much research into its origins in the baby and infant – needs careful study. It should be looked at from a contemporary and an archetypal set of images in the infant when they become available in projection in scribbling, doodling, drawing and painting.

Experimentation on memory systems should be much enhanced by the theory of the con-integrates and their related memory processes. Empirical work must contain the context that gave it its motivation for study: man's subjective experience of self and its ego-processes. The theory of the self objectivizes this subjective set of facts in a hierarchical construct – parsimonious and partially testable in that its postulates are open to falsification – which provides an exciting new orientation to ego psychology of great explanatory power.

What is the future of my ego-process model? Simon and Newell (1956) distinguish models from theories in three ways: (1) They are useful; they may or may not be true. (2) They are not too data-sensitive; disconfirming evidence does not necessarily damage a model as much as it may do a theory. (3) Models may make false claims more easily than a theory does. Obviously a model is aimed at a subtheory and tends to employ structural explanation in an abstract form.

Theories themselves tend to uncover areas of research that have become stagnant (for example ego psychology). Theory tends to

232   organize and collate unmanageable, disordered data where little
       coherence is evident (for example Freudian ego theory and its
       relation to Jungian ego theory). 'Theories are nets cast to catch
       what we call "the world": to rationalize, to explain and to master
       it' (Popper, 1959). They guide research and help to select certain
       experiments from an infinitude of possible experiments; they may
       bring order and coherence to material. Theories have a logical
       function which is often better expressed verbally; a schematic
       model often gives a psychological function clarity and is cast in
       the mode the theorist finds most *differential* to explanation.

       In my diagrammatic model of ego-process I try to explain the
       most with the least; this heuristic approach is an attempt to
       clarify ego-process and the dimension of focus at initial ego-
       development. In this it connects to the archaic past of the psyche
       in its archetypal images; it looks at closest stimuli, the mother
       and father or initial caretakers in an intrapsychic action to inner
       and outer dispositions and events.

       *The ego con-integrates are a molecular behavioural unit to the whole
       self/ego's molar achievement*, the product of the ego's life-activities;
       *this constructs a more suitable sublevel to begin to sort out the ego's
       function in its remote past, its distal and proximal stimuli and its
       intraorganismic function.* Con-integrate theory has parsimony,
       clarity and some testability. But does it have empirical support?
       My answer is that it does but it needs more and further empirically
       argued manipulation and manifestation. Then the theory would
       find an enhancement which would add to its fruitfulness to all
       schools and disciplines of human psychology.

       The con-integrates flow diagram, like a flow chart, shows a
       concern with a programme that governs total behaviour. I believe
       that the *ego-process delivers a process-programme in which the final,
       mostly unconscious governor is the self.* Ego-process uses feedback,
       as it causally relates to the baby's initial deintegration-reinteg-
       ration of self-match to outer/inner archetypal relatedness; then
       the self/ego-process achieves reabsorption to ego and its con-

integrates. Within this process a wide range of ego-flexibility is defined. That is why the hermeneutic method can exist for ego-interpretation, which relies on empathic intuition and conceptual analysis. This leads to the ultimate social question: What part does ego-process play in the social situation? But whether we refer to causal event or to a teleologically conceived subsequent event, *in ego we must first look at subsystems to know a little more about ego's process-structure.*

The ego's decisions concerning what is self and not-self could be the decisive question for human psychological survival, both personal and collective. Is it not time for self psychology, as paradigm, to refine its theory of its own initial ego process-structure?

Chapter VII

The con-integrates in a clinical case

Children's playings are not sports and should be deemed as their most serious actions.
Montaigne, *Essays* I, p. xxii

1. Introduction to 'David''s* case study

This chapter is a clinical example of depth interpretation of a child's symbolic projection in sand-play therapy from various self/ego con-integrates. It was chosen from my youngest patients' archives as a clear indication of ego-integrates in a child of less than four years old. It should be read at one sitting, if possible, to experience, with the child analyst, the considerable impact of this clinical approach in relation to the study of the con-integrates. This case study does not prove my theory in itself; however, it reveals the presence of con-integrates in a clear and arresting manner, showing the young child's self/ego ground as very present in my clinical observation.

I shall rename my young patient 'David'. David, a three-and-a-half-year-old boy was recommended to me for sand-play therapy by his mother's therapist. I was told that he was an adopted child. His real father, a black African from Ghana, and his real mother, a white European, put him up for adoption when he was six weeks old. Apparently the boy, although so young, had recently learnt that he had been adopted at six weeks by his

*The facts concerning the background of the child, here renamed 'David', but not the ideation of the case, have been completely altered to protect confidentiality. Therefore any similarity to an actual child is purely and strictly coincidental.

present caretaker-parents, chosen by the adoption agency to match the skin-colour of his genetic parents, the adoptive father an educated black man and the mother an energetic and intelligent European woman residing in London, with other children of their own. Since David had learnt he was adopted his parents had found him difficult to discipline, overactive and highly strung.

David and his adoptive mother arrived for the first session. The boy was a handsome mulatto with flashing black eyes. I welcomed them to my consulting room, which is next to a smaller sand-play room where two sand-boxes and about a thousand small objects on shelves allow patients to play and construct whole 'worlds' or sand-play 'scenes' in the sandbox. David had simply been told that I was a man who had a 'really nice' playroom.

David entered with his mother and immediately and repeatedly met my eyes directly. It was a cold autumn day and his mother helped him to remove his sportive outdoor coat, hat and gloves. There are ten chairs in my large consulting room, one of them disdained by David, as it is a low bamboo child's chair (which actually would have fitted him). While his mother and I exchanged pleasantries, David sped around the room bouncing in and out of each chair, finally staying on a modern chaise longue. He turned a backward somersault a few times, a ritual of high-spiritedness with a constant eye-check as to whether we had observed his prowess. I drew David obliquely into the conversation and soon asked him and his mother to come into the sand-play room.

I took the child's low chair into the room and placed it next to an adult's chair, in which his mother sat. I intuitively sat down on the small child's chair as a symbolic signal to David that I was entering this situation at his 'level' near the floor and observing him at his height. I was also playing by choosing a child's chair. He took a deep breath and sighed with delight when he saw the multicoloured shelves of miniature objects, and I assured him, when he asked, that he could play with anything he liked.

Three soft toys were on the floor: a stuffed camel, a donkey

236 and an elephant, which he quickly pushed aside. He put his hands
in the sand-boxes, one box having darker, wetter sand than the
lighter, dryer sand in the box next to it. He lifted a fistful of dry,
light sand and let it filter through his fingers. He exclaimed: 'It's
snowing, like last week', and without further instruction or
question began to place objects from the shelves behind him into
the dry sand-box.

The sand-play therapy of a distressed and confused three-and-
a-half-year-old boy had begun. David actively and excitedly built
his first sand-play (to be discussed below), checking to see that I
was observing him in my 'child's' chair at the side. He looked at
me less guardedly, for his fantasy went free and he seemed to be
showing me and his mother 'a thing or two' about life. His
symbolic attitude showed the almost instant ability that children
have to portray their unconscious wishes, fears and efforts directly
in the sand-box.

Two rituals preceded his entry to the fantasy of sand-play.
They became his thresholds of passage from his image of himself
as the adopted-mother's/father's-boy-but-my-parents-are-not-
really-mine-like-other-parents to the freely aggressive and joyful
omnipotent maker of sand-worlds. The first ritual was several
backward somersaults on the chaise longue next door, which
seemed to help David move into a space of action as nonverbal
bodily movement; then the sprinkling of a fistful of dry sand,
'like snow', on to the dry sand-box seemed to help him enter into
imaginative construction and unconscious projection.

To prepare to leave the symbolic world of play just before
finishing each of the six sand-plays he made, one each in six
sessions, David always offered me a 'pretend' cup of tea in mime,
then his visiting parent also received a cup of 'pretend' tea. Once
we had drunk the invisible cup of tea together David would put
the finishing touches to his sand-play and would declare that the
playtime was finished.

During the first two sand-plays his mother sat with me in the sand-room. Then, on the third visit, his father did so. After that, whichever parent brought David would wait in the next room with the communicating door open while he and I were alone in the sand-room. All these rituals held through all the sessions and the pretend cup of tea, near the sand-play's completion, would be taken by David into the next room to the waiting parent, after I had drunk mine. In this act of 'closure' he was acknowledging my presence as 'his guest', a reversal indicating that he knew 'more than play' was going on and that he wanted consciously to control aspects of the situation over which he had some but little power. In his tea-giving 'ceremony' he seemed partially to 'forgive' his adoptive parents for not being quite '*bona fide*' parents, and he was also showing gratitude to me for the absolute joy he felt in the sand-play space – free but protected.

In the first two sand-plays he remained silent, but at the third session he uttered my name for the first time as he handed me the pretend cup of tea – 'Here, Joel'. 'Thanks, David.' His transference to me and my countertransference to him deepened symbolically at that moment when he broke the silent tea ritual with words. This transference was to enable a healing process to occur, the first two sessions containing the sorting out of good/bad feelings about 'doing this with Joel'. Then, in the third sand-play, David moved more completely into a therapeutic process shared by child and therapist without fear, thus freeing psychic energy for the child's needed working through of problems in projection into the sand-box.

Verbal work with the very young shows that early objects are named by children only after they are noticed, picked up and carefully studied. In nonverbal sand-play the young child spends time with object-choices by taking up an object and turning it in every way to grasp its three-dimensional possibilities before rejecting it or deciding to put it into the sand-play.

David began his first sand-play by handling several objects that fascinated him. Ego-object delineation moves to both quiet and excited play, and experiment-sensing imaginary possibilities with increased handling of a toy object. Thus a child finds new ways of implementing action and expression in the sand-play.

From the first hour several favourite objects which David chose were to reappear in many of the six sand-worlds David made, which I will be discussing here. These objects become the fulcrum of symbolic play, being used by the child as an unconscious continuity. They included a pyramid (an ego-symbol in this case), an old-fashioned sailing boat with many sails (as the given world of the parents), a smaller yellow sailing boat (as David's initial self-object), a model petrol station which David consistently used for petrol stops with cars he chose as action-ego symbols within a given hour, the petrol station a symbol of his total psychic energy supply. A scene of a manger with the Christian Holy Family appeared in Sand-play 4, the developmental picture so essential to the reassertion of David's ego-world in a new omnipotence after the exuberance and confusion of his feelings in the first sand-play. A red Chinese house, also in Sand-play 4, was his self-transference object to me as his therapist as he parked his ego-car and a car he said was mine next to this house, when he remarked that 'Joel could now park there, too'. This was used in the crucial ego–self separation in Plate IV, on which the entire therapy was to hinge in terms of its healing function. David removed two cars from the picture just as he finished. This indicated that his transference and my countertransference could now be taken for granted. What an accurate and precocious child!

Before discussing the six sand-plays in detail, I want to introduce Jung's concept of the transcendent function as it appears in therapeutic sand-play. The transcendent function brings with it a confrontation between the opposites in the conscious and the unconscious. The data involved is mediated from warring opposites into a unity. Sand-play may reveal this through a reconciling symbol; if this is experienced consciously it comes in the form of new attitudes which transcend the earlier divided state or aspect of the self. The transcendent function might be described as a collaboration of conscious and unconscious which facilitates a transition from one attitude to another. Jung has remarked that conflicts are not so much solved as outgrown, but remember that new attitudes may lead on to fresh oppositions which require the transcendent function to continue its complex work to overcome this in new activity. Sand-play can help to embody this 'striving of the conscious for the light and the striving of the unconscious for substance' (see Jung, 1960).

In a dialectical process such as this, there are two main tendencies in dealing with material in fantasy productions: the aesthetic or artistic formulation and the way of understanding. Each has a danger which Jung points out:

> The danger of the aesthetic tendency is an overvaluation of the formal 'artistic' worth of the fantasy productions; the libido is diverted from the real goal of the transcendent function and sidetracked into purely aesthetic problems of artistic expression. The danger of wanting to understand the meaning is overvaluation of the content, which is subjected to intellectual analysis and interpretation, so that the essential symbolic character of the product is lost. (Jung, 1916, pp. 84–5)

2. The sand-plays

Sand-play 1 (see Plate I)

In exuberant joy alternating with thoughtful determination, David gradually filled the first sand-box with chosen objects he found of interest. A highly strung and precocious child, he was testing two boundaries when he added and added objects to achieve chaos. Would the sand-box hold and contain all his wishes, whims, experiments, angers, joys and fatigues? Would I, as the 'sand-play man', allow a chaotic scene as readily as a more conscious picture at the end of a session? With the learning process that these further-out boundaries were holding firmly, the four-sided sand-box (quaternity) became the holding *temenos* for the 'empty space' of David's confusion about being adopted. My calm, apparently unconcerned view as an adult of his chaotic picture, as the session ended, gave David the confidence to return to his second session with trust and he then started a more readable projection process which began a development at an unconscious level.

At the lower bottom centre of the first sand-play, note the small yellow sailing boat (a self-symbol) going upwards from the lower unconscious towards a higher position, but blocked by chaotic object-confusion. In this repressed chaos projected within this first sand-play we can glimpse the shadow con-integrate revealing many of its nonconscious personality aspects, which David simply threw together into a shadow-filled box. He could not at first separate good or bad objects as his excitement flowed into testing the materials at hand.

The older large sailing ship to the right, a more conscious position, represented an archaic self-ship trying to exit the box by pushing its forward sail over the bottom edge. A new self concept must be established and the smaller yellow sailboat, David's favourite 'me' object, needed space in which to sail onwards and upwards to a more conscious position, one in which the ego could join in with unison to break up the chaotic world David experienced at first. The older sailing boat, with its many hierarchically placed sails, suggested the adult world of differentiated energies catching the winds in many varying ways.

This suggests that the older sailing vessel was an ego-ideal con-integrate symbol, containing the parental archetypes. David knew he had only 'two child's sails' on his boat, a newer, smaller and more modern boat, but he longed to solve the mystery of his parenting, his parents' world and the world of his grandparents. He wished to use the forceful energies of his personality to make 'his world' and to have many sails with which to catch the winds of life. Thus the sand-play held powerful and transformative

energic possibilities for this child, and within the chaos the two
sailing boats give a glimpse of developments to be observed in
the subsequent sand-plays.

Sand-play 2 (see Plate II)
In the second sand-play the actual psychological projection
process continues, with a picture sharply divided into the left side
of unconscious chaotic contents from Sand-play 1 and a clear
image of symbolic content on the right side. The old sailing boat
faces left at the top centre, suggesting an ego-position in David
dealing with the pressures of repressed contents. The smaller
yellow sailing boat, David's favourite self-object, is almost
pushed out of the box at the upper left corner. A Swiss clock
featuring a man and a woman suggests gender fascination and a
huge African bird, black like his father's skin-tone, is present – as
is the petrol station, a symbol of libido and energic renewal. A
large blue castle, usually a symbol of archaic self (or archetypal
self) as contained in a fortified or self-defended home structure,
suggests the repression (beginning in the contents on the left side
of the sand-tray) of problematics within the boy's psyche, and on
the conscious right side of the picture a first clearly projected
picture of the boy's psychological dilemma.

On the right side there is a diamond-shaped constellation in
which sits a rectangular box-like imitation stone of numinous
quality for David. I noted that it was a mulatto colour of tan-
brown, similar to David's skin-colour. The top of the diamond-
shaped grouping is a stone on which sits a green bird, overlooking
the situation like an ego-position 'over and above' the sand-tray.
David's ego needed to be higher than, or to rise above, the scene
of his projected confusion and to be able to fly over the sand-box
to gain an overview of his muddled conscious feelings.

On the right below is a 'chimney sweep', a white man who
becomes black-looking from his task of clearing the chimney soot
away. Opposite him is a small white boy in a black suit. At the

242   bottom of the diamond-shaped grouping is an archaic furry black and white animal. David seems to be unconsciously suggesting that at animal or primal level, black and white have been mixed together. He does not yet consciously understand, however, why his father is actually black (like the phallic African bird on the unconscious side of the picture) and his own skin-colour nearer to white but more like the numinous mulatto-coloured stone. David turned this stone around in his hand many times, catching the light from the window in the sand-play room, before he placed it carefully near the black and white figures.

It seemed to me that the problem facing David was at least twofold. He needed to reconcile the idea of not having his real father and mother as the black-and-white primal union within him, and he needed to project the blackness and whiteness further forward into a conscious position concerning the acceptance of his adoptive father's black skin, his adoptive mother's white skin and how that emanated into his own mulatto-toned skin-colour.

David chose the wet sand-box for these first two sand-plays. The water or wetness, a feminine symbol, kept him quite fused to his mother, who attended these two sessions with him and protected him, through the considerable repression shown in Sand-play 2, from moving too quickly to a relief of his confusion about black and white. Was David the chimney sweep who always looked black but was actually white, or was he the white boy in black clothing which he could take off and change to another colour if he became more omnipotent?

David put an African lion at the bottom centre of the sand-box. This lion sits looking towards the left, unconscious side of the box. David wanted to become the king of the jungle (of life), in which he was trying to understand where his great old sailing ship (a symbol of heredity) could sail. This three-masted ship and the green bird to its right represented the mobility of ego that David longed to use more freely within the self.

At three-and-a-half, David was soon to move from a latency

Plate 1: Sand-play 1

Plate II: Sand-play 2

Plate III: Sand-play 3

Plate IV: Sand-play 4

Plate V: Sand-play 5

Plate VI: Sand-play 6a

Plate VII: Sand-play 6b

in fusion-to-mother to the omnipotent ego-stage of a freer ego-structure. But until a fuller self-constellation was projected into the centre of the sand-plays, he seemed stuck in his unconscious energies. When starting each of the first four sand-plays David would try to make a circular road and close it, like the Uroborus-snake eating its own tail. As the totality of the self-projection is held by the sand-box as a whole, we can take this attempt at closure of a circle as the ego's attempt to strengthen the defence-of-the-self con-integrate through the child's searching for greater ego-separation and freedom of ego from self in gaining 'I-ness'.

Sand-play 3 (see Plate III)
Again David began with an unclosed circular road, which he then rubbed out. His father sat with us during this sand-play; this seemed to quiet David into a considered and slower approach as he built up the sand-box.

He pushed down to the water-coloured bottom of the box near the lower centre of the picture, suggesting a firmer imaginative control of terrain as a landscape image and a digging deeper down into the unconscious waters.

The reader will recall that David always initially turned backward somersaults on a large chaise longue in my consulting room before coming into the sand-play room. This act, showing his deep links to the knowledge of play, or the play con-integrate, now expressed itself in object-identification. David chose a toy that has two high wooden railings on which a red-suited man rolls in backward somersaults from his built-out arms. This 'man-self' that David wanted to be – himself – was put in the right-hand centre of the sand-box as a self-representative in isolation. David was calming now into definite and clear projective material as his unconscious responded to the power of the sand-play process.

In the centre of the sand-box as a whole a wooden corkscrew stands as if a totem family symbol or, again, David's longing for

244 ego-omnipotence as phallic power, with both an empty bottle
and a large blue empty vase nearby, symbolic as the containers of
his ego-needs.

The Swiss clock, with its man and woman facing towards the
right – or towards consciousness – is backed by the sitting lion,
the king of David's inward jungle. Now the lion seems pacified
and becomes a spectator to the scene.

It was helpful that David's pleasant and intelligent adoptive
African father was also a relaxed and positive spectator for this
sand-play, as the paternal quest needed steadying. When David
gave me a 'pretend' cup of tea before giving his father one, I
realized that he was also using me as 'paternal-playroom man' in
a search for his root father. By daring to put me first, ahead of his
father, David showed that he now trusted the holding power of
the sand-play room and its total experience, which could 'allow'
symbolically putting someone momentarily ahead of his father.

David's self-ship, the small yellow sailing boat, was moored
in the lower left corner of the box. This deepest unconscious
corner often suggests an archetypal area of the psyche in projection. He stood a green spear upright there, on which a black
knight and the black-and-white furry animal seemed to be
pondering. (This green spear had been next to the numinous
mulatto-coloured stone in the upper right of Sand-play 2.)

Unconsciously David was moving deeply through his collective unconscious as he projected a psychological process now
moving rapidly, with clarity of projection, towards the next sand-
play. Black-and-white symbolism remained important to his
psyche.

Sand-play 4 (see Plate IV)
With this sand-play David at last, with a thrust of his left hand,
completed his circular imprint of a road, which he had been
unable to close in full circle before. In each previous sand-play he
had tried and had then obscured this path.

With this separation of ego from the totality of self, by closing a self-made circle, he moved from the latency period to the period of ego-omnipotence, the first complete ego-separation from self and from his need for fusion-with-mother. This transitional phase, here being acted out in sand-play construction, is clearly described in Winnicott's work (1965b) on the transitional period.

This spiral road was made in a clockwise direction, suggesting normal linear clock time as the 'now' of the process. The Holy Family as primal family sits at the upper left-hand bend of the ego-road, suggesting a rebirth or reconstellation of family. There is a ladder by which one can climb 'on top of this situation', the family scene, and perhaps understand it. In the top centre is a pyramid containing an enclosed green stone, which David said 'cannot be moved'. If David is locked into an adoptive family pyramid, here it takes on permanence. Anything metallic held within a pyramid 'sharpens' by natural force, so David seemed to be sharpening his own 'alchemical metal', his own true nature, his ego-within-selfhood.

Moving around the ego-circle counterclockwise, we next pass the petrol station, David's psychic energy centre, and beneath it a deep well, a symbol of new resource from the deeper layers of psyche, for nourishment and refreshment.

At the lower right-hand corner of the ego-circle road we have a free-standing windmill with a red fire engine behind it. The four winds can catch the windmills' propeller blades and gain energy momentum within the ego's newly found omnipotence; the danger of being overwhelmed by these new energies is unconsciously projected by putting a firefighting truck nearby, a symbol of control and repair against an out-of-control break-through of unconscious material.

Here David's psyche was experiencing warning of true danger from the fiery impact of his new ego-strength: a force, when it first goes free, of almost manic intensity in an already precocious, active and curious child. It suggests that the child was experiencing

246   an initiation or a *rite de passage* which, like all such developmental breakthroughs of new psychic possibility, is a dangerous moment of sheer archetypal change and requires much holding in its birth stages.

David's parents' presence, his therapist and the protection of the sand-play experience prevented some of the danger to his psyche from spreading into disintegration or severe regression.

In this sand-play the old three-masted sailing vessel, David's archaic family symbol, is moored just in front of and hiding the favourite yellow sailing boat. They are together now, moored in a peaceful harbour, suggesting a new ambience in David between self and archetypal inheritance.

A red Chinese house is introduced for the first time. 'This is Joel's house,' said David. So the therapist and the 'house of sand-play' are symbolized as a red, feeling-filled square house. Oriental objects are often used by Western children to 'orient' by, and David was skilfully using me and the 'sand-play house' for his new omnipotent ego-orientation. He placed an elephant nearby, an oriental symbol of far memory, implacable wisdom and service.

When David left this session – which his mother had attended, but staying out of the sand-play room in the adjoining room – she reported to me that he had surprised her when going home in the car by saying, 'I have known Joel in another life'.

I checked carefully to learn if David had met, heard or seen any Buddhist reference in person, or other reference in the media, to reincarnation. This was fully checked out and denied by his family. Thus on a psychological level David had substituted me, his therapist, as a friendly person from 'another life'. He now sensed that the sand-play room had an 'otherness' about it: something that drew his archaic side forward, as the sand-play process does, was in this play a part of the play con-integrate. The metaphysical aspect of David's statement is outside this study of therapeutic psychological ideation. It was something for me to ponder and to hold in silence.

I now decided that two more sessions would be required, during which I could defuse the powerful transference David had made to me during this time. I hoped these last sessions would enable the therapy to crystallize further. At the next session I told David I was going on holiday, so we would meet only once more. This was not said before he had given his own indication of his prior knowledge that we would not be meeting for very much longer!

Sand-play 5 (see Plate V)

David opened this session as he started to construct his sand-play by saying, 'I'm not going to live here much longer, am I?'

'No, David, soon I am going on holiday so the playroom will be closed, but would you like to come one more time, at least for now?'

'Oh yes, Joel!'

In this sand-play a regression into anger, fatigue and the pain of growth occurred which showed the ongoing depth at which David was now working. In revealing this fully in the sand, David was trusting me with his naked personal con-integrate. Here he unmasked the struggle that his new ego-power had cost his self-control, and indeed his parents now found it very difficult to control or discipline him at all. So psychological anger and destructive shadow con-integrate material were heaped together with a helpless yet determined fury and fatigue. My experience told me that this honesty might well lead to a healing and binding together of the work in the last session, so I had to endure the risk that – at this moment – David felt hopeless and again confused in what now became a search for whatever the sand-play might still have in store for him. I remained utterly calm, warm, accepting and quietly present, taking David's unmasking of his persona con-integrate as essential to his experience of life at this moment.

He moved the Holy Family towards the upper centre of the sand-box and put a small bird-in-a-cage left of it, tipped over in a despairing gesture. Was David the bird-in-the-family-cage and, if so, what family problem was he groping to understand? His adoption? Who had created him in the primal scene? The skin-colour of his father, his mother, himself? An empty bench looks over the scene from the upper left corner. Where is David now? He cannot sit down yet on the bench of life.

Then, in a fit of quiet rage, he crashed a bus on to a rooftop, threw down the beloved petrol station over some trees, turned a smaller bus upside down, overturned a waterwheel, played with a blue and green magnet (symbols of attraction) and threw them down, and left a lorry-cab upright in the bottom centre heading downwards. All this despair was placed on the left-hand uncon-scious side of the construction.

David was using the dry, lighter sand-box for this sand-play and – then – consciousness broke through. He took the darker, wet sand and put a few drops of it on the centre of the whiter sand. He was mixing the dark with the light colour. Suddenly his psyche knew how he came to be a mixture – it was like mixing the grains of sand to have a black father and a white mother. With a hugh sigh, David finished and abruptly swept past me omnipotently to go and put on his coat. He was beginning to accept his parents, both original and adoptive, and his own mulatto skin colour was going to be 'OK'.

Sand-play 6 (see Plates VI and VII)
The sixth and last sand-play session was a resolution. David arrived with his mother in a friendly mood. He delayed his first rituals of backward somersaults on the chaise longue and bounced about on all the chairs, as he had at the very first session. He was symbolically preparing himself for his final sand-play. Eventually he came into the sand-room and I took, as usual, the child's chair

and quietly awaited developments. (I always treat children as if they were visiting diplomats.)

David sprinkled dark sand into the dry, lighter sand-box and white sand into the wet, darker box. He placed the petrol station, his psychic energy, into the centre. To the conscious right, he placed a deep blue cube which he said was 'beautiful'. Here the aesthetic con-integrate came into play – his tribute to the world of sand-play, to his love of the many objects on the shelves to choose from, and perhaps an acceptance of himself as of a beautiful colour, the transformation of his different skin-colour still upper-most as problematic. To the left of the petrol station he placed the Swiss clock with the man and woman facing a small green tree, often a symbol of archetypal growth and of the natural world. A sand-covered upright piano completed the dry sand-box. (He had heard my wife practising the piano along the corridor that day.) He then broke out of the holding power of the one sand-box and moved to the left sand-box near it. He searched and searched among the shelves and then firmly placed a black London taxi alone in the second box.

This taxi represented a family vehicle, symbolically driven by his London-based adoptive black father. A vehicle of privilege, because expensive (David had paid the price of abandonment by his real forebears) yet a vehicle common, but special, among London's busy streets. Taxis get to their destination.

David's ego had at last transformed his confusion into a clear acceptance of a black father, symbolized as the ego-taxi of the family. Across in the more consciously constructed other sand-box, the essential symbol – the petrol station – proclaimed David's intact full psychic energy as he found understanding and transformation in finishing this sand-play process. He took two final fistfuls of sand, one dark, one lighter – and sprinkled these like a nourishing rainfall on to the two sand-boxes in a quiet and deep concentration. He was accepting the new meaning of black and white and of its mixture in him.

He returned to the consulting room and both unconsciously and consciously David and I were now at our farewell. He spied on my desk a torch (flashlight) which I was going to take on holiday. He took the torch and, turning it on, searched underneath each chair, pretending to be sure nothing more was hidden in the depths underneath all the chairs in my consulting room.

In this profound acting out of what the therapy had achieved – a searchlight upon David's unconscious or hidden areas at the floor of his psyche – the boy showed me he knew something of what the sand-play had been about. Satisfied that nothing more was hidden underneath my consulting-room chairs, he sighed in recognition and farewell, thanks and trust. We said goodbye quickly and simply, and David and his mother were gone.

3. Conclusions

The sand-play process had brought David six months in advance of the average child, to the full independence of ego-omnipotence separated from self but arising from it. A healthy, energetic and precocious boy now faced the world with a clearer focus of energy and a deeper acceptance of his adoptive parents, their skin-colours and his own.

David had also succeeded in making me feel a 'complete' therapist in his final gesture of that 'love which passeth understanding' – the *agape* or universal love which young children can know and communicate often more purely than adults to people who have enabled them to know themselves better. He had taught me much about psychological process and had revealed several of the con-integrates in a natural outflowing of personality.

The con-integrates that appeared in the sand-plays were the shadow con-integrate in Sand-play 1; both the ego-ideal con-integrate and the defence-of-the-self con-integrate in Sand-play 2; the play con-integrate in Sand-play 3 and by implication throughout the work; the persona con-integrate appeared in Sand-play 5, the aesthetic con-integrate in Sand-play 6.

This description of a sand-play process in a three-and-a-half-year-old boy does not claim to prove my thesis concerning the existence of the con-integrates. I hope it will stimulate other workers in the field to use the con-integrate theory to help clarify those ego-conglomerates which are vital support systems to the ego-processes. As these Gestalt-like complexes of deintegrates separate from self and then reintegrate into what I name the *con-integrates*, I believe the therapist can gain a clearer map, a surer insight into the ego of a child as it separates out partially from self in the step-by-step process of deintegration-reintegration which the con-integrates separate into conglomerates of special significance to the survival of the ego's effective performance and perception.

4. Thoughts for the reader

The end of this book is its beginning in two senses. The first sense of an end as a beginning is that it is a further continuation of a realization of ego and its subsystems of integration which must be made concrete by the empirical data of observation, experiment and analysis in child psychology; it contributes the assessment of the con-integrate theory and only begins with this theoretical formulation.

The second sense of the end as beginning would be to suggest to the student of psychology that the Preface, as threshold, now be reread to a fuller comprehension of what this book has actually been about. The author and the reader have then come 'full circle'.

Place of publication is London, unless otherwise specified

Abenheimer, K. (1968) 'The ego as subject', in J. B. Wheelwright, ed. *The Reality of the Psyche*. Barrie & Rockliffe.

Acheson, E. D. and Truelove, S. C. (1961) 'Early weaning in the aetiology of ulcerative colitis', *British Medical Journal* 2: 929–33.

Adler, G. (1951) 'Notes regarding the dynamics of the self', *Br. J. Med. Psychol.* 24: 97–105.

Ainsworth, M. D. S. (1967) *Infancy in Uganda: Infant Care and the Growth of Love*. Baltimore, MD : Johns Hopkins University Press.

Allport, G. W. (1961) *Pattern and Growth in Personality*. New York: Holt, Rinehart & Winston.

Anthony, J. (1958) 'An experimental approach to the psycho-pathology of childhood autism', *Br. J. Med. Psychol.* 31: 3–11.

Arnetz, B. B. *et al.* (1987) 'Immune function in unemployed women in Sweden', *Psychosomatic Medicine* 34: 6–12.

Bannister, D. and Agnew, J.(1976) 'The child's construing of self', in J. Cole, ed. *Nebraska Symposium on Motivation*. Lincoln, NB: University of Nebraska Press.

Bastian, A. (1860) *Der Mensch in der Geschichte*. Leipzig: Wigand.

Beloff, J. (1964) *Existence of Mind*. Citadel.

Bender, L. (1953) 'Childhood schizophrenia', *Psychiatric Quarterly* 27: 663–8.

—— (1959) 'Autism in children with mental deficiency', *American Journal of Mental Deficiency* 63: 81–6.

Bernfeld, S. (1949) 'Freud's scientific beginnings', *Am. Imago* 6: 163–96.

Bernheim, H. (1884) *De la suggestion dans l'état hypnotique et dans l'état de veille*. Paris: Doin.

—— (1888) *De la suggestion et de ses applications à la thérapeutique.* Paris: Doin.

Bettelheim, B. (1956) 'Schizophrenia as a reaction to extreme situations', *American Journal of Orthopsychiatry* 26: 507–18.

—— (1967) *The Empty Fortress: Infantile Autism and the Birth of the Self.* Collier-Macmillan.

—— (1982) *Freud and Man's Soul.* New York: Vintage.

Bion, W. R. (1955) 'Language of the schizophrenic', in M. Klein, ed. *New Directions in Psychoanalysis.* Tavistock.

Blackburn, T. R. (1971) 'Sensuous-intellectual complementarity in science', *Science* 172: 1003–7.

Bloom, L. (1973) *One Word At a Time.* The Hague: Mouton.

Börne, L. (1858) 'The art of becoming an original writer in three days', in *Collected Works.* Milwaukee, WI: Bickler.

Bowerman, M. (1974) 'Learning the structure of causative verbs', *Papers and Reports On Child Language Development* 8: 142–78. Stanford, CA: Stanford University Press.

Bowlby, J. (1969) *Attachment and Loss,* vol. 1. Hogarth.

Bradley, C. (1941) *Schizophrenia in Childhood.* New York: Macmillan.

Brain, W. R. (1950) 'The concept of the schema in neurology and psychiatry', in D. Richter, ed. *Perspectives in Neuropsychiatry.* H. K. Lewis.

—— (1951) *Mind, Perception and Science.* Oxford: Oxford University Press.

Braine, M. D. S. (1976) 'Children's first word combinations', *Monograph for Social Research in Child Development* 31: 1–92.

Breuer, J. and Freud, S. (1895) *Studien über Hysterie.* Leipzig and Vienna: Deuticke.

Bronson, G. (1965) 'The hierarchical organization of the central nervous system: implications for learning processes and critical periods in development', *Behavioural Science* 10: 7–25.

Brown, R. (1965) *Social Psychology.* New York: Macmillan.

Burch, P. R. J. and Burwell, L. G. (1965) 'Self and not-self', *Quarterly Review of Biology* 40: 3–21.

Burnett, M. (1962) *The Integrity of the Body.* Oxford: Oxford University Press.

Burt, C. (1921) *Mental and Scholastic Tests.* London County Council.

—— (1934) *How the Mind Works.* Arno.

—— (1959) *A Psychological Study of Topography.* Cambridge: Cambridge University Press.

—— (1961) 'The structure of the mind', *British Journal of Statistical Psychology* 14: 145–70.

254   —— (1968) 'Brain and consciousness', *Bulletin of the British Psychological Society* 1: 29–36.

Cairns, D. (1976) *Conversations With Husserl and Fink*. The Hague: Nijhoff.

Campbell, F. W. and Robson, J. G. (1968) 'Application of Fourier analysis to the visibility of gratings', *Journal of Physiology* 197: 551–66.

Chasseguet-Smirgel, J. (1985) *The Ego Ideal*. Free Association Books.

Chomsky, N. (1966) *Cartesian Linguistics*. New York: Harper.

—— (1968) *Syntactic Structures*. The Hague: Mouton.

Clark, E. V. (1978) 'From gesture to word: on the natural history of deixis in language acquisition', in J. S. Bruner and A. Garton, eds *Human Growth and Development*. Oxford: Clarendon.

Cohen, L. J. and Campos, J. J. (1974) 'Father, mother and stranger as elicitors of attachment behaviours in infancy', *Developmental Psychology* 10: 146–54.

Condon, W. S. and Sander, L. W. (1974) 'Neonate movement is synchronized with adult speech', *Science* r83: 99–108.

Creak, M. (1961) 'Schizophrenic syndrome in childhood', *Cerebral Palsy Bulletin* 3: 501–4.

—— (1963) Childhood psychoses: a review of 100 cases', *British Journal of Psychiatry* 109: 84–9.

Critchley, M., O' Leary J. and Jennet, B., eds (1972) *Scientific Foundations of Neurology*, vol. 5. Philadelphia, PA: F. A. Davis.

Delafreshaye, J. F., ed. (1954) *Brain Mechanisms and Consciousness*. Oxford: Oxford University Press.

de Sanctes, S. (1925) 'La neuropsychiatrica infantile', *Infanzia Anormale* 18: 633–61.

Descartes, R. (1911) *Passions of the Soul: Philosophical Works*, E. S. Haldane and G. R. T. Ross, trans. New York: Cambridge University Press.

Despert, J. L. (1938) 'Schizophrenia in children', *Psychiatric Quarterly* 12: 366–71.

—— (1940) 'A comparative study of thinking in schizophrenic children and in children of preschool age', *American Journal of Psychiatry* 97: 189–213.

—— (1947) 'The early recognition of childhood schizophrenia', *Medical Clinics of North America (Pediatrics)* 31: 660–87.

—— (1951) 'Some considerations relating to the genesis of autistic behaviour in children', *American Society of Orthopsychiatry* 21: 335–50.

—— (1955) 'Differential diagnosis between obsessive-compulsive neurosis and schizophrenia in children', in P. H. Hoch and J. Zubin, eds *Psychopathology of Childhood*. New York: Grune & Stratton.

Despine, P. (1868) *Psychologie naturelle*. Paris: Savy.   255

de Villiers, J. G. and de Villiers, P. A. (1978) *Language Acquisition*. Harvard University Press.

Diatkine, R. (1960) 'Reflections on the genesis of psychotic object relations in the young child', *Int. J. Psycho-Anal.* 41: 4–5.

Dixon, N. F. (1971) *Subliminal Perception: The Nature of a Controversy*. McGraw-Hill.

Dorer, M. (1932) *Historische Grundlagen der Psychoanalyze*. Leipzig.

Du Bois-Reymond, E. (1892) *Ueber die Grenzen des Naturerkenness*. Leipzig: Viet.

Eccles, J. C. (1964) *The Physiology of Synapses*. New York: Academic.

Edinger, E. F. (1960) 'The ego-self paradox', *J. Analyt. Psychol.* 5: 3–17.

Efron, R. (1966) 'The conditioned reflex', *Perspectives in Biology and Medicine*. 9: 488–514.

Ehrenzweig, A. (1967) *The Hidden Order of Art: A Study in the Psychology of Artistic Imagination*. San Francisco: University of California Press.

Eimas, P. D. *et al.* (1971) 'Speech perceptions in infants', *Science* 171: 303–6.

Einstein, A. (1933) *On the Method of Theoretical Physics*. New York: Oxford University Press.

Ekstein, R. (1955) 'Vicissitudes of the "internal image" in the recovery of a borderline schizophrenic', *Bulletin of the Menninger Clinic* 19: 86–92.

Ellenberger, H. F. (1970) *The Discovery of the Unconscious*. Allen Lane.

Ende, R. N. and Harrison, R. J. (1972) 'Endogenous and exogenous smiling systems in early infancy', *Journal of Child Psychology and Psychiatry* 2: 177–200.

Erdelyi, M. H. (1974) 'A new look at the new look: perceptual defence and vigilance', *Psychological Review* 81: 1–25.

Erikson, E. H. (1964) *Childhood and Society*. Hogarth.

Escalona, S. K. (1963) 'Patterns of infantile experience and the developmental process', *Psychoanal. Study Child* 18: 197–244.

—— (1969) *The Roots of Individuality: Normal Patterns of Development*. Tavistock.

Evans, J. St B. T. and Wason, P. C. (1976) 'Rationalization in a reasoning task', *British Journal of Psychology* 67: 479–86.

Exner, S. (1894) *Entwurf zu einer physiologischen Erklärung der psychischen Erscheinungen*. Vienna: Deuticke.

Fairbairn, W. R. D. (1954a) *An Object-Relations Theory of the Personality*. New York: Basic.

256   —— (1954b) 'Observations on the nature of hysterical states', *Br. J. Med. Psychol.* 27: 105–25.

Fantz, R. L. (1963) 'Pattern vision in newborn infants', *Science* 140: 296–7.

Flourens, M. J. P. (1842) 'Recherches expérimentales sur les propriétés et les fonctions du système nerveux dans les animaux vertébrés'. Paris.

Flügel, J. C. (1955) *Studies in Feeling and Desire.* Duckworth.

Fordham, M. (1944) *The Life of Childhood.* Routledge & Kegan Paul.

—— (1947) 'Integration, disintegration and early ego development', *Nervous Child* 6: 266–77.

—— (1951) 'Some observations on the self in childhood', *Br. J. Med. Psychol.* 24: 83–96.

—— (1957) *New Developments in Analytical Psychology.* Routledge & Kegan Paul.

—— (1958a) 'Individuation and ego-development', *J. Analyt. Psychol.* 3: 115–30.

—— (1958b) *The Objective Psyche.* Routledge & Kegan Paul.

—— (1960) 'Ego, self, and mental health', *Br. J. Med. Psychol.* 33: 249–53.

—— (1963) 'The empirical foundation and theories of the self in Jung's work', *J. Analyt. Psychol.* 8: 1–24.

—— (1969) *Children as Individuals.* Hodder & Stoughton.

—— (1976) *The Self and Autism.* Heinemann Medical.

Fraiberg, S. A. (1968) *The Magic Years.* Methuen.

French, J. D., Verseano, M. and Magoun, H. W. (1953) 'A neural basis of the anaesthetic state', *American Medical Association Archives of Neurology and Psychiatry* 69: 519–29.

Freud, S. (1895a) *The Origins of Psychoanalysis. Letters to Wilhelm Fliess. Drafts and Notes.* Imago, 1954.

—— (1895b) *Project for a Scientific Psychology,* in James Strachey, ed. *The Standard Edition of the Complete Psychological Works of Sigmund Freud,* 24 vols. Hogarth, 1953–73, vol. 1 (1966), pp. 281–397.

—— (1908) 'Civilized sexual morality and modern nervous illness'. *S.E.* 9.

—— (1914a) 'On narcissism: an introduction'. *S.E.* 14.

—— (1914b) 'On the history of the psychoanalytic movement', in *Collected Papers,* 1925b.

—— (1920) 'A note on the prehistory of analysis'. *S.E.* 18.

—— (1924) 'The economic problem of masochism'. *S.E.* 19.

—— (1925a) *An Autobiographical Study. S.E.* 20.

—— (1925b) *Collected Papers,* vol. 2. Hogarth.

—— (1926) *Inhibitions, Symptoms and Anxiety*. Hogarth.

—— (1927a) *The Ego and the Id*. Hogarth.

—— (1927b) 'The question of lay analysis', *Int. J. Psycho-Anal.* 8.

—— (1938) 'Splitting of the ego in the process of defence', *S.E.* 23.

—— (1939) *Moses and Monotheism*. Hogarth.

—— (1949) *The Outline of Psychoanalysis*, J. Strachey, ed. and trans. Hogarth.

—— (1953) *On Aphasia, A Critical Study*, E. Steugel, trans. New York: International Universities Press.

—— (1959) *Beyond the Pleasure Principle*. Hogarth.

Freud, S. and Jung, C. G. (1974) *The Freud/Jung Letters*, W. McGuire, ed. Bolligen Series XCIV: Princeton University Press.

Friedman, S. (1972) 'Habituation and recovery of visual response in the alert human newborn', *Journal of Experimental Child Psychology* 13: 339–49.

Galton, F. (1879) 'Psychometric experiments', *Brain* 2: 149–62.

Geleerd, E. K. (1963) 'Evaluation of M. Klein's narrative of a child analysis', *Int. J. Psycho-Anal.* 44: 493–501.

Gell, P. G. H. (1957) 'On the nature of some hypersensitivity reactions', in B. M. Halpern, ed. *Psychopathology of the Reticulo-Endothelial System*. Oxford: Blackwell.

Good, R. A. (1984) 'Immunologic aberrations: the AIDS defect', in K. M. Kahill, ed. *The AIDS Epidemic*. Hutchinson.

Gottlieb, G. (1970) 'Conception of prenatal behaviour', in L. R. Aronson, E. Tobach, D. S. Lehrmann and J. S. Rosenblatt, eds *Development and Evolution of Behaviour*. San Francisco: W. H. Freeman.

Groddeck, G. (1949) *The Book of It*. Vision.

—— (1951) *The Unknown Self*. Vision.

—— (1977) *The Meaning of Illness*. Hogarth/Institute of Psychoanalysis.

Guntrip, H. J. S. (1971) *Psychoanalytic Theory, Therapy and the Self*. Hogarth.

Harmon, R. J. and Ende, R. N. (1971) 'Spontaneous REM behaviours in a microcephalic infant', *Perceptual and Motor Skills* 34: 827–33.

Harrison, J. E. (1908) *Prolegomena to the Study of the Greek Religion*. Cambridge: Cambridge University Press.

Hartmann, H. (1964) *Essays on Ego Psychology*. New York: International Universities Press.

—— (1975) *Ego Psychology and the Problem of Adaptation*. Hogarth.

Head, H., Rivers, W. H. R., Holmes, G., Sherran, J., Thompson, T. and Riddoch, G. (1920) *Studies in Neurology*. Frowde & Hodder.

Hegel, G. W. F. (1931) *The Phenomenology of Mind*, J. P. Baillie, trans. Allen & Unwin.

258 —— (1975) *Introduction to Aesthetics*, T. M. Knox, trans. Oxford: Clarendon.

Heimann, P. (1955) 'A contribution to the re-evaluation of the Oedipus complex', in M. Klein, ed. *New Directions in Psychoanalysis*. Tavistock.

Heller, T. (1930) 'Über dementia infantalis', C. W. Hulse, trans. *Journal of Nervous Mental Diseases* 119: 671–82.

Helm, G. (1904) *Die Theorien der Elektrodynamik nach ihrer geschichtichen Entwicklung*. Leipzig: Viet.

Hernández-Peón, R. (1969) 'Neurophysiologic aspects of attention', in E. Venken and C. Bruyn, eds *Handbook of Clinical Neurology* 3: New York: Wiley.

Herrick, C. J. (1963) *Brains in Rats and Men*. Chicago: University of Chicago Press.

Hilgard, E. R. (1973) 'A neodissociation interpretation of pain reduction in hypnosis', *Psychological Review* 80: 396–411.

Holt, R. R. (1965) 'A review of some of Freud's biological assumptions and their influence on his theories', in N. Greenfield and W. Lewis, eds *Psychoanalysis and Current Biological Thought*. Madison, WI: University of Wisconsin Press.

Hubert, H. and Mauss, M. (1898) *Sacrifice: Its Nature and Function*. Cohen & West, 1964.

Hume, D. (1896) *Treatise*, Bks I and II, D. Selby-Bigge, ed. Oxford: Clarendon.

Husserl, E. (1948) *Experience and Judgement*. Routledge & Kegan Paul.

—— (1960) *Cartesian Meditations*. The Hague: Nijhoff.

Isaacs, S. (1948) *Childhood and After*. Routledge & Kegan Paul.

Jackson, M. (1960) 'Jung's archetype: clarity or confusion?', *Br. J. Med. Psychol.* 33: 83–94.

Jacobi, J. (1962) *The Psychology of C. G. Jung*. Routledge & Kegan Paul.

—— (1976) *Masks of the Soul*. Darton, Longman & Todd.

Jaffé, A. (1972) *From the Life and Work of C. G. Jung*. Hodder & Stoughton.

Jahoda, M. (1977) *Freud and the Dilemmas of Psychology*. Hogarth.

Jakobson, R. (1968) *Child Language, Aphasia and Phonological Universals*. The Hague: Mouton.

Janov, A. and Holden, E. M. (1975) *Primal Man: The New Consciousness*. New York: Crowell.

Jeans, Sir J. (1942) *Physics and Philosophy*. Cambridge University Press.

Johnson, M. (1948) *Science and the Meanings of Truth*. Faber & Faber.

Jones, E. (1953–57) *S. Freud, Life and Work*, 3 vols. Hogarth.

Jung, C. G. (1912) 'Transformations and symbols of the libido', in Sir H. Read, M. Fordham and G. Adler, eds *The Collected Works (C.W.)* Routledge & Kegan Paul, vol. 2.

—— (1916) 'The transcendent function'. *C.W.* 8.

—— (1918) *Studies in Word-Association.* New York: Moffat, Yard.

—— (1919) 'Instinct and unconscious'. *C.W.* 8.

—— (1921) *Psychological Types. C.W.* 6.

—— (1923) 'On the relation of analytical psychology to poetry'. *C.W.* 15.

—— (1928) 'The relations between the ego and the unconscious'. *C.W.* 7.

—— (1934) *The Archetypes and the Collective Unconscious. C.W.* 9, part I.

—— (1936) 'The concept of the collective unconscious'. *C.W.* 9.

—— (1938) 'The Terry lectures'. *C.W.* 11.

—— (1939) 'Die psychologischen Aspekte des Mutterarchetypus', *Eranos Jahrbuch* 8: 79–91. Zurich: Eranos.

—— (1940) *The Integration of the Personality,* W. S. Dell, trans. Kegan Paul.

—— (1944a) 'The holy men of India: introduction to Zimmer's *Der Weg sum Selbst'. C.W.* 11.

—— (1944b) *Psychology and Alchemy. C.W.* 12.

—— (1946) 'Der Geist der Psychologie', *Eranos Jahrbuch* 15: 385–490.

—— (1949) 'Prolegomena', in C. G. Jung and C. Kerenyi, eds *Essay on a Science of Mythology.* Princeton, NJ. Bolligen Series.

—— (1950) *Gestaltungen des Unbewussten.* Zurich: Rauscher.

—— (1951) *Aion. C.W.* 9, part II.

—— (1953) *Two Essays on Analytical Psychology. C.W.* 7.

—— (1954) *The Development of Personality. C.W.* 17.

—— (1955) *The Secret of the Golden Flower* (with R. Wilhelm). New York: Harcourt Brace.

—— (1956) *Symbols of Transformation. C.W.* 5.

—— (1958) *Psychology and Religion: West and East. C.W.* 11.

—— (1959a) 'The psychology of the child archetype'. *C.W.* 9, part IV.

—— (1959b) *Flying Saucers.* Routledge & Kegan Paul.

—— (1960) *The Structure and Dynamics of the Psyche. C.W.* 18, part I, part III.

Kalff, D. M. (1980) *Sandplay.* Boston: Sigo.

Kanner, L. (1944) 'Early infantile autism', *Journal of Pediatrics* 25: 211–17.

—— (1948) *Child Psychiatry.* Oxford: Blackwell.

—— (1954) 'To what extent is early infantile autism determined by constitutional inadequacies?', *Association for Research in Nervous Mental Diseases* 33: 378–85.

260   Kant, I. (1788) *The Critique of Pure Reason*, T. K. Abbott, trans. Longmans, 1909.

Kellogg, R. (1969) *Analysing Children's Art*. Palo Alto, CA: National.

Kelly, G. A. (1955) *The Psychology of Personal Constructs*. New York: Norton.

Kerenyi, C. (1951) *Gods of the Greeks*. Thames.

Kernberg, O. F. (1974) 'Contrasting viewpoints regarding the nature and psychoanalytic treatment of narcissistic personalities', *J. Amer. Psychoanal. Assn* 22: 255–67

Kerner, J. (1819) *Das Bilderbuch aus meiner Knabengeit, 1786–1804*. Braunschweig: Viehweg.

Khan, M. M. R. (1974) *The Privacy of the Self*. New York: International Universities Press.

Kintsch, W. (1970) *Learning, Memory and Conceptual Processes*. New York: Wiley.

Klatzky, R. L. (1975) *Human Memory: Structure and Processes*. San Francisco: W. H. Freeman.

Klein, M. (1930) 'The importance of symbol formation in the development of the ego', in *Contributions to Psychoanalysis*. Hogarth, 1948.

—— (1932) *The Psychoanalysis of Children*. Hogarth.

—— (1946) 'Notes on some schizoid mechanisms', in *New Developments in Psychoanalysis*. Tavistock, 1952.

—— (1948) *Contributions to Psychoanalysis (1921– 45)*. Hogarth.

—— (1952) *New Developments in Psychoanalysis* (with P. Heimann, S. Isaacs and J. Rivière). Hogarth.

—— (1957) *Envy and Gratitude*. Tavistock.

—— (1961) *Narrative of a Child Psychoanalysis*. Hogarth.

Kline, P. (1972) *Fact and Fantasy in Freudian Theory*. Methuen.

Koestler, A. (1968) *Drinkers of Infinity*. Hutchinson.

—— (1972) *The Roots of Coincidence*. Hutchinson.

Kohut, H. (1977) *The Restoration of the Self*. New York: International Universities Press.

Kris, E. (1954) *Introduction to the Origins of Psychoanalysis*. Imago.

—— (1955) 'Neutralization and sublimation: observations on young children', in R. Eissler, A. Freud, H. Hartmann and E. Kris, eds *The Psychoanalytical Study of the Child* 10: 30–46.

Kuhn, T. S. (1962) *The Structure of Scientific Revolutions*. Chicago: University of Chicago Press.

—— (1963) 'The essential tension: tradition and innovation in scientific research', in C. W. Taylor and F. Barron, eds *Scientific Creativity*. Wiley.

Lacan, J. (1966) *The Language of the Self*, A. Wilden, trans. Baltimore, MD: 261
Johns Hopkins University Press.

Lakatos, I. (1970) 'Falsification and the methodology of scientific research programmes', in I. Lakatos and A. Musgrave, eds *Criticism and the Growth of Knowledge*. Cambridge University Press.

Lambert, K. (1981) 'Emerging consciousness', J. Analyt. Psychol. 26: 1–9.

Langer, S. K. (1942) *Philosophy in a New Key*. New York: Howard.

Lashley, K. S. and Colby, K. M. (1957) 'An exchange of views on psychic energy and psychoanalysis', *Behavioural Science* 2: 231–40.

Leboyer, F. (1975) *Birth Without Violence*. New York: Knopf.

Leibeskind, J. C., Guilbrand, C., Besson, J. M. and Oliveras, J. L. (1973) 'Analgesia from electrical stimulation of the periaqueductal grey matter in the cat', *Brain Research* 50: 441–6.

Leibnitz, G. W. von (1717) *A Collection of Papers, 1715–1716*.

Levinger, G. and Clark, J. (1961) 'Emotional factors in the forgetting of word associations', *Journal of Abnormal Social Psychology* 62: 99–105.

Lewis, M. and Brooks-Gunn, J. (1979) *Social Cognition and the Acquisition of Self*. Plenum.

Libby, F. (1965) 'Man's place in the physical universe', in J. R. Platt, ed. *New Views of the Nature of Man*. Chicago: University of Chicago Press.

Light. L. L. and Carter-Sobell, L. (1970) 'Effects of changed semantic context on recognition memory', *Journal of Verbal Learning and Verbal Behaviour* 9: 1–11.

Lipps, T. (1903) *Aesthetik: Psychologie der Schönen und der Kunst*. Leipzig: Voss.

Luria, A. R. (1966) 'L. S. Vygotsky and the problem of functional localization', *Soviet Psychology* 5: 53–60.

Lynkeus (pseudonym of Joseph Popper) (1899) *Phantasien eines Realistin*. Dresden: Reissner.

Macfarlane, A. (1975) 'The first hours and the smile', in R. Lewin, ed. *Child Alive*. Temple Smith.

Macfarlane, J. W., Allen, L. and Honzig, M. P. (1954) *Behaviour Problems of Normal Children*. Los Angeles: University of California Press.

MacIntyre, A. C. (1958) *The Unconscious*. Routledge & Kegan Paul.

Mackie, J. L. (1974) *The Cement of the Universe*. Oxford: Clarendon.

Magoun, H. W. (1952) 'The ascending reticular activating system', *Research Publication of the Association for Research in Nervous and Mental Disease* 30: 480–92.

262 Mahler, M. (1969) *On Human Symbiosis and the Vicissitudes of Individuation.* Hogarth.

Mahler, M. and Gosliner, R. J. (1955) 'On symbiotic child psychosis', *Psychoanal. Study Child* 10: 195–212.

Mahler, M., Pine, F. and Bergman, H. (1975) *The Psychological Birth of the Infant.* Hutchinson.

Mainx, F. (1955) 'Foundations of biology', in O. Neurath, R. Carnap and C. Morris, eds *International Encyclopedia of Unified Science* 1: (2). Chicago: University of Chicago Press.

Marr, D. (1976) 'Early processing of visual information', *Philosophical Transactions of the Royal Society London* B 274: 483–534.

McDougall, W. (1938) 'Fourth report on a Lamarckian experiment', *British Journal of Psychology* 28: 321–45.

Medawar, P. B. (1957) *The Uniqueness of the Individual.* Methuen.

Meltzer, D. (1974) 'Mutism in infantile autism, schizophrenia and manic-depressive states', *Int. J. Psycho-Anal.* 55: 397–404.

—— (1975) 'The psychology of autistic states and of post-autistic mentality', in D. Meltzer, ed. *Exploration in Autism.* Clunie.

Merlan, P. (1949) 'Brentano and Freud', *Journal of the History of Ideas* 6: 375–7.

Meyer, A. and McLardy, T. (1950) 'Neuropathology in relation to mental disease', *Recent Progress in Psychiatry* 2: 284–323.

Meynert, T. (1889) *Klinische Vorlesungen über Psychiatrie auf wissenschaftlichen Grundlagen.* Vienna: Braumüller.

Millar, S. (1968) *The Psychology of Play.* Harmondsworth: Penguin.

Miller, G. A., Galanter, E. and Pribram, K. H. (1960) *Plans and the Structure of Behaviour.* New York: Holt.

Mischel, W. (1973) 'Toward a cognitive social learning reconceptualization of personality', *Psychological Review* 80: 252–83.

Nagel, E. (1953) 'Teleological explanation and teleological systems', in H. Fiegl and M. Brodbeck, eds *Readings in the Philosophy of Science.* New York: Appleton-Century-Crofts.

—— (1961) *The Structure of Science.* New York: Harcourt, Brace and World.

Nelson, K. (1976) *The Conceptual Basis for Naming.* New Haven, CT: Yale University Press.

Neumann, E. (1954) *The Origins and History of Consciousness.* Princeton, NJ: Princeton University Press.

—— (1955) *Narzissismus, Automorphismus und Urbeziehung.* Zurich: Rascher.

—— (1959) 'The significance of the genetic aspect for analytical psychology', *J. Analyt. Psychol.* 4: 125–38.

Nisbett, R. E. and Wilson, T. (1977) 'Telling more than we know: verbal reports on mental processes', *Psychological Review* 84: 231–59.

Ostow, M. (1962) *Drugs in Psychoanalysis and Psychotherapy*. New York: Basic.

Parke, R. D. (1979) 'Perspectives on father–infant interaction', in J. D. Osofsky, ed. *Handbook of Infant Development*. New York: Wiley.

Parrish, W. E. (1966) 'Antibody to sperm', *International Medical Tribunal of Great Britain* 1: 29–41.

Pauli, W. (1955) 'The influence of archetypal ideas on the scientific theories of Kepler', in Pauli and C. G. Jung, *The Interpretation of Nature and Psyche*. Routledge & Kegan Paul.

Pavlov, I. P. (1927) *Conditioned Reflexes*. Oxford: Oxford University Press.

Penfield, W. (1958) 'The excitable cortex in conscious man', *Sherrington Lecturers* 5. Liverpool: Liverpool University Press.

Perlmutter, M. and Lange, G. (1978) 'The developmental analysis of recall-recognition distinction', in P. S. Ornstein, ed. *Memory Development in Children*. New Jersey: Erlbaum.

Perry, J. W. (1957) 'Acute catatonic schizophrenia', *J. Analyt. Psychol.* 2: 137–52.

Piaget, J. (1923) *The Language and Thought of the Child*. New York: Humanities Press, 1952.

—— (1951) *Play, Dreams and Imitation in Childhood*. Routledge & Kegan Paul.

—— (1953) *The Origin of Intelligence in Childhood*. Routledge & Kegan Paul.

—— (1972) *Insights and Illusions of Philosophy*. Routledge & Kegan Paul.

Piaget, J. and Inhelder, B. (1973) *Memory and Intelligence*. New York: Basic.

Pokorny, J. (1959) *Indogermanisches etymologisches Worterbuch*. Berne: Franke.

Popper, K. R. (1959) *The Logic of Scientific Discovery*. Hutchinson.

—— (1963) *Conjecture and Refutations*. Routledge & Kegan Paul.

—— (1965) *Of Clouds and Clocks*. Oxford University Press.

Popper, K. R. and Eccles, J. C. (1977) *The Self and Its Brain*. Springer-Verlag.

Pribram, K. and Gill, M. (1976) *Freud's Project Reassessed*. Hutchinson.

Rapaport, D. (1960) 'The structure of psychoanalytic theory – a systematizing attempt', *Psychological Issues* 2: 2–12.

Redfearn, J. W. T. (1977) 'The self and individuation', *J. Analyt. Psychol.* 22: 125–41.

264

Reeves, J. W. (1965) *Thinking About Thinking*. Secker & Warburg.

Ricoeur, P. (1970) *Freud and Philosophy*. New Haven, CT: Yale University Press.

Rimland, B. (1964) *Infantile Autism*. New York: Appleton-Century-Crofts.

Rodrigue, E. (1955) 'The analysis of a three-year-old mute schizophrenic', in M. Klein, ed. *New Directions in Psychoanalysis*. Tavistock.

Rogers, C. (1961) 'Two divergent trends', in R. May, ed. *Existential Psychology*. New York: Random House.

—— (1967) *On Becoming a Person*. Constable.

Rosch, E. (1973) 'On the internal structure of perceptual and semantic categories', in T. E. Moore, ed. *Cognitive Development and the Acquisition of Language*. New York: Academic.

Russell, B. (1940) *An Inquiry Into Meaning and Truth*. Allen & Unwin.

Rychlak, J. F. (1976) 'Is a concept of self necessary in psychological theory, and if so why?', in A. Wandersman, P. J. Poppen and D. F. Ricks, eds *Humanism and Behaviourism*. Oxford: Pergamon.

Ryle, G. (1949) *The Concept of Mind*. Hutchinson.

Salzman, L. (1967) 'Review of Dieter Wyss's depth psychology: a critical history', *Psychiatric and Social Science Review* 1: 12–17.

Sartre, J.–P. (1956) *Being and Nothingness*. New York: Philosophical Library.

Schaffer, H. R. (1971) *The Growth of Sociability*. Harmondsworth: Penguin.

Schaffer, H. R. and Emerson, P. E. (1964) 'The development of social attachments in infancy', *Monographs Society for Research in Child Development* 19: 1–77.

Schlick, M. (1953) 'Philosophy of organic life', in H. Feigl and M. Brodbeck, eds *Readings in the Philosophy of Science*. New York: Appleton-Century-Crofts.

Schneirla, T. L. (1945) 'Levels in the psychological capacities of animals', in R. W. Sellars, V. J. McGill and M. Farber, eds *Philosophy in the Future: The Quest of Modern Materialism*. New York: Macmillan, 1949.

Schopenhauer, A. (1819) *The World as Will and Representation*, E. F. J. Payne, trans. New York: Dover, 1966.

Schwartz, F. and Rouse, R. G. (1961) 'The activation and recovery of associations', *Psychological Issues* 3: 1–140.

Scott, C. (1948) 'Some embryological, neurological, psychiatric and psycho-analytic implications of the body schema', *Int. J. Psycho-Anal.* 29: 141–55.

Seaborn-Jones, G. (1968) *Treatment or Torture*. Tavistock.

Sears, R. R. (1942) 'Repression', in S. G. M. Lee and M. Herbert, eds *Freud and Psychology*. Harmondsworth: Penguin, 1970.

Segal, H. (1957) 'Notes on symbol formation', *Int. J. Psycho-Anal.* 38: 391–7.

Shaffer, D. and Dunn, J., eds (1979) *The First Years of Life*. Chichester: Wiley.

Sherrington, C. S. (1900) *Textbook on Physiology*. Edinburgh: Pentland.

—— (1906) *The Integrative Action of the Nervous System*. Constable.

—— (1951) *Man on His Nature*. Cambridge: Cambridge University Press.

Shevrin, H. and Toussieng, P. (1965) 'Vicissitudes of the need for tactile stimulation in instinctual development', *Psychoanal. Study Child* 20: 310–39.

Simon, H. A. and Newell, A. (1956) 'Models: their uses and limitations', in L. D. White, ed. *The State of the Social Sciences*. Chicago: University of Chicago Press.

Singer, C. (1959) *A Short History of Scientific Ideas to 1900*. Oxford: Oxford University Press.

Skinner, B. F. (1931) 'The role of the reflex in the description of behaviour', *Journal of General Psychology* 5: 427–58.

—— (1938) *The Behaviour of Organisms*. New York: Appleton-Century-Crofts.

—— (1953) *Science and Human Behaviour*. New York: Macmillan.

—— (1969) *Contingencies of Reinforcement*. New York: Appleton-Century-Crofts.

—— (1971) *Beyond Freedom and Dignity*. New York: Knopf.

—— (1975) 'The steep and thorny way to a science of behaviour', in R. Harré, ed. *Problems of Scientific Revolution*. Oxford: Oxford University Press.

Smith, Sir Grafton Elliot (1933) *The Diffusion of Culture*.

Spitz, R. (1955) 'The primal cavity: a contribution to the genesis of perception', *Psychoanal. Study Child* 10: 215–40.

—— (1957) *No and Yes*. New York: International Universities Press.

—— (1965) *The First Year of Life*. New York: International Universities Press.

Spitz, R., Ende, R. N. and Metcalf, D. (1970) 'Further prototypes of ego formation', *Psychoanal. Study Child* 25: 417–41.

Stallibrass, A. (1974) *The Self-Respecting Child*. Thames & Hudson.

Stayton, J. J. and Ainsworth, M. D. S. (1973) 'Individual differences in infant responses to brief, everyday separations as related to other infant and maternal behaviours', *Developmental Psychology* 9: 226–35.

Stein, L. (1951) 'On talking or the communication of ideas and feelings by means of mainly audible symbols', *Br. J. Med. Psychol.* 13: 113–14.

——— (1957) 'What a symbol is supposed to be', *J. Analyt. Psychol.* 2: 73–84.

——— (1967) 'Introducing not-self', *J. Analyt. Psychol.* 12: 97–114.

Stern, Wilhelm (1924) *Psychology of Early Childhood*, A. Barwell, trans. London.

Storr, A. (1955) 'A note on cybernetics and analytical psychology', *J. Analyt. Psychol.* 1: 93–5.

Strawson, P. F. (1966) *The Bounds of Sense*. University Paperbacks.

Sullivan, H. S. (1953) *The Interpersonal Theory of Psychiatry*. Tavistock.

Sulloway, F. (1979) *Freud, Biologist of the Mind: Beyond the Psychoanalytic Legend*. Busnett/Deutsch.

Taine, H. (1871) *On Intelligence*. Reeve.

Tinbergen, N. (1951) *The Study of Instinct*. Oxford: Oxford University Press.

Toulmin, S. (1953) *The Philosophy of Science*. Hutchinson.

Tulving, E. and Thompson, D. M. (1973) 'Encoding specificity and retrieval processes in episodic memory', *Psychological Review* 80: 352–73.

Turnbull, L. and Hawk, R. (1966) *World Medicine*, 19 July: 23.

Tustin, F. (1972) *Autism and Childhood Psychosis*. Hogarth.

Tversky, A. and Kahneman, D. (1974) 'Judgement under uncertainty: heuristics and biases', *Science* 184: 124– 31.

Valentine, C. W. (1962) *The Experimental Psychology of Beauty*. Methuen.

Valentine, E. (1978) 'Perchings and flight! Introspection', in A. Burton and J. Radford, eds *Thinking in Perspective*. Methuen.

Volcan, V. D. (1973) 'Transitional fantasies in the analysis of a narcissistic personality', *J. Amer. Psychoanal. Assn* 21: 351–76.

——— (1975) *Primitive Internalized Object Relations: A Clinical Study*. New York: International Universities Press.

von Schubert, G. H. (1837) *Die Symbolik des Traumes*. Leipzig: Brockhaus.

Vygotsky, L. S. (1962) *Thought and Language*, E. Haufmann and G. Vakar eds and trans. New York: Wiley.

Walker, R. C. S. (1978) *Immanuel Kant*. Routledge & Kegan Paul.

Wandersman, A., Poppen, P. J. and Ricks, D. F., eds (1976) *Humanism and Behaviourism: Dialogue and Growth*. Oxford: Pergamon.

Wason, P. C. and Evans, J. St B. T. (1975) 'Dual processes in reasoning', *Cognition* 3: 141–54.

Watkins, M. J. and Tulving, E. (1975) 'Episodic memory: when recognition fails', *Journal of Experimental Psychology: General* 1: 5–29.

Weismann, A. (1893) 'The germ-plasm: a theory of heredity', *Contemporary Science Series*, p. 477.

Weygandt, W. (1933) 'Dementia praecocissima and dementia infantiles',   267
    Medical Weekly: 1053–55.

Weyl, H. (1949) *Philosophy of Mathematics and Natural Science.* Princeton,
    NJ: Princeton University Press.

WHO Workshop (1987) 'Immunological aspects of the prevention of viral
    disease', *Bulletin of the World Health Organization* 65: 1–11.

Whyte, L. L. (1962) *The Unconscious Before Freud.* Tavistock.

Wiener, N. (1948) *Cybernetics or Control and Communication in the Animal
    and the Machine,* second edition, 1961. New York: MIT.

Wilhelm, R. and Jung, C. G. (1935) *The Secret of the Golden Flower.*
    Routledge & Kegan Paul.

Wilkinson, F. R. and Carghill, D. W. (1955) 'Repression elicited by story
    material based on the Oedipus complex', *Journal of Social Psychology* 42:
    209–14.

Wilkinson, J. J. G. (1887) *Correspondences.* Speirs.

Wilson, W. R. (1975) 'Unobtrusive induction of positive attitude', Univer-
    sity of Michigan Library doctoral dissertation (Ann Arbor, Michigan).

Winnicott, D. W. (1953) 'Transitional objects and transitional phenomena.
    A study of the first not-me possession', *Int. J. Psycho-Anal.* 34: 89–97.

—— (1955) 'A case managed at home', in *Collected Papers.* Tavistock,
    1958.

—— (1958) 'Psychoses and child care', in *Collected Papers.* Tavistock.

—— (1965a) 'A clinical study of the effect of failure of the average expected
    environment on a child's natural functioning', *Int. J. Psycho-Anal.* 46:
    81–7.

—— (1965b) *The Maturational Processes and the Facilitating Environment.*
    Hogarth.

—— (1967) 'The location of cultural experience', *Int. J. Psycho-Anal.* 48:
    368–72.

—— (1971a) *Therapeutic Consultations.* Hogarth.

—— (1971b) *Playing and Reality.* Tavistock.

Wittgenstein, L. (1945) *Philosophical Investigations.* Oxford: Blackwell.

Wolman, B. B., ed. (1968) *Historical Roots of Contemporary Psychology.*
    New York: Harper & Row.

Worringer, W. (1908) *Abstraction and Empathy.* Routledge & Kegan Paul.

Yakovlev, P. I. (1962) 'Morphological criteria of growth and maturation
    of the nervous system in man', *Mental Retardation* 39.

Yakovlev, P. I. and Lecours, A. R. (1967) 'The myelogenetic cycles

268   of regional maturation of the brain', in A. Minkowski, ed. *Regional Development of the Brain in Early Life*. Oxford: Blackwell.

Young, R. M. (1986) 'Freud: scientist and/or humanist', *Free Assns* 6: 7–35.

Note. Only authors mentioned more than twice have been included.

Index

Index

self-defence 64, 93, 228–30
self/ego-integrates theory: need for 9–12; *see also* con-integrates theory
self in early childhood *see* autism; con-integrates theory; Freud; Jung; physiology; psychology
self-knowledge 79
self-love *see* narcissism
self-object *see* object relations
self–other 80
self-prediction 15
self-regard 11, 77
self-regulating system 26–7
series of theories 165, 188–90
sexuality 54, 77, 82, 91, 93, 105, 119–20
'shadow' premises 193
Skinner, B. F. 170, 175, 191
smiling 14, 227–8, 229
somatic system *see* physiology; psyche-soma
speech 89; and autism 132, 134–7; and con-integrates theory 64, 212–16; lack of 134–6, 137; *see also* language
Stein, L. 35–6, 67, 145, 155
steric shape 156–7
stimuli 29, 148–9, 176–7; *see also* reflexes
stress 161
sublimation 77
subliminal perception 44–5
Sullivan, H. S. 9–11, 101
superego *see* id and ego and superego
symbol/symbolization: definition 35–6; Freudian view of 70–4, 83, 129; mythology and 35–7; objects in formation of 70–4; *see also* archetypal image; art
system-ego theory 102

Taine, H. 83–4, 91, 92
T-cells 159, 160
teleology 10
Thanatos *see* death: instinct
theory 18–19, 34, 75, 231–2; abandoned 48–51; cognitive experimental 191–5; in psychology 164–95; *see also* autism; falsifiability
therapy *see* art; sand-play
totality 3, 4, 16–17, 20, 178; Freudian view of 107–8, 124–6; Jungian view of 31–2, 37–45, 48–51, 62, 128
transcendental function 16, 41
transitional object 72–3, 114, 119, 142, 245
transpersonal phenomena 23–4; *see also* collective unconscious
trauma 152–3, 155, 217
true self *see* real self
Tustin, F. 131–4, 138–9, 140

unconscious 7, 11; and con-integrates theory 199, 204, 216, 223; Freudian view of 80–2, 91; *see also* collective unconscious; consciousness; personal unconscious; reflexes
undifferentiated memory store 201, 207–8, 209–10, 211

variable 191–2
vitalism 86, 99–100
voluntary movement 174

whole self 94, 104, 107–9, 124–6; *see also* totality
Winnicott, D. W. 20, 60, 76, 118, 196; and environment 55–6, 124, 128–9, 138, 139; and real and false self 102, 111–16; and transitional object 72, 114, 119, 142, 245

This first edition of
The Self in Early Childhood
was finished in February 1988.

It was phototypeset in 10½/15pt Bembo
on a Linotron 202 and printed by
a Crabtree SP56 offset-litho press
on 80 g/m² vol. 18 Supreme Antique wove.

The book was commissioned by Robert M. Young,
edited by Karl Figlio,
copy-edited by Gillian Beaumont,
designed by Carlos Sapochnik,
indexed by Ann Hall
and produced by David Williams and Selina O'Grady
for Free Association Books.